PLEASE SCREAM QUIETLY

D1605655

DIVERSE SEXUALITIES, GENDERS, AND RELATIONSHIPS

Series Editors

Richard Sprott, PhD, California State University, East Bay
Elizabeth Sheff, PhD, Sheff Consulting

The Diverse Sexualities, Genders, and Relationships Series highlights evidence-based approaches to understanding and serving diverse individuals and families whose relational or sexual practices or identities have been marginalized and understudied; reports of emerging empirical research on these topics; and analyses of the latest trends in cultural and societal developments on the status and place of diverse sexualities, genders, and relationships. Books in the series emphasize the intersections of race, culture, age, social class, (dis)ability, and other factors that shape the social locations of relational, sexual, and gender minorities as they intersect with institutions in fields such as education, law, medicine, religion, and public policy.

The books in this series will serve as sound and critical resources for the training and continuing education of professionals directly serving diverse communities, professions such as counseling, marriage and family therapy, social work, healthcare, criminology, human service, and education. They will also be useful for educators teaching undergraduate and graduate level university courses in anthropology, cultural studies, gerontology, psychology, sexuality studies, sociology, and women's and gender studies. Finally, these books will interest educated laypeople who wish to better understand diversity among relational, sexual, and gender minorities.

Titles in Series

Love and Freedom: Transcending Monogamy and Polyamory by Jorge Ferrer

Please Scream Quietly: A Story of Kink by Julie L. Fennell

Mental Health Practice with LGBTQ+ Children, Adolescents, and Emerging Adults in Multiple Systems of Care by Cristina L. Magalhães, Richard Sprott, and G. Nic Rider

The Handbook of Consensual Non-Monogamy: Affirming Mental Health Practice edited by Michelle D. Vaughan and Theodore R. Burnes

PLEASE SCREAM QUIETLY

A STORY OF KINK

JULIE FENNELL

Gallaudet University

ROWMAN & LITTLEFIELD
Lanham • Boulder • New York • London

Acquisitions Editor: Mark Kerr
Acquisitions Assistant: Sarah Rinehart
Sales and Marketing Inquiries: textbooks@rowman.com

Credits and acknowledgments for material borrowed from other sources, and reproduced with permission, appear on the appropriate pages within the text.

Published by Rowman & Littlefield
An imprint of The Rowman & Littlefield Publishing Group, Inc.
4501 Forbes Boulevard, Suite 200, Lanham, Maryland 20706
www.rowman.com

86-90 Paul Street, London EC2A 4NE

Copyright © 2022 by The Rowman & Littlefield Publishing Group, Inc.

All rights reserved. No part of this book may be reproduced in any form or by any electronic or mechanical means, including information storage and retrieval systems, without written permission from the publisher, except by a reviewer who may quote passages in a review.

British Library Cataloguing in Publication Information Available

Library of Congress Cataloging-in-Publication Data
Names: Fennell, Julie, 1981– author.
Title: Please scream quietly : a story of kink / Julie Fennell, Gallaudet University.
Description: Lanham : Rowman & Littlefield, [2022] | Series: Diverse sexualities, genders, and relationships | Includes bibliographical references and index.
Identifiers: LCCN 2022014056 (print) | LCCN 2022014057 (ebook) | ISBN 9781538168752 (cloth) | ISBN 9781538168769 (paperback) | ISBN 9781538168776 (epub)
Subjects: LCSH: Sexual dominance and submission. | Bondage (Sexual behavior) | Sadomasochism.
Classification: LCC HQ79 .F45 2022 (print) | LCC HQ79 (ebook) | DDC 306.77/5—dc23/eng/20220503
LC record available at https://lccn.loc.gov/2022014056
LC ebook record available at https://lccn.loc.gov/2022014057

∞™ The paper used in this publication meets the minimum requirements of American National Standard for Information Sciences—Permanence of Paper for Printed Library Materials, ANSI/NISO Z39.48-1992.

CONTENTS

ACKNOWLEDGMENTS

This book would never have been possible without the many, many kinksters who were willing to share their lives with me, whether through conversation or photographs. At every stage in this process, I was overwhelmed by the generosity of total strangers who were willing to share some of their most intimate and vulnerable moments with me—and, through me, the world.

I also must thank Sara Cohen for her support and comments; my editors Elisabeth Sheff and Richard Sprott; and the publishing team of Mark Kerr, Ivy Roberts, and Alden Perkins.

My department chair, Sharon Barnartt, provided incredible support for me as a junior untenured faculty member when I embarked on this research, and I thank her too.

DEDICATION

For all my partners, past and present, whose stories are here—whether in the text or between the lines of it, who have put up with me working on this massive project for nine years. But most of all, for my poor husband, Jonathon Walker, who supported me through graduate school and made this all possible.

INTRODUCTION:
"YOUR FANTASY IS MY REALITY"

NOT YOUR STANDARD DEVIANT

The summer of 2012 was brutally hot at Camp O-Town, where I conducted much of my fieldwork and many of my interviews studying the pansexual BDSM (Bondage and Discipline/Dominance and submission/Sadism and Masochism) subculture. In the 100+ degree heat, it didn't seem particularly strange to sit in the shade, naked and dripping with sweat, with a recorder on a table between me and my interviewee, having a long conversation about how they became involved in this interesting lifestyle.

Professional sociologists don't usually come straight out and admit on the first page of their books, "I interviewed respondents naked, occasionally," but professional sociologists have mostly nervously eschewed researching explicitly erotic environments. Consequently, there aren't solid methodological precedents for proper research conduct and procedure in the kinds of contexts where interviews might get interrupted by a violent fake "kidnapping" stampeding through it (this actually happened during one of my interviews). There was, quite simply, nothing that was remotely "normal" about my research experiences, and I might as well warn you on page 1 that there's not really much that's normal about me as a person, either. In a subculture full of oddballs, I eventually rose through the ranks to become a respected and even odder oddball (or, as my friend Alex put it, "not just a standard deviant"). I'm not going to pretend to an objectivity I don't possess: I'm going to tell you the story of my people and the kooky social world they built for themselves to celebrate their deviance. This book is a collective autobiography of the BDSM subculture from 2010 to 2017, as told by its self-appointed chief recorder and analyst—me.

Another reason I've bluntly confessed from the start that I conducted some of my interviews naked is that I want to make it abundantly clear that I consider myself an enthusiastic participant in Jason Orne's (2017) project of *carnal sociology*. Beginning with Alfred Kinsey (1948), scholars of

1

sex and sexuality have generally sought to distance themselves from the more salacious aspects of their research in what often looks like a desperate bid for legitimacy and respect. From Michel Foucault (1990) to Judith Butler (1990), and continuing to most recent scholarship, this tendency to disregard the carnal and corporeal pleasures of fucking in favor of the theoretical pleasures of sesquipedalian verbosity has typically left me with the impression that scholars have taken one of the most interesting subjects in the world—SEX—and made it as tedious as tallying gall wasps (Gathorne-Hardy, 2004). In a conspicuous exception to this trend, Orne (2017) makes a sort of call to arms for other sexual sociologists to join him in doing "carnal sociology," and putting fucking and carnal sense back into the study of sex. There is a corporeal world of physical, emotional, and social pleasure in the BDSM subculture, and it is sweaty, orgasmic, emotional, tearful, agonizing, joyful, compassionate, and many other things besides. My top priority in writing this book is to convey to you at least some hint of that intense and pleasurable reality.

RESEARCHING UNDER ABNORMAL CONDITIONS

In the summer of 2012, one might easily have mistakenly imagined that the BDSM subculture wasn't quite so peculiar because BDSM appeared to be going mainstream, thanks to the unfathomable success of *Fifty Shades of Grey* (James, 2011). These three novels, which eventually became three movies, about a supposedly not-kinky woman's (Anastasia) relationship with a very kinky man (Christian) were jaw-droppingly successful. Though BDSM as a fantasy might have been headed mainstream, the Scene (which is what pansexual kinksters call the BDSM subculture) definitely *wasn't*. The Scene consists of a vast array of purely social events ("munches" and happy hours), evening parties where BDSM activities ("play") are allowed, educational events where people learn about various aspects of BDSM, and days-long BDSM "events" that take place in hotels and campgrounds; additionally, a great deal of BDSM socializing happens online. The pansexual BDSM Scene is so-called to differentiate it from the separate but slightly overlapping gay/lesbian BDSM subculture (often called the Leather subculture) and also from the slightly more overlapped dyke + trans BDSM subculture described by Bauer (2014). The pansexual Scene (hereafter just referred to as "the Scene" or "the BDSM subculture") primarily consists of straight/heteroflexible cis men,

2

and bi/pansexual cis women who tend to be in heteroromantic (meaning opposite-sex) long-term relationships; members of the Scene refer to themselves as *kinksters*. In the social world of the pansexual Scene, the specter of the Other for kinksters is definitely not our kinky gay/lesbian/queer brethren: it's the Normal People—"vanillas"—who we imagine live monogamous lives with their two children in cookie-cutter suburban houses surrounded by white picket fences. During the summer of my fieldwork, many kinksters worried that *Fifty Shades* would inspire hordes of these outsiders to come in and ruin everything that was "cool" about the Scene.

Many kinksters I spoke with that summer invoked the "threat of a soccer mom invasion" (a phrase often repeated verbatim) to signify the doom of the Scene at the gormless hands of sexually unsatisfied, not-"really"-kinky housewives. Yet the predicted invasion never occurred because the Scene (which is by no means culturally unified) has always been, and remains, a relatively secluded "home" (kinksters' own term) for social misfits. In truth, the Scene is fueled by participants' deep desire not to be normal and their awareness of themselves as weird much more than by their desire to consensually hit each other with whips and floggers. It's a place where largely white, well-educated geeks come to "play"—meaning, with the consent of all parties, that they do things from flogging to rope bondage to sticking needles in each other all the way up to the aforementioned brutal "kidnapping," and occasionally have public sex while they do. "Consent" is fundamental to the way kinksters approach what they do, with many hours of education and community discussion devoted to the idea that people need to make well-informed decisions to ensure that what they do is "BDSM" and not "abuse." (The system is far from perfect, but the subculture at least makes an earnest attempt.) In the case of Camp O-Town, 800–1,200 people converge several times a year on a private campground to do these things together for several days at a time in a utopian space where vanillas rarely tread and where vanilla rules don't apply. The Scene as a whole, and Camp O-Town especially, are intentionally designed to make "normal" people feel unwelcome, regardless of how alluring they find the idea of orgasming from being hit in the clitoris with a riding crop.

In a social world that views normalcy in Durkheimian (Durkheim & Swain, 2008) terms as *profane* (which is to say, the antithesis of what is cherished or valued in the culture), following conventional expectations for research professionalism would certainly have worked against me. I was fully embedded personally in the local BDSM Scene by early 2010, identifying myself, as so many in the Scene do, as polyamorous, kinky, pansexual, and Pagan (all words I'll explain). When I began planning my research project in 2011, all the published sociological research on the pansexual BDSM subculture had been conducted by people who either were very conspicuously *not* kinky (Newmahr, 2011; Weiss, 2011) or were completely obscuring their involvement in the community (whom I won't cite for obvious reasons). Reading these accounts, I was frustrated by what I perceived as a lack of social science empathy for and understanding of this group that society at large already misunderstands. In short, the literature begged for an insider's perspective to balance so many writings from outsiders, and I nominated myself for the job.

Conspicuously absent from that earlier sociological writing is acknowledgment of and compassion for the dark undercurrent of shame that runs through the BDSM subculture and the experiences of kinky people. As a self-identified kinkster, I understood what it meant to crave pain at a basic physiological level for my entire life, and in the classic terms of Goffman's (2009) conceptualization of stigma, I also understood how much that craving tainted their/my credibility within mainstream society. I recognize that my telling you that I spend much of my free time going to camps where people consensually tie and beat each other up for pleasure, with an outdoor gangbang here and there for added excitement, might have already made you suspect that I may be in need of psychological help and that my research might be inherently compromised. My university's ethics board was initially disgusted by my proposed research, with the head of the board arguing that it was unethical to stand by while people were being hurt and doing nothing to stop it. She became speechless when I challenged: "Even when that person is having an orgasm?" My status as a community insider ultimately worked to my advantage, since the board was obviously uncomfortably aware that when they said that what kinksters did was bad, they were also saying that what *I* did was bad. I shamed the university into not only approving it but also giving me funding. Those kinds of suspicions and disgust are stigma in action, and I understood all too well what social stigma against kinksters felt like in a way that outsiders to kink really didn't seem to.

Closely connected to that undercurrent of shame is a sea of medicalization. *Medicalization* refers to the way that doctors and other medical professionals pathologize conditions that might otherwise be perceived as normal or healthy, which tends to result in stigma against the people being medicalized (Lin, 2017). For years, psychologists pathologized BDSM; thanks to extensive activism from kinksters, the *Diagnostic and Statistical Manual* (DSM), which psychologists use to diagnose mental illness, modified the pathology of "sexual sadism" in the early 2000s to exclude people who derive sexual pleasure from *consensually* hurting other people (Krueger, 2010; Lin, 2017). The stigma of medicalization was so strong that it seemed to even affect the vocabulary choices of sociologists and anthropologists, who until recently usually wrote about "SM" and "sadomasochism" years after people within the community had begun referring to "S&M," "BDSM," and "kink" (see, for example, Harviainen, 2011). Kinky people call *themselves* "kinky," but social scientists seemed afraid to use this label themselves, as if they were ashamed of the very people they were studying. This hesitation parallels the way that social scientists kept writing about "homosexuals" (who psychologists also thought had a mental illness until 1973), long after the so-called homosexuals had started calling themselves "gays" and "lesbians" (Peters, 2014). As a result, kinksters are understandably leery of social scientists, and my position as an insider gave me serious advantages in terms of access in this normally very research(er)-unfriendly context.

I didn't have to pretend to be an insider; at most of the events I attended the summer of my fieldwork, I interviewed people all day and then played all night. But I consciously invoked my insider status when engaging with actual and potential participants to gain their trust. I started dyeing my hair bright Manic Panic colors, as many kinksters do, and showing up for interviews wearing whatever was appropriate for the context, from street clothes to nothing. As a result, even when I was doing interviews outside of kink events in settings like coffeehouses, I still looked more like "one of our people" (a joking phrase kinksters sometimes use when identifying one another in the outside world). All told, I collected 70 interviews with a wide range of kinky folks, including people who had never been to events, people who were at their first-ever event, and people who had been in the Scene for 20 or more years. Throughout, I went out of my way to make sure my respondents perceived me as being like them—which wasn't hard, because I generally was.

There are so few guidelines for how to conduct research in these types of deviant contexts because historically, even when sociologists have done qualitative research with deviant communities like the Scene, both the larger culture and academic circles have expected the sociologists either to be visiting outsiders or to politely hand wave at their level of personal involvement (for example, Becker's [2008] seminal study of the marijuana subculture of the 1950s glossed over his personal involvement in it [Gopnik, 2015]). In contrast to other sociologists who were trying to obscure their own levels of involvement in deviant subcultures, I made a personal, political, and academic commitment when I began studying the BDSM subculture to be the first "out" American sociologist to do so. (For a discussion of what it means to be "out," see Orne [2011].) At no point in my research process have I ever hidden the fact that I was personally involved in the BDSM community for several years before I began studying it, and I have remained heavily involved in it since the completion of my official fieldwork in the fall of 2012.

You might worry that my position as an insider means I'll be less critical of the Scene. It's true that I'm less critical of some things than most of the outsiders I have read. However, I am also very critical of *different* things, because rather than imposing the judgment of an external observer, I apply the classical standard of a good ethnographer: I judge the Scene's ability to achieve its goals based on its own values (Adler, 1993). In general, I have found that as long as I hold onto my sociological imagination (Mills, 1959)—that is, an analytical awareness of the larger social context of individual experiences—my position as an insider actually provides me with *better* opportunities to frankly critique the social construction of meaning and values in the BDSM Scene. As you read this book, imagine how condescending some of the critiques of the Scene I offer would sound coming from an outsider versus how they sound coming from an insider. There is, after all, a world of difference between saying, "We made a mistake," versus "They made a mistake." That difference is my biggest asset as an insider.

That said, I think I have had one serious disadvantage as an insider, which is simply that I am white. As I will explain, the Scene is extremely white, and I was obviously unable to attend social events that were specifically for people of color. Even though I dated, played with, and befriended Black people in the Scene—and went out of my way to disproportionately interview them—I rarely found people who were eager to talk about race with me much (Asians are also rare in the mid-Atlantic Scene, and nonwhite Hispanics even more so). I would like to think this hesitancy on the part of others wasn't a personal problem with me, as I certainly found a few Black friends who were delighted to talk about race with me. But the general attitude among everyone in the Scene mostly seems to be, "Don't talk about race if we can avoid it." In particular, as a white kinkster, I learned quickly by watching others that anything I said in a public forum about race would almost certainly offend and anger many people (especially many people of color), and I was better off keeping my mouth shut. I have not been able to escape that training in writing this book, and I hope readers will understand my hesitancy in talking about race to be an awkward product of my social position as a white woman in the Scene rather than a product of simply not noticing or not caring.

HOBBY OR PROFESSION? 2013–2017

Over the four years after I concluded my official fieldwork, my involvement in the Scene changed greatly. People asked me what the difference was between doing fieldwork and just going to parties, and I joked that I wasn't taking notes when I was just going to parties. In reality, this was only half true; I could never stop taking notes with my eyes, and it's not like I could just turn my sociological imagination off. You know how in the TV show *Sherlock*, they show him going into rooms and compulsively noticing details about the way things are placed and mentally cataloging them? That's what a trained sociologist like me does in a social environment, but instead it's mental notes about the gender dynamics of how people interact, their race, their dress, their language use, and their collective social values.

By 2014, I was traveling all over the United States and Canada to teach kinksters how to do kink. The BDSM subculture focuses heavily on education, and my day job as a sociology professor who researched the Scene lent me serious cachet as a BDSM educator. Teaching so many classes in so many places had the important side benefit of allowing me to observe kinksters in most major American cities in their natural habitat. Although my original research site focused exclusively on the mid-Atlantic Scene, in subsequent years I traveled from Texas to Toronto and even taught BDSM in Iceland. My observations in these different places confirmed something I already knew from my original research: BDSM subcultural norms have much in common throughout the United States and Canada, but the Scene is fundamentally a loosely networked set of microcultures (Stephens, Leach, and Taggart, 1998). That means there are conspicuous differences in Scenes based on cities, and even often based on the people who usually attend a specific party, event space, or meetup.

By early 2017, I felt like my observations weren't quite enough to achieve my research goals (and they didn't seem to be sufficient for reviewers, either, who were concerned that my insider position was "biased" rather than "extremely well-informed"). I wanted to confirm my loose and brief observations about the differences in Scenes between cities and states, and I needed a lot of data to do that. Moreover, interviews really are inadequate to tell you everything about a group when their behaviors and attitudes don't match, or when people aren't always consciously aware of their attitudes. So I fielded a survey in April 2017 to allow me to measure the scope of many attitudes, beliefs, and behaviors in the Scene in ways that had never been published before.

The timing for my survey was unintentionally perfect. By June of 2017, the #MeToo movement—which had not yet acquired a name or hashtag and which wouldn't appear in the broader culture for another two months—began stampeding through the Scene with the force of a rampaging elephant. High-status (within the Scene) men were publicly shamed and systematically shunned ("banned") for alleged consent violations against women. Given that men run most of the events in the Scene (at least as figureheads), many events ceased to exist when their organizers were banned. As you'll see throughout this book, the Scene depends on a complex system of trust, negotiation, and reputation to function, but in the wake of these bleak revelations all these systems became increasingly anomic (Merton, 1938), meaning that the conventional rules and norms had broken down. Kinksters (reasonably) lost faith in the social institutions that had supported the Scene, and alternative institutions didn't really emerge. People were angry, sad, anxious, afraid, and—worst of all—staying home. I hope that anyone researching the Scene after me can use this book as a guide to figuring out why this crisis occurred and developing hypotheses about how the subculture might change (or fail to) in the wake of such a large-scale social panic.

Because of the cataclysmic changes that bookend the period from 2010–2017, this book is, for all intents and purposes, a sociological present-day history of the pansexual BDSM Scene during that time (with a focus on North America and the mid-Atlantic in particular). In addition to the social changes in 2017, the Scene had also changed radically in 2009 (just before I arrived) when the social networking behemoth website FetLife appeared. (FetLife is like Facebook for kinky people, only for that period it was even more important and ubiquitous.) Before FetLife, people had to go out of their way to learn about the existence of the Scene, its ways, and the parties and events that were happening. After FetLife, the entire Scene was basically organized through FetLife, and literally *everyone* in the public Scene was on it. New people joined every day and immediately had access to the kinds of

Scene information (and gossip) that used to take months or even years of in-person interaction to acquire.

FetLife exploded rapidly. By February of 2010, when I attended my first kink event, it was already normative to put your FetLife nickname on your event name badge. By early 2013, I had numerous conversations with people about their Fetlife user ID number, which was attached to profiles and ordered by when a person had joined; anything under a million was considered a status symbol that one had been around a long time, and I knew one eccentric fellow who actually talked of having his FetLife number tattooed on him. It was no coincidence that I got into the Scene (along with so many other people) in the post-FetLife internet explosion. It was pure luck that I fielded my survey only a month before the Scene radically changed again in the midst of its own #MeToo movement. So I am fortunate to be able to tell a fairly complete story of the Scene during the Fetlife era, especially since the other three books (Bauer, 2014; Newmahr, 2011; Weiss, 2011) about the Scene discuss it pre-FetLife. Although I won't focus much on FetLife itself here (in large part because the website is extremely nervous about researchers), remember as you read that the changes it brought to the Scene are always part of the background social context of the Scene, even when kinksters themselves had forgotten about it.

YOUR FANTASY IS MY REALITY

There's a popular shirt in the Scene that quips, "Your fantasy is my reality." That one shirt summarizes the values of much of the Scene, which tends to smugly present itself as a group who have had the courage to do what everybody wants to do but is too scared to. I regularly had debates with kinky friends who insisted that life in the Scene was what everyone wanted but mostly lacked the will or social resources to achieve. I remain very skeptical of this perspective, but statistics support the idea that most Americans at least *fantasize* about the life the Scene encourages. Lehmiller's (2018) book was the first to broadly study Americans' sexual fantasies, and he found that we overwhelmingly fantasize about consensual nonmonogamy and BDSM, which are by far the top two most popular fantasies for both men and women. However, there's a pretty big gap between "fantasizing" and "doing," and an even bigger gap between doing privately and doing something usually defined as private in front of a bunch of people you don't know well.

This book explores that gap between the fantasy of BDSM and the reality of doing it publicly in a highly complex subculture, seeking to answer two main questions: if BDSM is such a popular fantasy, why do so few people become involved in the Scene? And once they do, how does the Scene shape their perspective on BDSM and relationships? I'll answer these questions chapter by chapter, but the short answer is that the BDSM subculture is a true sub-culture with a specific set of core values and norms that are only tangentially related to BDSM itself, and the vast majority of people who fantasize about BDSM probably don't fit in well with those other values and norms. The Scene teaches people to understand, interpret, and practice BDSM in ways that probably don't appeal to the majority of people who occasionally fanta-size about kink, and it attracts and maintains people who want to build an entire kinky life for themselves.

If we think of the BDSM subculture as a place whose *manifest function* (Merton, 1938)—which is to say, its official social purpose—is to create a social space where common sexual fantasies can become manifest in improb-able ways, we have to remember that while BDSM fantasies are extremely common, they are not the number-one spot on Lehmiller's list: consensual nonmonogamy is. Consensual nonmonogamy (CNM), which is more often called "ethical nonmonogamy" by people who aren't academics, refers to re-lationships in which people openly agree to some type of nonmonogamous arrangement, from a single night's threesome to a long-term arrangement as polyamorous (meaning multiple romantic relationships with the consent of all involved parties). I'll explain a lot more about CNM in chapter 3, but for now, suffice it to say that the Scene's focus on maximum fantasy fulfillment means that a heavy focus on CNM is inevitable, since it's an even more common fantasy than BDSM. When people from the Scene say, "Your fantasy is my reality," they're not just referring to the partner they have who can orgasm from being bitten (these people aren't mythical, I assure you; I've bitten some of them myself): they're referring to the fact that they have a wife *and a girlfriend* who can.

This was very much my reality during the summer of 2012, when I was living the hedonistic dreams of the Scene to the hilt. I had (and have) a hus-band who had (and has) a girlfriend, and I was dating a collection of people of various genders who will make brief appearances throughout the rest of this book. Many of my exploits were a bit ludicrous, even by the generous standards of the Scene. In between driving all over the mid-Atlantic to con-duct face-to-face interviews and attend various dayslong BDSM events, I undertook a deeply personal journey that echoed much of what you'll see from the people I interviewed. BDSM—and even more importantly, the Scene—went from being a background interest to a central aspect of my social, romantic, and sexual life. No matter how critical I became of the Scene later as its problems became increasingly large and as I watched in heartbreak as two of my partners from that summer were eventually "banned" from it, I remain keenly aware of and grateful for the opportunities it created for me to have intense experiences most people don't even know to fantasize about. Yet no matter how much my life started to feel like I was walking through tangible porn (albeit porn with a lot less makeup, way better dialogue, and much smaller dicks), I was still constantly surrounded by real life, with real-life problems of gossip, breakups, jealousy, and insecurity. Throughout this book, I'm going to try to foreground this contrast between fantasy and reality because I think understanding it is fundamental to fully understanding life in the Scene.

WHAT EXACTLY IS "THE SCENE"?

The term "the Scene" is mostly used for convenience; there are pockets of related groups of people who do BDSM, and kinksters label the collection of them that mostly falls under the "pansexual" umbrella "the Scene" and "the Lifestyle." While they have much more in common than not, norms still vary among geographical areas and even among specific groups within the same area. A single charismatic individual often holds extraordinary sway over their own little fiefdom within this conglomerate. Kinksters themselves often make much of the differences and variations between groups (and as an insider, I tend to think that some of these differences are quite important as well), but I don't think many outsiders would even notice a lot of these differences, which I'll discuss more in chapters 5–7. The majority of kinksters never go far beyond their own little Scene microcosms and are often unaware of the variations between them.

There are many formal and informal BDSM organizations throughout the country (the more formal ones have cards and small membership dues). The most formally organized of these have volunteer boards of directors, but most of them are just groups of people who got together and decided to try to run "something" for the community. The things they run tend to take the form of social gatherings, classes, public parties, immersive daylong events that combine all those things, and sometimes private parties. Social gatherings, often called "munches," generally consist of meeting at places like a restaurant or bar and taking over a large room or table, or sometimes the entire venue. Although some of these gatherings allow BDSM play, there's usually an expectation that the play will be pretty light, and sex is almost never allowed. The focus of these gatherings is meeting, networking, and socializing, although many also include some kind of education. Classes and workshops are usually between one and two hours, focusing on some aspect of BDSM, and may be in the form of lectures, discussion sessions, demonstrations, or hands-on learning experiences. It's normal to see classes on everything from blow jobs to single-tail whips to bondage to relationship strategies (mostly for polyamorous people). Typically, group organizers reach out to others they think might like to teach, but sometimes the potential teachers reach out to the organizers.

"Public parties" usually happen at a local standing dungeon (BDSM club) or sometimes at a temporary location in a warehouse. Public parties are usually available to anyone who wants to go who hasn't been banned from the organization for some reason. Most kinksters learn about these parties from friends who are going or through FetLife. Most dungeons only occasionally throw parties of their own; usually, they work out some sort of arrangement with other local groups allowing those groups to throw parties at the dungeon. "Private parties," confusingly, also often happen in local dungeons but usually are much more selective in terms of who is allowed to attend. Groups may restrict attendance to people who are formal members of their groups or to people who've attended a specific series of classes. Private parties are sometimes advertised on FetLife; many happen in the homes of kinksters who have personal dungeons, and those are often exclusively invite-only from the host rather than being run by an organization or group. As there are entire large cities that have historically been unable to sustain a standing public dungeon for a variety of reasons (Boston was especially notorious for this at the time of my research), private parties have become the norm in those areas. Unsurprisingly, these Scenes have a reputation for being cliqueish and disconnected; for several years, there was a running joke in other Scenes about "waiting for the annual collapse of the Boston Scene" in a mass of infighting (think *Mean Girls* with collars).

Dayslong events take place either in hotels or on secluded campgrounds. They pretty much always include a wide array of educational programming and networking events, with parties every night. Hotel events tend to be much more restrained because of space and legal limitations. The police can raid hotel events at any time (although they rarely do), and people usually have to put on clothes and get on crowded public elevators to get from their dungeon play in hotel ballrooms to their rooms to shower. As many more extreme BDSM activities are pretty messy (from violent anal sex to peeing on people), things tend to be a bit tamer at hotel events. Also, most hotel events don't have much or any public play space during the day, and most of the play spaces at night are heavily supervised by hotel security. Camp events, on the other hand, tend to be much more private, with basically no vanilla supervision, and are much farther away from the eye of the law. There are usually very few limitations on types or times of play at these events. Hotel events have an air of propriety about them that is entirely absent from the kinky, free-for-all spirit of most camp events.

Many social gatherings are basically free or charge a nominal fee ($5 or so) to get in, although there's often an expectation that people will buy food or drink once they're there. Most public dungeon parties cost anywhere from about $20 to $45 per person to attend for a night, so the cost of regular attendance can add up quickly. Most private parties held in public dungeons cost about the same, but house parties are often free, donation/potluck affairs, or very cheap. Dayslong events average about $400 a person for admission and lodging, not including food, with hotel events generally costing more than camp events. If you're committed to getting to lots of dayslong events, you almost always have to travel pretty long distances as well, because even in the Baltimore area—which has by far the most in the country—there are usually only five or six major events in any year.

The people who are the most involved, however, usually aren't paying for all (or even most of) the events they go to. Most of the major BDSM organizations are run entirely by volunteers who are compensated ("comped") by gaining admission for free into the parties and events where they work. Weekend dungeon parties require volunteers to work as event monitors, greeters, and snack bar salespeople, so many folks do those jobs in exchange for free admission to the party. The labor force required for dayslong kink events is much larger, and there are many opportunities for comps to these events by doing everything from cleaning bathrooms to building/taking down dungeon furniture to teaching to performing to working the registration desk. Many of these events have scaled comps so that people who do a lot of work also get free rooms or cabin spaces and sometimes free food as well.

Unsurprisingly, people who are highly involved in organizations tend to burn out quickly, so turnover is high and continuous institutional knowledge is often weak. Working setup and takedown for many large events sometimes involves one to two days of additional labor on both ends of a three-to-five-day event, so people who want to become involved that way need to have a lot of free time. Although there are a few very skilled professionals who happen to get a lot of time off and become highly involved in the Scene, the vast majority of people at higher echelons of organization, volunteer staffing, and teaching are mostly underemployed. Essentially, a large body of much more loosely involved—usually richer—kinksters funds the involvement of a core group who often pay little or nothing. Although kinksters on the whole are a fairly well-educated lot, they really only average out to "middle-class," even though the most involved ones tend not to be very well off. Most upper-class and upper-middle-class jobs don't allow for the kind of leisure time required to make a lifestyle out of BDSM.

Regardless of level of involvement, once you put so much as a toenail into the BDSM subculture (usually meaning that you've found yourself reading a blog or community website), it will start trying to throw rules and norms at you. I'll go over all of these in great depth in later chapters, but always keep in mind that the first and last principle that guides life in the Scene is that the term "consensual kink" is basically redundant: if it's not consensual, it's abuse. Everything about life in the Scene is structured and organized around trying to make behaviors that society says are always unethical and/ or downright illegal (e.g., slapping your partner across the face or having sex with someone while they say they don't want to) ethical and legal-ish, under specific circumstances. It turns out that the lines between "consensual" and "nonconsensual" are sometimes really, really fuzzy, but the Scene tries incredibly hard to keep things as consensual looking as it reasonably can, both at the micro and macro levels.

DEVIANT PRIVILEGE

The general social response toward the extreme differentness of the Scene is not neutral. During the course of my fieldwork, a prominent local party promoter was instantly demoted in the military when a coworker outed him as kinky, and one of my interviewees, a high-ranking official in a major government agency, had her job threatened when her superiors decided that she was essentially engaging in conduct unbecoming by presenting at kink events. The legality of BDSM is constantly in question (White, 2015), and its deviant status is sometimes at stake in child custody issues (Meepos, 2013).

Sociologists usually define *deviance* as behavior that violates social expectations and is viewed negatively, and that seems to be a fair characterization of life in the Scene. The path to a deviant lifestyle (sometimes called *career deviance* [Matza and Blomberg, 2017]) differs widely depending on the type of deviance, and we'll look more at the paths people take to the Scene in the next chapter. Most theories of deviance, which are closely related to theories of crime, assume that people become deviant either because they don't have much to lose or because economic or social necessity drives them to it (Matza and Blomberg, 2017). In contrast to many other deviant subcultures, which are often motivated by depression, disillusion, or perceived or real deprivation (such as gangs, many drug subcultures, or Neo-Nazi groups), the BDSM subculture seems like a pretty cheerful voluntary association. Williams (2009) has argued that the BDSM subculture should be understood as a *deviant leisure* activity, meaning that people do this for fun and social enjoyment, in spite or because of its deviance. Newmahr (2010) goes further, arguing that the BDSM subculture is *fundamentally* about "serious leisure," meaning that it is an intense social hobby and not really focused on sex or sexuality at all.

Meanwhile, Weiss (2011) and Sheff and Hammers (2011) focus on materialism and privilege in the BDSM subculture, noting that the Scene is extremely disproportionately white and upper/middle class. As I will discuss further in chapter 5, while it might be tempting to think that the Scene's whiteness is a product of unusually high levels of individual or structural racism within it (e.g., several reviewers of my own work have suggested that the "legacy of slavery" in both BDSM language and aesthetics of Dominance/submission and Master/slave relationships accounts for the low presence of people of color in the Scene), I do not think these arguments really explain the low numbers of people of color in the Scene. All of the Scene's adjacent subcultures—none of which carry any "legacy of slavery"—are also extremely white. Although the Scene is hardly a race utopia, it has an extremely low tolerance for racist ideology, and interracial dating is very normalized there (note that it's not really "encouraged" per se, because to encourage it would require calling much more attention to race than is the Scene norm). Rather, I think the whiteness of the Scene is more a product of participation in the BDSM subculture being (1) a leisure activity and (2) a *deviant* leisure activity. As a deviant leisure activity, unlike many other forms of deviance, privilege is actually an *enabling* factor for involvement in the Scene. In exactly the same way that many of the first gays and lesbians to come out were people with high status (Orne, 2011), privilege means that people can potentially afford the economic and social costs of the stigma of kink. In essence, a major part of why the Scene is so white is because *society* is structurally racist and because society stigmatizes BDSM. Moreover, the Scene is a voluntary association, and the overall structural racism of society means that voluntary associations in America tend to be extremely racially segregated (DiPrete et al., 2011), especially churches (Dougherty, 2003)— and the Scene is no exception.

The demographic composition of the Scene closely resembles that of its adjacent sub/countercultures: the gaming/geek subculture (Gilsdorf, 2010), the Renaissance festival subculture (Rubin, 2012), the Pagan subculture (McClure, 2017), and the polyamorous subculture (which it so heavily overlaps as to be difficult to distinguish itself from [Sheff and Hammers, 2011]). All of these subcultures are largely populated by very liberal, disproportionately well-educated, hetero-coupled/interested, Pagan or religiously unaffiliated people under 50. Almost by sociological default, these characteristics mean that their members are largely white and upper/middle-class, but most people who are not still fit the rest of that profile. The Scene selects for my initially listed characteristics first, and those characteristics uncoincidentally happen to associate with white, upper/middle-class people, thus inevitably reinforcing the race/class homogeneity of the Scene. The crossover between the above listed subcultures is extremely high, with many of my interviewees recounting stories of entering the BDSM Scene through one of these other groups. All of which is to say that *kinky* may very well be a sexual orientation that is more or less randomly distributed within the population (at least when it comes to a preference for persistent and/or relatively intense kink). Yet because the BDSM subculture is first and foremost a social group, there's no reason to imagine that all kinky people are involved in it, any more than it's reasonable to expect that all gay men are involved in the gay men's club culture described by Orne (2017)—and indeed, statistics strongly suggest that most gay men are not (Rosenberg et al., 2011). Participation in the

BDSM Scene is not required to be "kinky" any more than participation in gay men's club culture is required to be "gay."

As best I can define it, broadly speaking, "kinky" people enjoy a vaguely defined set of practices known as BDSM with mutually consenting partners, whereas people who prefer ambivalent consent for similar practices might be described as abusive and people who clearly want victims who have not consented for similar practices might be described as torturers (Taylor and Ussher, 2001). Throughout the rest of this book, I'll mostly talk about "kinksters" and "people in the BDSM subculture," and please do not misunderstand that to mean "all kinky people" or "all people who desire BDSM." There are *many* BDSM communities, including the aforementioned gay and lesbian Leather communities (Nordling et al., 2005; Rubin, 2000) and the dyke + trans BDSM community (Bauer, 2014), as well as a community of spankers (Plante, 2005), and even a small community of people who engage in Christian Domestic Discipline (DeGroot, Carmack, and Quinlan, 2015). *All* of these communities overlap, at least a little, with the pansexual BDSM subculture that I am shorthanding to "the Scene" and "the BDSM subculture." Even aside from all these people who are part of BDSM-related social communities, there are almost certainly many, many more people who engage in BDSM privately (Bezreh, Weinberg, and Edgar, 2012), and those privately kinky people's values, norms, and practices probably have relatively little to do with the people and social world I'm describing. In short, "BDSM practitioner" does *not* mean that someone is in the Scene, but basically everyone in the Scene is a BDSM practitioner.

I have a little bit of information about "privately" kinky people, but all of the people I have information about were publicly kinky enough to be willing to take a survey targeted at "people who considered themselves part of the BDSM subculture" or volunteer to do an in-depth interview with a researcher investigating BDSM, so I'm more inclined to say they're in a grey area between public and private kink. Even "Scene involvement" itself can be a very ambivalent concept, as many people join, leave (sometimes for years at a time), and then come back. There are, at any given time, far more people who are hazily involved in the Scene than people who are clearly involved in the Scene. Throughout this book, I will explicate the values, norms, and practices of this core group of highly and consistently involved members and describe their effects on kinksters who are more peripheral in the Scene.

HOW TO READ THIS BOOK

No sociologists have published a book about the post-FetLife, post–*Fifty Shades* Scene; for that matter, nonacademic books explaining the social world of the Scene are pretty scarce, too. So I'm optimistically assuming that the audience for this book is going to be somewhat eclectic, and I'm likewise assuming that what you take away from this book is going to inevitably reflect why you came to it.

For Sociologists

Since the earliest days of sociology with Durkheim's (1897) classical study of suicide, one of the founding principles of sociology is that society and culture can profoundly affect even the most intimate and seemingly individualistic aspects of people's lives. In this study, I show how the BDSM subculture differs significantly from mainstream culture in its understanding, interpretation, and experience of the physical, emotional, and relational aspects of BDSM. This subcultural influence is so strong that it can (re)shape people's basic physical experiences of pain and pleasure. I also explicate the many rules and norms the Scene employs to try to regulate members' behavior and resist drifting into actual criminality—in spite *and* because of its status as a highly stigmatized deviant community.

For Sexuality Scholars

As discussed earlier, this book enthusiastically participates in Orne's (2017) project of carnal sociology by explicitly discussing sex, sexuality, and pleasure as corporeal experiences. It does not delve deeply into theoretical development. Following the principles laid out by sociologist Robert Merton (1967), who argued that data must be the foundation of all good theoretical development (an argument more recently picked up by Besbris and Khan [2017]), I argue that our data on BDSM are too rudimentary to support intense theoretical exploration. Instead of pretending to a level of data sophistication that simply does not exist in this area of study, this book provides rich empirical information from multiple data sources to inform future theoretical development once we have a better understanding of this supercomplicated and nebulous thing that is BDSM. This book will publish the first large-scale survey findings about the American BDSM subculture, with more than 1,600 respondents, and contains the largest interview sample (70 interviewees) as well as the most geographically diverse ethnographic observations to date.

For Mental Health Professionals and Social Workers

It is very difficult at present to find a picture of what BDSM relationships look like outside of a highly dysfunctional clinical context or the often somewhat rosy and idealistic portrait many BDSM advocates provide. This book will give you a more realistic sense of how kinksters imagine themselves, what they aspire to in their identities and relationships, and some of the common places where a mismatch appears between ideals and realities. You should have a good sense from reading this book of what "the average kinkster" is like and what "an average kinky relationship" is like.

For Undergraduate and Graduate Sociology Students

This book aims to provide a rich methodological experience as you contemplate some of the weird challenges of doing insider interviews and ethnography as a member of a sexually explicit subculture. Along the way, I'll provide an overview and introduction to some of the core principles in the sociological studies of deviance, sexuality, and gender.

For the Privately Kinky and Kink-Curious

Yes, we have a label for you in the Scene (taken from the term *bicurious* for heretofore hetero- or homosexual people interested in exploring sexual experiences with the other side). Maybe you're sitting on the fence, wondering if you "really are kinky" and if you should take the plunge and show up for a kink event near you. Maybe you were a fan of *Fifty Shades of Grey* and want to know what real BDSM lives look like. You'll find a lot about real-world kink identities, relationships, and experiences in the Scene in this book that should help you make up your mind. But be warned: I haven't sugarcoated things here to make them easier to digest for you here the way many introductory BDSM educators will. This is the nitty-gritty of the Scene, not its rosy face for newcomers.

For Interested "Vanillas"

As I'll explain in the next chapter, the line between kinky and vanilla is a thin one that the Scene maintains largely for its own convenience. I expect that some of you will be reading this because your kinky family member or friend wanted you to better understand their lives. I have striven in this book to fairly and accurately represent us, and what I most hope you will learn from this book is the truth about the extravagant pleasures and staggering mundanity that is life in the Scene. I hope that you will read with an open mind.

For My Fellow Kinksters

The greatest moments of sociological insight are the ones that take us outside ourselves, making the familiar strange. I hope that this book opens your eyes to aspects of the Scene that you never noticed or never had words to explain before. And I want us to be honest about our problems, even as we celebrate the things that make our lives so much fucking fun. And for you, a different word of caution: nothing in this book is intended to be representative of *everyone* in the Scene, so if your experience differs wildly from something or many things you see here, please don't assume that I have made an error—maybe you're just unusual or in a different place.

For everyone reading, I'll show how this deviant subculture tries to regulate and influence intensely personal behaviors in an unusually public context. It not only regulates how kinksters *do* BDSM in a practical sense, but it also regulates the relationship contexts they do it in and the meaning they find from it, and teaches them how to *perform* BDSM. Additionally, I'll show how the subculture sometimes fails to regulate behavior in patterned ways. I don't know that the crisis of the Scene in 2017 was really predictable, but it is traceable back to some key conflicting values and norms in the Scene leading up to it. However, to make this book purely a story of failure would be a great disservice to all the kinksters who found—and still find—a home in the Scene. Sociology, by its nature, tends to be grimly analytical because it's a problem-oriented discipline. It's hard to make a sophisticated-sounding argument about joy, so I'm not going to try; instead, I'll simply say at the outset that most of the kinksters I interviewed in 2012 were pretty darned happy with their lives in the Scene. Thus I've made a scholarly choice to emphasize happiness and pleasure in this book, because that's what kinksters talked about.

The arc of this book will take you from the micro (individual) toward the more macro (community/social) level of life in the Scene. I'll start with identities, then move to relationships, and then to group norms and rules.

In chapter 1, I'll explain how kinksters learn to define "kink/BDSM" and "kinky," and to construct socially meaningful identities for themselves as kinksters. Chapter 2 tackles the complex question of what kinksters get out of doing BDSM, with a particular focus on how they experience BDSM as sexual or not. Chapter 3 examines the way the Scene teaches kinksters to do relationships in a specifically consensually nonmonogamous/polyamorous way. Chapter 4 looks at the way kinksters do BDSM relationships. Chapter 5 explains Scene demographics as well as behavioral and attitudinal norms. Chapter 6 describes the real-life world of dungeons and the Scene's style of performative BDSM. Chapter 7 looks at how the Scene constructs positive and negative social status for members. And the conclusion reflects on the Scene's world of BDSM versus the somewhat speculative world of BDSM outside of it.

So with that plan in mind, let's start with an important social question of definitions: namely, who gets to decide what it means to be "kinky" in the first place?

CHAPTER ONE

BECOMING "KINKY"

EVERYONE'S A LITTLE BIT KINKY . . .

My friend Alex—who is, to use the popular parlance of the Scene, "kinky as fuck"—loves to tell a story about a ballerina they once had sex with. Knowing about Alex's love of kink, the ballerina initially refused to sleep with them, insisting that she was vanilla. Alex assured her that they didn't need kink to have a good time and that they really just love sex, too. So she agreed to have sex with them. Once they started having sex, laying on her back, she crossed her legs onto her chest and encouraged Alex to push her legs down. She kept encouraging Alex until they were eventually *choking her with her own ankles* while fucking her. And so, Alex likes to conclude, they had some of the kinkiest sex of their life with a "vanilla" girl.

The story plays well at BDSM parties because (1) by the standards of the Scene, it sounds like really hot sex, and (2) it supports one of the favorite beliefs of folks in the Scene: everyone's a little bit kinky (although even by the standards of the Scene, getting choked by one's own ankles while having sex is probably more than a "little bit" kinky). One of the women I interviewed, Mila, articulated this perspective particularly well, saying,

> I honestly think that if you delve deep enough into anybody's sexual relationship, with very few exceptions, you will find that there's at least a little something that would be considered kink. When you think about it, there is a power dynamic that exists in every single relationship. You don't have to call that kinky. However, when you're thinking about how you relate to your partner in bed, there's someone that's the top, there's someone who consistently kind of drives the sex—that's a little bit kinky. When you climb on top of somebody else and fucking ride them, that's a little bit kinky. Vanilla sex is the missionary position. That is what that is. Anything aside from that is a little bit kinky. If you enjoy giving blow jobs, that's a little bit kinky.

23

Mila's view is common among folks in the Scene: many kinksters argue that if you scratch the surface of just about any sexual relationship, you'll find a dynamic that defies social constraints and expectations about what sex is supposed to be and include. According to this perspective, society has a notion of what "normal" sex is supposed to be and look like, but most people don't come close to meeting it. In this chapter, I'll begin by exploring the very ambiguous larger cultural context that shapes the definition of *kinky*, and then explain how the BDSM subculture shapes kinky identities within the Scene. I'll conclude by describing why those identities are so important to the kinksters who cherish them.

More than most people, kinksters tend to be extremely aware that *kinky* is a very subjective label—a cultural product of social time and space. Most people in or out of the Scene agree that there are things that are *obviously* kinky in the sense that society says that they're sexual or sexual-like things that are way outside of the acceptable norms of sex and desire. Despite social labeling, many people still find some of these things arousing. For example, studies consistently find that around 50 percent of all women show signs of physical arousal from reading graphic accounts of rapes, and fairly large numbers will even say they're aroused (Critelli and Bivona, 2008; Suschinsky and Lalumière, 2011). To most kinksters, that sounds pretty kinky. Tellingly, to the best of my knowledge, despite years of research about women's rape fantasies, no one bothered to research men's rape fantasies (as victims) until Lehmiller (2018) did so, finding that 50 percent of men also said they fantasized about being raped (while two-thirds of women did; p. 27). (And just to bypass any curiosity or concerns, let me hasten to add almost no one *actually* wants to be raped. These are just fantasies.) In order to manifest these types of fantasies in a relatively safe and regulated way, the Scene has constructed an entire set of practices that it euphemistically labels "consensual nonconsent" (CNC) to try to avoid the negative connotations of rape. Even in the Scene, CNC and "rape play" are considered "edgeplay"—that is, *very* kinky (Bezreh, Weinberg, and Edgar, 2012; Newmahr, 2011). But if something that's very kinky by everyone's standards arouses the literal majority of men and women occasionally, then "very kinky" desires are actually statistically normal.

You might reasonably counter with, "But most women and men don't actually engage in 'rape play' or even want to, so that hardly seems like a convincing argument for the idea that 'kinky' is 'normal.'" If I subsequently point out that the millions of women who bought *Fifty Shades of Grey* probably weren't reading it for its in-depth character studies and that Lehmiller's

(2018) study shows that BDSM fantasies are some of *the* most common sexual fantasies, you might still reasonably counter that most of those consumers and fantasizers aren't actually entering into the kinds of "owner-submissive" relationships at the heart of *Fifty Shades*. There's obviously a lot of room between fantasizing about something and actually engaging in it, and at most, these numbers show widespread kinky desires, not widespread kinky activities. The frequency of these fantasies inevitably raises the question of what is stopping people from manifesting them. My own research and that of others allows me to answer only the complementary question, which is: What conditions facilitate people manifesting those desires in a fairly public social context?

Yet it's not just the disconnect between fantasy and behavior that makes kink feel less common than it really is: kink also feels less common because the standards for what's kinky are constantly changing. Society cheats here, because as something becomes more common, society stops thinking of an activity as kinky and thus gets to ignore how kinky we're collectively becoming. Consider how oral sex was considered kinky in the 1950s, but now it's considered normal (Kinsey, 1948; Chambers, 2007); likewise, anal sex used to be considered pretty kinky but is slowly finding its way into mainstream sexual practices (Kaestle and Halpern, 2007). Bondage is still technically defined as kinky (and it's the first word in the BDSM acronym), yet the Spencer's store at my local mall has started selling increasingly high-quality rope and handcuffs that were once sold only in the basements or back rooms of windowless sex shops. No longer zoned to the decrepit side of town, sex shops themselves have gone mainstream (Brents and Sanders, 2010). The bright glass storefronts of feminist sex shops openly sell a colorful variety of vibrators, dildos, and other toys (Comella, 2017)—all of which were once considered kinky. Biting and hickeys appear pretty popular in the mainstream, too, but they seem at least a little bit kinky to me (in the Scene, some of the most impressive bruises are from biting). What's kinky is just a matter of perception, and that perception tends to change fast. Yet no matter how you define *kink*, statistics indicate that Americans and people in most other developed countries have gotten increasingly experimental in their sexual lives during the last 50 years (Twenge, Sherman, and Wells, 2015). Much like punk culture (Hebdige, 1979), it feels like kink is perpetually getting mainstreamed, then having to go in a different direction to stay edgy.

Although society tries to label some things kinky and other things not, in reality, small-scale social interactions are much more important than broader social norms in shaping personal identity with regards to kink. We learn a lot about sex from pornography, movies, books, and our friends (Guttmacher Institute, 2017), but in the end, what we learn from our partners generally seems to vastly outweigh almost anything we learn from those other contexts, *especially* for people dating outside of conventional heterosexual ("heteronormative") contexts (Lamont, 2017). Dating happens in an unusually private social context, which complicates the social construction of kink because a single partner can have a powerful influence on your attitudes, perceptions, and behaviors (Giordano, Longmore, and Manning, 2006). Thus, if you date someone who thinks everything you like to do is normal, it doesn't feel so kinky to you, even if most people think it's really kinky.

For some people, especially members of strict religious groups like Mormons or Hasidic Jews, society's judgment in the bedroom might be very loud; for these groups, regulating sexuality and sexual expression is an important aspect of social control (Farmer, Trapnell, and Meston, 2009). But if you're from a more liberal background and you and your partner are basically in accord about what you want, then "kinky" can start to feel "normal" very quickly. My husband, who had a collared submissive and a collection of sex toys that causes even most kinky folks' eyes to go big, loves to joke, "What you do is kinky. What I do is perfectly normal"—and he says the same thing whether he's talking to kinksters or vanillas. It's a good joke because it's the actual (unarticulated) attitude of so many people, especially people outside the Scene. Lehmiller's data (2018) seem to support the belief that most people have a few "weird" things that turn them on, with only 4 percent of women and 7 percent of men never having had a BDSM fantasy (p. 190), and a whopping 45 percent saying they have fantasized "about fetish objects—objects that one relies on for feelings of sexual arousal" (p. 42). People just aren't in the habit of talking about their weird kinks or admitting how weird their kinks really are—to themselves or others. But in order to make the transition to actually identifying as kinky and joining the BDSM subculture, a person *does* have to admit that to both themselves *and* others.

SO WHAT IS "REALLY" KINKY?

The only way to know what is "really" kinky—that is, sexual activities that really are abnormal—would be to have reliable data on what most people actually do in bed. We don't. So the next best way to figure out what's really kinky is to see what people who call themselves kinky like to do. FetLife logs the most popular things self-identified kinky people say they're into. Discounting oral sex (#2) and anal sex (#5), the 10 most popular fetishes are: bondage, spanking, hair pulling, blindfolds, biting, talking dirty, hand-cuffs, discipline (which is every bit as vague as it sounds, but basically means systematically shaping someone else's behavior), collar lead/leash, and lingerie. In my opinion, none of those things seem shockingly kinky; I'd wager that the majority of you reading this have done at least two, if not more, of the things on that list, even if you don't self-identify as kinky. So are these things *really* kinky? The FetLife list continues with: candle wax, masturbation, toys, Master/slave, ass play (which includes, but is not limited to, anal sex), roleplay, erotic photography, mutual masturbation, high heels, and dildos. Although I will definitely concede that Master/slave relationships seem pretty far outside the norm, aside from that, most of the things on this list don't seem shockingly kinky.

It's only when we get into the 20s on the list that some of the items sound kinkier: sex in public, vibrators, breast/nipple torture, pain, strap-ons, whips, humiliation, rough sex, bare-bottom spanking, and exhibitionism. There was undoubtedly an era where vibrators seemed kinky (Maines, 2001), but it's hard to think of them that way in 21st-century America. Conversely, sex in public was probably normal for most of human history (privacy is something that few people had historically and a significant chunk of the world's population still lacks) (Ryan and Jetha, 2010), and thus has only come to be considered kinky in the last couple of hundred years. But I'm guessing that most people would still agree that nipple torture, whips, and blatant exhibitionism (in the BDSM world, "exhibitionism" is defined as actively enjoying people watching you engaging in BDSM or sex or showing off your body, not the medical definition of "flashing" people) are still pretty kinky. Meanwhile strap-ons, rough sex, and bare-bottom spanking would probably fall into the "fairly kinky" category (with the caveat that strap-ons generally seem to be kinkier to straight people than to women who have sex with women).

In short, without good scientific data about what's normal to do or even much about what's *perceived* as normal, nobody really knows what makes a person, their proclivities, or their activities "really kinky" because there is no standard of "vanilla" to clearly measure against. When it comes to judging what's kinky, as the US Supreme Court has said about pornography (Hagle, 1991), the best metric we have is that "we know it when we see it."

Alternatively, we could argue that it's kinky if kinksters say it is, but I don't know who has more power to decide what's kinky: kinksters or mainstream society. And we're always left with the question of whether the things that self-described kinksters like to do are really *that* different from what vanillas like to do. My suspicion is that the answer is yes, but no one is in a great position to say for sure.

EVERYONE'S A LITTLE BIT KINKY . . . BUT MAYBE NOT QUITE LIKE THAT

Despite the common belief in the Scene that "everyone's a little bit kinky," kinksters tend to imagine themselves, their lives, and their relationship practices as being very different from those of so-called vanillas. But if kink is so hard to define, and everyone's little bit kinky, what really distinguishes people in the BDSM Scene from the supposed vanillas outside the Scene? A vanilla acquaintance of my friend Alex accidentally summarized the answer when he said, "Sure, I like to do kinky things with my wife in our bedroom—but that doesn't mean that I want to pay money to spend my Friday nights doing it in clubs, wearing leather, and talking about it." His comment highlights the subtle and not-so-subtle differences between kinksters and vanillas, which mainly come down to: (1) scales of kink, (2) public display/exhibitionism, (3) subcultural values, and (4) the financial and social value of these to (potential) participants. I'll explain the first two here, and the other two in chapter 5.

My phrase "scales of kink" refers to the way that people who participate in the Scene heavily tend to have a taste for more extreme versions of what many people outside the Scene do casually. For example, although literally almost everyone in Lehmiller's (2018) sample reported having had BDSM fantasies, most of them were "quick to clarify their limits" with modifiers like "gentle spanks" and "just rough enough . . . but not enough to inflict real pain" (p. 25). Kinksters often distinguish between "slap-and-tickle"—the type of lightly kinky activity vanillas engage in—and the kink they themselves engage in. Phrases like "gentle spanks" and "not enough to inflict real pain" aren't very popular in the Scene, where people are much more likely to say things like my interviewee Luke, who rhapsodized about "enduring" the pain of having hundreds of needles in his body and the possibility of being "punished" with "physical pain" as an act of "submission."

Similarly, Lehmiller (2018) reports that three-quarters of his respondents had ever had bondage fantasies (giving or receiving), and one-third said they have them often (p. 21). Kinksters generally assume that outside the Scene, bondage mostly involves a person tied to a bed, using polyester "love ropes" purchased at a local sex shop, presumably for sex. In the Scene, bondage is usually much more elaborate, only sometimes explicitly sexual, and typically uses handmade ropes made from natural fibers such as hemp and jute (which Scene bondage enthusiasts mostly consider superior to machine-made polyester ropes). Beginning around 2010, bondage in the Scene became increasingly focused on "suspensions," which range from mildly uncomfortable to excruciating ways of using rope to constrict someone's body and then mostly or completely suspend them in the air. My survey results and observations indicate that bondage in the Scene usually *doesn't* include sex and is often not even obviously erotic.

The same concept of scale holds true for many other kinks as well. Lehmiller (2018) reports that the most popular types of sadomasochistic fantasies reported by his respondents were (light) spanking, biting, and whipping (p. 25). But while biting and hickeys may be considered vanilla activities, people in the Scene will sometimes allow themselves to be covered in serious bruises from heavy biting all over their bodies. Similarly, the "light spanking" that seems to be common for vanilla sex often looks very different when self-identified kinksters do it, engaging in much harder or more frequent spanking play. For instance, I interviewed a man named Bill who primarily identified as a spanking "fetishist" (meaning spanking was his main kink). He explained that he had had a partner who wanted to quit smoking and had encouraged him to discipline her by spanking her whenever she smoked. He said that he ended up spanking her at "breakfast, lunch, dinner, and before going to bed," adding with a wicked grin, "You wouldn't believe how naughty she is." Many kink events include a "best bruises" competition, and it's common for people who have "just" been spanked to be so bruised that their asses and thighs are twenty different colors, with enormous bruises literally covering the entire area.

Of course, self-identified kinksters do more than just extreme versions of the same lightly kinky things that vanilla people do. Self-identified kinksters also often enjoy doing things that are considered much more extreme by their very nature. These kinds of activities are difficult to admit to liking without at least some kinky identification, regardless of whether one actually participates in the public BDSM Scene. These activities include fairly common (in the Scene) things like single-tail whips, which are both very painful and require a lot of practice to use well; breast/nipple torture, which involves everything from using nipple clamps to poking needles through nipples to suspending a person's entire body primarily by ropes tied around their breasts; and cock and ball torture, which involves everything from stepping on or kicking testicles to encasing a penis in metal or cages to inserting medical grade metal rods called sounds into the urethra. These are not activities that fit social criteria for normal sexual or pleasurable behaviors, and engaging in them almost necessitates some self-identification as kinky. It's difficult to learn to do these things safely without at least accessing BDSM websites, but it's usually easier to learn them from kinky experts teaching classes in the Scene. Enjoying and actually engaging in these activities usually requires having a partner who also enjoys them, and it's much easier to find such people through the Scene than outside of it. Consequently, a taste for these types of "extreme" activities usually eventually leads people to the Scene, and the taste for extreme kinks is culturally self-reinforcing. Since the types of people who are culturally "forced" to participate in the Scene because of their tastes are more likely to have a taste for "extreme" kink, the Scene comes to define itself culturally by a taste for extreme kink, even though that's not necessarily the defining taste of its members.

BECOMING A KINKSTER

Many years ago, I was at a Pagan event that was semifurtively hosting a ritually consecrated private BDSM dungeon. The organizer of the dungeon, who knew me a little but not well, came up to me to let me know about it and invite me. "That's okay, thanks," I told him smiling. "I'm not really kinky."

He still (understandably) occasionally mocks me about this exchange via FetLife posts.

How does a person go from saying they're "not really kinky" to being a well-known kinky teacher, writer, and player in just a few years? Having had graphic sadomasochistic fantasies since I was five, I'm hard-pressed to explain how I managed to say that I wasn't kinky, when asked. At the same time, I wonder if highlighting those fantasies is a way to support a kinky identity that came to be very important to me—to create "narrative continuity" in my own life (Johnston, 2013). My story is funny, but it's not that unusual in the Scene. My interviews showed that there are two main paths into the Scene. In one, people meander into it and find a home there, then grow an identity as kinky based on latent desires and uncovering new ones. In the other, they identify as kinky and actively seek the Scene out. Note that there's a palpable difference between the following phrases: "I have kinky tastes," "I'm pretty kinky," and "I identify as kinky." The first statement describes something the person likes to *do* (presumably sometimes); the second uses it as an adjective to describe the *person* themselves in a broader sense; and the third takes it all the way to a matter of personal/subcultural identity—and presumably a more fixed quality of the person themselves. Outside the BDSM subculture, an identity as kinky is largely meaningless, and *kinky* is just an adjective to describe something you like to do, not a way to describe your *self*. But in the Scene, *kinky* often becomes much more than a description of tastes, expanding to become a subcultural identification and signifier for in-group status and "people like us."

LEARNING TO IDENTIFY AS KINKY

The journey to identifying as kinky sometimes starts long before entering the Scene and sometimes starts very young. Kinksters often tell stories of kinky childhood shenanigans with great amusement, implying that they were always kinky. For example, my interviewee Dylan claimed that he did his first BDSM "scene" when he was six years old, consensually binding a girl with a belt and tickling her. Many kinksters tell these kinds of stories, often invoking "born this way"–style rhetoric to describe their experiences and insisting that they can't remember a time when they weren't kinky. Yost and Hunter (2012) found that these "essentialist" constructions of kink identity were common in their survey of BDSM practitioners (in and out of the Scene). As we'll see in the next chapter, some kinksters even name "kinky" as their fundamental sexual orientation.

There's no statistical way to know how normal these kinds of kinky childhood antics are, because studies of actual sexual behavior in childhood are basically nonexistent. It's entirely possible that lots of people who grow up to have pretty vanilla tastes tied up their friends when they were younger, or perhaps they didn't—scientifically, we have no real idea. Given how subjective the labels "normal" (or "vanilla") and "kinky" are, people have to be taught to interpret them to mean that their desires—and they themselves—are kinky.

The Scene teaches kinksters to remember these kinds of childhood experiences as signs of early kinky desires. Without that social influence, kinksters can easily just assume that whatever they did was normal for everybody (and several of them told me that growing up, they assumed their behavior was normal).

Though many self-identified kinksters tell these stories of apparently kinky childhood tendencies, there was wide variation among my interviewees regarding the age at which they started to realize their interest in BDSM. Several people told stories of realizing an interest in BDSM in early puberty. Some said they didn't realize an interest in BDSM until young adulthood, typically around college age. Most of these people said that they had some vague interest in BDSM for years before they were able to manifest that interest in the Scene. And then a few others said they didn't think of themselves as having any interest in BDSM until they were full-fledged adults. For example, Mike said he had "no clue. I did not think about sex, really, in high school—until well after college. I lost my virginity at 21, and there was never some kind of hidden path that when I look back at it now tells me that I was kinky."

Identity development questions are too complex to measure well on a 1,600-person survey, so I have to rely on my much smaller (and probably much less representative) 70-person interview sample to look for patterns in the kinky identity development process. Men and women (I didn't have enough gender-nonconforming folks in that sample to make conclusions about them) appeared about equally likely to come to an identity as kinky in childhood or young adulthood versus arriving at the identity as full-fledged adults. People who were barely involved in the Scene were more likely than people who were more involved to say they'd arrived at a kinky identity later in life. However, many people who became heavily or moderately involved still arrived at kink identities later as well. The factor that showed up as by far the most prominent was age: people who were 35 or older at the time of our interview in 2012 were much more likely to say they had realized a kinky identity far later than younger folks, thanks to the internet. Because of the ages at which Americans gained access to the internet, people who were 35 in 2012 (who were 20 in 1997 when internet access became much more widely available) were less likely to have been exposed to BDSM via the internet when they were young, and almost no one older than 40 had been.

DISCOVERING THE COMMUNITY

Regardless of whether or not interviewees identified as kinky before coming to the Scene, my interviews in 2012 showed that there were several ways kinksters found the Scene. The most common one involved having a long-term partner with a shared interest in the Scene and BDSM. Polyamory was probably the second most common gateway into the Scene, as people who were interested in polyamory (which is almost always just abbreviated to "poly" in the Scene) often found that poly events functionally cross-listed with BDSM events. The third most common route was the internet. Interviewees often had vague stories about learning about the Scene through "the internet," but didn't remember particular sites or interactions. People were more likely to remember specifically becoming involved via online dating. I rarely heard of anyone using the Scene to develop a serious relationship with someone they met through online dating; rather, these dating websites were mostly just another form of social networking. While the internet as a route to the Scene obviously applied far more to people who had become more recently involved, it was not exclusive to them. Older kinksters told stories about kinky online networking via bulletin board systems (BBS) in the days before the modern internet. Many kinksters have speculated that the Scene's ties to the geek community arose partly because only geeks had such early access to the internet, which allowed them to network with fellow kinksters. However, older interviewees had also often arrived in the New York and DC Scenes via newspaper and magazine advertisements. Another common route to the Scene was through professional Dominants (people, usually women, paid to hurt and dominate others, usually men). This route worked both for people who had been employed as professional Dominants, as well as men who patronized them. And then there were women and former women who had taken the long and meandering path from the lesbian community to the lesbian Leather community to the pansexual Scene. Basically all the kinksters I spoke with in the pansexual Scene who had been through lesbian Leather communities had grown frustrated by what they perceived as the community's failure to accept trans people and bi/pansexual/queers.

Connection to any of the BDSM-adjacent communities—geek, Ren Faire, swinger, and especially Pagan or poly—often led people to the Scene as well. Many kinksters were so connected via all or most of these communities that they were hard-pressed to explain exactly how they came to be involved in the Scene. They told long and winding tales where it was basically impossible to separate out which community had ultimately led them to the Scene. For people involved with *all* these communities, participation in the Scene starts to feel almost inevitable, even if the person feels they "aren't that kinky."

Even after people discover the Scene, membership in it is not a black-and-white proposition. People usually dip their toes in, and some of them instantly become passionately and wholeheartedly involved, while others take to things much more slowly—or promptly leave. Some kinksters go to parties, socials, and weekend-long events all the time, then graduate to teaching classes and/or organizing their own gatherings. Others are more reserved, attending a few things here and there, and sometimes attending nothing for months at a time. In order to capture this gradation, my survey used a variety of measures to look at how involved respondents were in the public Scene, and I scaled responses to low (which was usually functionally none), medium, and high levels of involvement. Depending on the outcomes, sometimes the only thing that mattered was being involved in the Scene at all (medium/high versus low), while sometimes each of the three levels of involvement was significantly different from the other.

THE PERFORMANCE: FROM PUPPIES TO "RAPE"

Many factors determine whether people get involved in the Scene and stay in it. Though people on the kinkier end of the scales-of-kink spectrum mentioned earlier are almost certainly more attracted to the Scene, their level of kinkiness is perhaps secondary to one of the key factors differentiating people in the Scene from those who stay home with their kinks: a penchant for exhibitionism/voyeurism. I'm not using those terms, as a diagnosing psychotherapist might, to refer to someone's tendency to engage in illegal acts of sexual or physical display/invade others' privacy; on the contrary, the structure of the Scene intentionally creates a consensual performance space for people to enjoy watching and being watched as they engage in sex and BDSM. The label *Scene* is no coincidence: the public BDSM Scene heavily focuses on utilizing flamboyant costumes, crafting personas, and creating a sexy and kinky performance. Public dungeons usually function in part as stages for people to create intimate kinky "performances" and others to openly and guiltlessly enjoy watching them do it.

One of my interviewees, Alice, explained the spectrum of these performances well. She described in detail a comedic but vicious gang-rape scene she had witnessed at a party, involving a Jacuzzi and five people violently and rather absurdly fucking a girl I'll call Jezebel:

> She was being held under the water, and they were fucking her with dildos on a stick and still being kind of ridiculous and parodic about it, like, "That's what you get, dick on a stick." So it was sort of a comedic performance. But at the same time it was being, like, a very brutal thing. And so she came up out of the water, and she just started wailing. It wasn't a quiet cry—it was loud, shrill, prolonged, and at that point I was, like, shuddering pretty hard, seeing her come up and react like that. And she collapsed in the whirlpool, and everybody was gathered around her, and being very soothing and whatnot. And so at that point I left because I felt like . . . it was a public scene, but I felt like that moment was a little too personal to have witnesses. I remember that was the very first kink party I ever took my boyfriend to.

Jezebel's "rape" scene was a local Scene legend, and I've heard several people's accounts of it through the years. As an entertaining performance that was also conspicuously emotionally meaningful, it embodied much of what the Scene values. It was well known that Jezebel, who had previously been a victim of sexual assault, deliberately created the scene for cathartic purposes—a practice that therapists are investigating (Lindemann, 2011). This potent blend of kinky performance and emotional intensity, which straddles a line between public and intimate, is what kinksters often most admire in BDSM scenes. And yet Alice, like many kinksters, still felt the subtle distinction between the kinky performance and the more private, intimate emotional catharsis.

At the other end of the exhibitionist spectrum are lighthearted role-plays that people perform in a highly interactive fashion. Alice went on to explain:

> And then the next party I took my boyfriend to was one where my friend Amy was doing her puppy play thing and bounced up to him in puppy mode. And he ruffled her hair, and she was panting at him and being all cute. After those two parties, I was like, "Now you've witnessed the spectrum of the kink community: puppies and 'rape.'"

Puppy play can take many forms, from silly to sexy. *Photo: Torsive; Model: Ripley*

Puppy play is one form of pet play, which involves people taking on the roles of a variety of animals (the most popular being puppies and ponies). People taking on animal form usually have some type of "handler" to figuratively or literally hold their leashes. Handlers will sometimes encourage other people to feed "kibble" (cereal) to the pets, scratch their ears, or throw toys for them. Acting as a pet sometimes involves elaborate costuming gear—especially for ponies, who may wear leather body harnesses, headdresses that resemble manes, butt plugs with tails, and even special hooflike covers for their hands and feet. Lucy, who worked as a "groom" and "trainer" for pony players for many years, explained that as a groom, her job was to take care of "whatever accoutrement they have to make the person feel more pony-like, because pony play is all about someone taking on the persona of a pony and acting in that way as much as they want. Some people go really, really deep into it and really become a pony." Pet play is usually not particularly violent (although it can be) and rarely culminates in complex scenes. Kinksters seem to value it in large part for its whimsy and fun, as well as the intimate interactions that can occur between "owners," who are often Dominants (people who seek to control), and their pets, who are often submissives (people who seek to be controlled). Pet play involves deeply taking on a role; performing partly for the amusement of others, partly for the fulfillment of self; and informally interacting with others while maintaining that role.

Even for the Scene, pet play often involves exceptionally elaborate performances and roleplay. Many people who participate heavily in the Scene create less elaborate kinky personae or roles for themselves. Kinksters often use "Scene names" for themselves, in much the same way that burlesque performers, strippers, or porn stars traditionally take alternative names (Colosi, 2017). The tradition of Scene names originally began as a means of protecting people's real names and identities so that they could stay safe from being "outed" in professional contexts (which is a very real concern for many). Although some people have strong professional or personal motivation to protect their real names and identities, many people just seem

Pony play usually involves elaborate costumes, and like all pet play, can be serious or very playful. *Photo: SiRoberto; Models: Willow and MartiPaige*

to enjoy adopting an identity that allows them to basically become a cooler version of their normal, everyday selves. People frequently acquire signature styles, symbols, or looks to accompany their kinky personae, from lab coats to elaborate garter belts to rainbow tutus to superhero backpacks to elf ears to three-piece suits. (I personally know people who habitually come to events in each of these.) These costumes and identities may become integrated into people's kinky scenes: a girl in superhero underwear may be suspended in ropes so as to appear to be flying, or a man in a suit may wear a tie that functions as a leash. Zoe, who had been involved in the Scene for only a few weeks when I interviewed her, explained that one of her many pleasures from it came from "the freedom to just display yourself and have a little bit of exhibitionism and voyeurism as well. Because, really, where else are you going to get that?" An important difference between the kinds of people who just want to do kinky things at home and the kinds of people who want to join the Scene is their interest in this type of elaborate kinky public performance, roleplay, and identity.

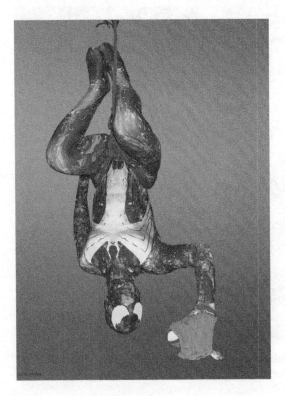

Spider-man suspensions are a costumed classic for kinksters. *Model and Photo: Cinephile87*

Bondage performances are sometimes very elaborately staged and costumed, like this Little Mermaid–themed one at Folsom Street Fair. *Photo: The Silence; Rigger and model: Bliss; Model: Mermaid Renegade*

One of the most common reasons people I interviewed who self-identified as kinky but didn't participate in the public Scene gave for their nonparticipation was, "My partner/I don't like to play in public." Without strong exhibitionistic or voyeuristic motivations, even very kinky people often feel like they don't have a good reason to pay $20 to $45 to attend kink parties unless they're looking for a partner or opportunities to socialize. (People who are looking for a partner but don't like to play in public frequently use the Scene to find partners and then basically leave). People who want their kinks to stay private don't do them loudly in semipublic places.

CAPITAL AND LOWERCASE PEOPLE

As new kinksters learn to adopt identities as kinky, create Scene names, and establish some sort of personae or presence in the Scene, Scene culture also expects them to adopt a label to describe their own BDSM role. FetLife allows you to put in your BDSM role, and the four things it shows about you constantly on the site are your username, age, gender, and BDSM role. In general, these kink roles fall into three basic umbrella categories: tops, bottoms, and switches. Tops are people who cause sensations, while bottoms are people who receive sensations; switches (people who enjoy a variety of roles) are complicated, and I'll explain them separately. New kinksters, who often just want to experiment in an unrestricted way with various types of BDSM, frequently find themselves shunted into one role or another, and which role they are encouraged to try depends on their gender identity. Women are usually encouraged into bottoming, men into Topping, and genderqueers into switching. For actual identity labels, kinksters tend to pick from a long list of power-related titles and roles that fall within these respective categories. The most common Top titles, usually gendered, are Master/Mistress, Dominant(Dom)/Domme, and Daddy/Mommy. The most common corresponding bottom titles, which are much more rarely gendered, are slave, submissive(sub), and boy/girl. Kinksters tend to generically use "Dom" and "sub" to refer to all these different roles and abbreviate the relationship pairings to D/s.

Traditional subcultural orthography capitalizes the titles associated with Tops but not the titles associated with bottoms. In extremes, people who identify as submissives and slaves will sometimes not capitalize "i" when referring to themselves in kinky writings (and occasionally capitalize pronouns when referring to their Top). Many kinksters adamantly *never* capitalize these titles and incessantly mock people who do, but because the majority habit is capitalization (less for Tops than for Doms and Masters), I'm following the cultural trend for this ethnography. Although people can theoretically also identify as Tops or bottoms, or sadists (almost never capitalized), masochists, or sadomasochists, my observations and survey data show that they rarely do. The Scene regards Topping/bottoming and sadism/masochism much more as activities focused on sensation than personal identities and values the relationship potential of "power exchange" relationships focusing on Dominance and submission much more; consequently, kinksters are much more likely to identify as Doms and subs than Tops and bottoms.

The Scene has historically had little conceptual room for switches, although it has grown much more flexible in this regard over time. When I first started teaching workshops on switching at kink events in 2014, several of them rapidly turned into group therapy sessions in which the switches present complained about how the Scene ignored the reality of their identities; within just a few years, participants were usually much more laid back. Discussions constantly happen in the subculture about what it means "be a Dom" or to "Dominate," "be a sub" or "submit," but almost never focus on what it means to "be a switch" or "to switch." This skepticism continues partly because the Scene defines "switches" and "switching" so vaguely that it's correspondingly easy to define them out of existence (although conversely it's easy to argue that "everyone is a switch," but it's not a popular argument).

Switches include people who enjoy taking on submissive and Dominant roles in relationships as well as people who enjoy the actual changing of roles in and of itself. Theoretically, switching applies to changing between Topping and bottoming, sadism and masochism, and various types of power exchange; in practice, people ambiguously use the term to refer to all three. To further confuse the category, many people who identify as switches do not, in fact, switch within their relationships; they simply happen to enjoy both Dominance and submission in general or with different partners. Most importantly for these purposes, there's almost no popular concept of what "switch relationships" look like in the kink subculture. Although many people *have* switch relationships, the subculture does little to promote, explain, or encourage them. My interviewee Lucy admitted that it took her years to finally "come out as a switch," and that it was actually more difficult for her than coming out as Queer was. She says she didn't like admitting that she likes to hurt people, and complained that "switches get a bum rap." Many events have color-coded bracelets, ribbons, or tags so that people can label themselves as Tops, bottoms (the more generic terms associated with Dominance and submission), and sometimes switches, but people often avoid the switch tag. "Kinky speed dating" events are common at many large events, with the goal of helping people find BDSM play at the event (not usually long-term partners). I have attended many of these sessions, at many events around the country, and they always have the same structure: Tops sit on one side of an aisle of chairs, bottoms sit on the other and rotate—and switches are told to just pick a side. In short, Dominance and submission and *being* a Dominant or a submissive are central to Scene culture, so central that people who prefer switching in the Scene often compare their experiences of invisibility in it to the experiences of bisexuals in the larger culture.

Those same kinky speed dating events also make it abundantly clear that D/s roles are incredibly gendered in the Scene: having a line of Tops and a line of bottoms mostly means having a line of men and a line of women, dotted with a few exceptions. Yet, as other sociologists have observed (Martinez, 2018; Simula and Sumerau, 2019), kinksters tend to be strangely reluctant to acknowledge the deeply gendered reality of these roles in the Scene. Scene ideology insists that anyone can be anything and doesn't like to admit how much Topping/Dominance are tied to masculinity and bottoming/submission to femininity. In fact, when I published the results of my survey on FetLife with regards to these roles, several kinksters openly mocked my findings as clearly incompetent because I found so few women Tops and men bottoms. Their mockery was telling, since anyone can see how severely gendered these roles are, and statistical analyses of BDSM roles that don't account for gender are uninterpretable.

Previous research with small samples found that cis men are mostly Dominants, cis women mostly submissives, and genderqueers mostly switches (Martinez, 2018). My findings with a much larger sample confirm these findings, adding a further layer of complexity by separating gender-nonconforming people with vaginas from those with penises. As you can see in table 1.1, when we break the roles out in detail, when asked, "Which of the following best describes your BDSM role/relationship dynamic preference?" women and men are about twice as likely to identify as subs and Doms, respectively, as they are to identify as bottoms and Tops, while more than 50 percent of both groups of gender-nonconforming people identify as switches. I'll discuss a lot more about the nuances of these trends in chapter 4, but for now, just remember that D/s roles are deeply tied to both kink identity and gender identity in the Scene, so new kinksters' experiences depend on how easily they fit into those gender/BDSM role expectations.

TABLE 1.1. BDSM Role Identity by Gender for Medium/High Scene Involvement

Gender	Women		GNC-Vag		GNC-Pen		Men	
	%	N	%	N	%	N	%	N
BDSM Role								
Top	3%	18	5%	8	6%	8	21%	94
Dom/Master	6%	42	10%	15	8%	10	41%	183
Switch	34%	231	58%	91	50%	64	30%	133
Bottom	16%	105	6%	10	9%	11	4%	16
Sub/Slave	41%	277	21%	33	27%	34	5%	22

LEARNING TO LOVE THE SCENE: "DID YOU READ THAT IN A NOVEL?"

Faced with a series of questions about desires, motivations, and roles many have scarcely contemplated before, new kinksters are often overwhelmed by their initial exposure to BDSM. Their stories about their first exposure to public BDSM at kink parties often take on the same sort of rapturous, excited, and confused tones people have when they talk about losing their virginity (Carpenter, 2005). They glow as they talk about the new kinks they're exposed to for the first time in real life. Even for people who'd been doing BDSM privately for years, first play parties tend to be full of things that people have only read about or watched in porn before, often making a pretty serious impression as a result. Some kinksters nervously stand on the sidelines for a long time, while others immediately dive in and begin playing with friends who brought them or total strangers they've just met that night. Perhaps the most paradoxical are people who end up staying in the Scene for years who weren't all that impressed with it initially. For example, Mike, who had been in the Scene for decades, said that he was initially extremely bored, and Liz complained that she initially found the level of intimacy of play in the Scene to be extremely shallow (a complaint I also shared when I first entered the Scene). Yet both Liz and Mike ultimately said that the Scene helped satisfy deep sexual and kinky desires they couldn't fill anywhere else—so they stayed and learned to love it.

People's initial experiences of the Scene aren't always a great predictor of their futures in it. You might reasonably expect that people who instantly dive in all the way become the Scene's most devoted long-term members, but that turns out to be at best half true. If I narrow my (much larger) survey sample down to people who've been involved in the Scene for five or more years, only 38 percent of organizers and educators (who I'll call "core members") report "consistently high" involvement since entering in the Scene, and most of the rest of them (32 percent) report steadily increasing or increasing to a plateau levels of involvement. Additionally, for people who stay in the Scene for more than four years, becoming a core member is the most common *outcome* of those two levels of involvement, with half of the steadily increasing folks becoming core members and 68 percent of the consistently high-involvement folks becoming core members. The trends aren't that different with the full sample (not restricted by years of involvement), where all told, a third of people who had initially high levels of involvement left the Scene and a further 21 percent were currently on the lower end of medium involvement—meaning that the literal majority (54 percent) of people with initially high involvement become a lot less involved. By contrast, only 31 percent of people whose involvement steadily increased were now in these lower categories of involvement. To summarize: initial high involvement is no guarantee that someone will stay in the Scene, and steadily increasing involvement often results in a longer-term commitment to the Scene.

There is a process of falling in love with the Scene that is related to, but distinct from, the process of falling in love with the BDSM practices of the Scene. The Scene is a subculture, and for the people who love it, it can become a place of wonder. As people fall in love with the Scene, their descriptions tend to emphasize a sense of wild and seemingly infinite possibilities that parties provide them, and their tales are full of the feeling that amazing and unexpected things could happen out of the blue. For example, Mila described attending a party for the first time and almost instantly becoming the habitual submissive partner of a man there, then coming back to volunteer at the party "naked and covered in glitter" every month as the highlight of her month. Lane described how at her first dayslong BDSM event, not long after she had entered the Scene, a woman picked her up to play later while they were in line to register to get into the event. Lane said that she ultimately had "a really, really intense sadistic scene with this woman, which was the furthest I had gone on that. Which was kind of—it was weird. Mostly I flogged her and spanked her and used various thuddy implements, and she was screaming and covered in bruises." New kinksters' stories tend to emphasize a pervasive sense that intense, weird, and unexpected experiences can pop up at any moment.

On the other hand, more experienced kinksters' stories often foreground friendship, self, and relaxation, while colorful kinky sights and experiences start to fade to the background. For example, Mary, who was now much older, described her experiences of Camp O-Town when she was younger as an idyllic paradise where she could just be her kinky self in the company of people she cared about:

> You would be with your friends and family in a cabin, and we would always do [wax play for other people]. It was this beautiful, like, cabin with a big porch around some trees, and the wind would blow through the gauze room dividers. So I loved that weekend immersion of not having to wear clothes, of just being with everybody, and being in role [of kinky person] for the whole weekend.

As kinksters gain experience, rather than describing a sense of overwhelming newness, they talk more in terms of serenity, companionship, and just general good times.

However, sometimes that weird background still gets thrust into the foreground, and they're sharply reminded that things that have started to feel normal objectively really aren't. Connor, who had been in the Scene for many years when I interviewed him at Camp O-Town, said,

> But then again, when I tell certain [vanilla] people about events like the ones we're at now, I'm just like, "Oh yeah, so I went to this one, and there were these women being crucified, and they were screaming, and it was really awkward because I was trying to eat my ice cream in peace," and people just look at me and go, "Did you read that in a novel?" And I'm like, "No, it's in September . . ."

Returning to the theme of the introduction that "your fantasy is my reality," kinksters who stick around learn to revel in the sense that they're doing something that just doesn't feel very likely—something that feels stranger than fiction.

US VERSUS THEM: KINKY VERSUS VANILLA

Over time, kinksters learn to identify themselves as "kinky" as a subcultural identification—not just as an adjective to describe something they like to do for kicks. As they learn to think of themselves as kinky in this context, the Scene teaches them to differentiate themselves from "others"—in this case, "vanillas." Kinksters often characterize vanilla (sometimes called "normal") people as boring, sexist, bad at communicating, unsuitable partners for kinksters, and even rather unlikely friends. For example, Lane said that she still had friends outside of the Scene but that her vanilla friends looked to her for information on kinky sex, saying, "I've given several of [my vanilla friends] lessons on how to do things. My best friend from grad school started dating this kinky woman. She says she's so vanilla she's flavorless. So I was like, 'Okay, here are things that you can do that will not be scary for you but okay for her. Also, here's how you fist someone.'" It's common for highly involved kinksters' entire voluntary social network (meaning people they see by choice, not for work or family obligation) to be fellow kinksters. Pat, a longtime BDSM educator, explained that he only had "like five or six real hard, dyed-in-the-wool, vanilla friends. And that's because we have other really strong interests in common. But even then, they'll be like, 'All right, I'm

done! I don't want to hear any more about your thing and the weird stuff!'"
The idea that kinksters mostly associate with other kinksters is so deeply
ingrained that a kinkster's vaguely mentioned "friend" is often assumed to be
a fellow kinkster unless they are described as "vanilla."

Kinksters' skepticism about the success of romantic/sexual relationships
with vanillas is less surprising than their skepticism about friendships with
vanillas. One of the first questions kinksters will ask a friend in the Scene
upon learning they're in a new relationship is, "Are they in the Scene?" If the
answer is no, kinksters often respond with doubts, especially if the newly
partnered kinkster has been in the Scene for a long time. Although several
of my older male interviewees were in long-term relationships with vanilla
women, three of them were cheating on their wives/partners, which certainly
lends some credence to the Scene's general subcultural skepticism about the
success of kinky/vanilla relationships. Brian, who was only just beginning to
explore the Scene, had arrived in it because he wanted to "try new things"
after having finally left his marriage, which he characterized as "very vanilla,
very . . . not much excitement. The same thing over time." Ben, who had
been in the Scene for many years, spoke with exasperation about his 17-year
relationship with a vanilla woman, jokingly describing it as "*real* S&M"—
meaning that one of the most frustrating and sadomasochistic things a
person could do was be in a relationship "with somebody who is not kinky
when you're kinky. I've done vanilla, and I've done kink. I couldn't give up
kink if I met the vanilla girl of my dreams. I couldn't do it."

Liz said that the mismatch for her with a previous vanilla partner was
deeper than mismatched desires; she framed him as also too bad at communicating for her to have a successful relationship with him. She explained,

> The vanilla guy I was with before—we had a completely open relationship,
> but he never took advantage of the openness [i.e., he never had sex with
> anyone else]. And it was almost as though his kink was me being with other
> guys, but I didn't learn that until almost the end of our relationship. So I
> never knew what I was supposed to tell him. Like, he didn't really give me
> the rules of communication about what happened, just that it was allowed.
> I really felt like I was taking advantage of his sweet vanilla niceness—"I'm
> going to go off and do all these things [with other people]," and the dynamic
> ended up feeling uncomfortable for me.

In Liz's description, "the vanilla guy"—who in fact, maybe had what is
known in the Scene as a cuckolding kink (meaning he gets off on her having

sex with other people when he's not allowed to)—couldn't own up to his kink, couldn't clarify his communication boundaries, and/or was letting her take advantage of him by sleeping with other people. These are the kinds of problems kinksters learn to expect to have in relationships with vanillas.

The kinkster/vanilla dichotomy that kinksters construct embodies an attitude of skepticism and derision toward vanillas and pride in the culture of the Scene. The quote that best encapsulated this attitude for me was one I heard from a BDSM event organizer who told me, "In my opinion, 'vanilla sex' is any sex that's poorly negotiated." I have quoted this to many fellow kinksters since, and the general reaction is, "That seems really harsh." But I think it only seems harsh because of its blunt phrasing. Tony, who echoed what many kinksters often say, said the same basic thing more gently:

I feel like if I could manage to ["be sexual with a lot of people"] in the normal world by what I perceive as the normal rules, I would feel shitty about myself. I mean, because it's just this sort of game of roulette that you're playing with consent and with sort-of just, like, trying to feel the situation out and subtly inch toward it.

Many kinksters like Tony perceived the "normal world" as lacking real value for consent and communication. In general, kinksters see vanillas as bad at consent, bad at talking about what they want sexually, bad at communication in general, and bad at managing their relationships—and see themselves as better at these things. Creating these lines between themselves and vanillas helps to perpetuate feelings of in-group pride and identity among kinksters, while also encouraging them to mostly choose kinky sexual and romantic partners from the Scene, and thus sustaining their involvement.

THE SCENE IS GREAT FOR KINKY PEOPLE'S SELF-ESTEEM

Feeling better about themselves is a crucial theme in many kinksters' journey to the Scene. Many of my interviewees reported growing up with a sense of shame around their kinky desires. For example, Doyle, who grew up in a conservative religious family and originally figured out he was kinky by reading fiction, said he repeatedly threw away and repurchased Anne Rice novels due to his own conflicted feelings about the desires they aroused in him. Ashley said she realized she had kinky desires when she was 17, but that it was a long time "until I was comfortable with telling people about that" and even longer "before where I could comfortably act those fantasies out." Given the shame and discomfort so many kinky folks feel, we might reasonably imagine that finding a community of people to provide support would be good for them. When I went to test this hypothesis, I was staggered by how true it was. I found large (much larger than I expected), statistically significant differences in reported self-esteem from kinky people with no/low Scene involvement compared to those with medium involvement, and between those with medium involvement versus high involvement. For low involvement, 57 percent of people agreed or strongly agreed with the statement, "On the whole, I feel like I have good self-esteem"; that number increased to 65 percent for people with medium involvement and increased even more, to 76 percent, for people with high involvement.

When I broke those numbers out by gender, sexual orientation, and BDSM role, I found that while the numbers between each of those groups differ a lot, the *relative* differences by level of Scene involvement held pretty constant across them. For example, as we'll see more in chapter 4, submissive women have much lower self-esteem than most other groups, but they still have higher self-esteem when they have greater Scene involvement. The major exception to this trend is for bisexual men, who have radically better self-esteem when they participate in the Scene. *All* of the 6 bisexual men with low involvement felt they had poor self-esteem, but only 13 percent of the 26 bi men with medium involvement did.

Some of this difference in self-esteem seems to be the product of what sociologists call a "selection effect": in this case, that means people with higher self-esteem are more likely to join and become more involved in the Scene in the first place. My data provide some support for this idea, because people with higher levels of Scene involvement were also more likely to agree with the statement, "Since I was a teenager, I feel like I have had good self-esteem." However, the differences here by level of involvement, while still statistically significant, were smaller than those for current self-esteem. Moreover, that selection effect doesn't account for most of the differences in self-esteem. Thirty-three percent of those who were highly involved strongly agreed with the statement, "When I entered the BDSM Scene, it really improved my feelings of self-worth," versus only 20 percent of those with medium involvement. (The numbers for "agree" were basically the same for each, at 40 percent and 42 percent, respectively.) Since the majority of kinksters with both medium and high levels of involvement reported that it had really improved their feelings of self-worth, these numbers strongly suggest that the Scene both attracts kinky people with higher self-esteem *and* does a good job of improving the self-esteem of its target members.

SHADES OF GRAY

Most kinksters tend to think that the defining dimension of the Scene is an interest in kink. They usually assume that all really kinky people will eventually find their way into the Scene and love it once they get there. For example, I've often found that kinksters display skepticism about the happiness and compatibility of my marriage because my husband so rarely goes to events, even though I go all the time. When I try to explain that he's at least as kinky as I am, they're often perplexed: kinksters generally assume that all kinky people want to be in the Scene, forgetting that many (like my husband) just aren't very excited about public play.

Though it's almost certainly true that most kinky people aren't in the Scene, it's a little more plausible to say that most "very kinky" people are. People who enjoy kinks that are way outside the norm would need or want a group of people to support them and their interests (especially since most of those activities require special tools and training to do safely and well). My sense from interviewing people is that there are probably still more people outside or at the edges of the Scene who are very kinky (even by the standards of the Scene) than there are in the Scene. But it's very difficult to assess how kinky someone is. For example, I used to jokingly say that my partner Curtis was "kinkier than me, even though I'm really kinkier than he is." That sentence sounds illogical, but he and I both agreed to the truth of it: he *needs* kink much more than I do in order to enjoy intimate sexual-type interactions, but I love doing things that are much more extreme than what he was willing or interested in doing. So who's kinkier? I don't think anyone could ever really say. Deciding what is and isn't kinky isn't a black-and-white matter: kinky is a complex, ever-changing spectrum that really just comes down to shades of gray.

Ultimately, the defining feature of the Scene is not the nature of its kinky practices, its members' need for kink, or their desire for exhibitionistic/voyeuristic performances. Although kink culture tends to frame BDSM as the defining feature of the Scene, kinksters' social lives in it tend to be much more important, with about a fifth of my interviewees spontaneously commenting that kinky social life was their favorite part of their lives in the Scene. If I had to summarize the social world of the Scene in one sentence, I would say, "Come for the beatings, stay for the friends." Most kinksters spend most of their time at happy hours, parties, or events *not* engaging in BDSM play—they just hang out with their friends. Yet BDSM is still the background tie that binds this loose social world together, and as we'll see in the next chapter, the Scene spends a lot of cultural resources teaching kinksters how to understand, interpret, and create meaning from their own and others' BDSM experiences.

CHAPTER TWO

"DOES THIS LOOK SEXUAL TO YOU?"

Why Kinksters Do BDSM

"THERE ARE MORE THINGS IN HEAVEN AND EARTH . . ."

In the 2002 kinky romantic comedy *Secretary*, the penultimate sequence
has the film's protagonist seated at a desk for days, exhausted, hungry, and
peeing herself as she endeavors to prove her worthiness and desire to become
the full-time submissive of her boss, who has ordered her to keep her hands
on the desk and then abandoned her. Her ex-fiance mocks her, "Are you
doing something sexual right now?" and she furiously retorts, "Does this
look sexual to you?" He responds frustratedly, "I don't know!" which pretty
much summarized my own response the first time I watched the film, years
before I ever got into the Scene.

Personally and professionally, I remain fascinated by the answer to that
question. When I got into the Scene, I was constantly confused by the way
that most of the parties and events I went to allowed sex, but little that even
fit a queer-friendly and expansive definition of "sex" (e.g., strap-on sex,
oral sex, fingering, blow jobs) was happening. I often heard people (usually
women) admired for engaging in blatantly exhibitionistic sex, and there was
frequently a tone of wistfulness in that admiration, as if many kinksters themselves longed to unite BDSM and sex but hadn't quite figured out how. The
longer I stayed in the Scene, the more convinced I became that it deliberately teaches kinksters to view BDSM as being about "more than just sex" (a
phrase often repeated verbatim [Simula, 2019a]) for three main reasons. First,
desexualizing BDSM theoretically makes it more palatable to sex-negative
mainstream culture, and the Scene likes to try to keep its image relatively
"clean" for public relations purposes and to attract new members—particularly new members who are focused on BDSM as much as or more than sex.
Second (and relatedly), many BDSM clubs at least claim that local laws and
law enforcement restrict them from permitting sex. Third (and I think most

importantly), the more reasons kinksters have for wanting to do BDSM, and the more meaning they find in it, the more likely they are to continue participating in the Scene. In this chapter, I'm going to explain how the Scene teaches and encourages kinksters to find a wide variety of meanings from BDSM, even though most kinksters still say that BDSM is mostly sexual for them most of the time. Along the way, I'm going to continue to explore some of the ambiguity around the concept of *kinky* as well as some of the ambiguity in the concept of *sexual*. It turns out that it's pretty hard to say whether BDSM is sexual because it's pretty hard to say what exactly "sexual" is.

Academics took up the question of the relationship between sex and BDSM in earnest after Newmahr (2010) and Williams (2009) proposed that BDSM was "really" a "serious leisure" activity for people in the Scene, rather than a sexual activity. Newmahr (2010, 2011) went so far as to propose that "BDSM is not inherently sexual," a take that Bauer (2014)—who was an insider in the dyke + trans BDSM Scene—criticized harshly. I, too, find Newmahr's desexualized perspective problematic. I feel like Newmahr was trying to "rescue" BDSM in the eyes of mainstream society by comparing it to any other serious hobby and reassuring her readers that her research (which largely consisted of her doing BDSM with a lot of different people as a bottom) hadn't really involved anything "sexual." To be fair, Newmahr studied the Scene before a lot more events and parties started allowing sex in the early 2000s, and the New England BDSM Scene she studied is still quite conservative about sex relative to many other areas around the country. However, Newmahr lacked the larger national context to understand the geographical variation among BDSM microcultures, and thus to know that not all BDSM Scenes were as desexualized as the one she studied; nor did she seem to realize that the types of kinksters who were willing to play with and be interviewed by a researcher who was only willing to *do* nonsexual BDSM were inevitably going to have different attitudes about BDSM sexuality than the types of kinksters who expected to fuck their play partners.

Ultimately, I've come to the conclusion that Newmahr was correct that BDSM is a serious leisure activity for many kinksters, but it's preposterous to suggest that sex is simply irrelevant to it. She was somewhat right that BDSM isn't "inherently sexual," because I'm not sure BDSM is inherently *anything*. Given that BDSM is basically just an amorphous and frequently unrelated collection of activities thrown together for labeling convenience, it's not easy to clearly say what BDSM is or isn't. BDSM is an extremely subjective experience that participants interpret and feel completely differently about depending on who they are, what they're doing, and who they're doing it with. That said, all of my data indicate that the majority of kinksters seem to experience BDSM in sexual or erotic terms most of the time, and there are definite patterns in the way that people at the core and the periphery of the Scene interpret BDSM experiences.

But let's start by considering what it means for anything to be "sexual," because once you shed a heterosexist paradigm that "sex = penis in vagina," defining what is and isn't sexual gets tricky fast (Simula, 2019a). Is it only things that are arousing? Is it only things that involve genitals touching? Is it only things that result in orgasm? These days, I usually define *sex* for myself as "any activity that could reasonably be expected to potentially result in orgasm for most people," but even that definition is just a weak starting point. In the Scene, I've brought women to orgasm by kicking their genitals, and I've watched women orgasm from being whipped, and even just from being hypnotized and told to. I personally know women who have orgasmed in nonkink contexts from normal acupuncture and nongenital tattoos—but I don't think I've ever personally seen a man orgasm without some sort of direct penile or anal stimulation (for more on these sorts of gender differences, see Simula [2012]). And yet if we were ever foolish enough to define the sexuality of BDSM entirely in terms of orgasm, we'd run up against the problem that I've encountered far more women than men in the Scene who say they can't orgasm at all or have great difficulty doing so.

Overall, any attempt to judge the sexualness of BDSM is going to keep running up against a problem *Hamlet* pretty well summarizes: "There are more things in heaven and earth, Horatio, than are dreamt of in your philosophy" (I, v, 165–67). Human sexuality is mind-bogglingly diverse, and our society as a whole isn't remotely prepared to understand that; our social context constrains even our social and physical scientists, and they don't necessarily have the experiential breadth and vocabulary to begin to make sense of it all. There are a lot of actions and behaviors that are sexual that aren't really sex, and many not-very-sexual experiences that feel and look like sex. As a society, we're in the habit of defining experiences that might look sexual—like massages or gynecological exams (Kapsalis, 1997; Oerton, 2004)—as nonsexual because it suits our purposes. There's even an entire subcategory of experiences that society almost entirely defines as nonsexual— like cupping (a traditional Chinese medicinal technique that involves suction cups), wrestling, and waterboarding—that kinksters co-opt for their own purposes as BDSM. The kinky versions of these activities all look very different from their vanilla origins, with cupping focused on pain rather than therapy, wrestling lacking any system of scoring, and waterboarding being done voluntarily. These activities almost never involve sex in any way at BDSM events, but they feel palpably different when kinksters do them. I wish I could put that difference into words, but the best I can say is that these things feel "charged" in their BDSM contexts, and the intentionality affects how kinksters perform and receive those acts. Underneath all of them, even waterboarding, is a glimmer of something that I can only call *pleasure*, but *thrill* might work as well. Even kinksters themselves have never developed a good language for describing these complex physical, emotional, sensual, and sometimes sexual experiences.

BDSM AS ACQUIRED TASTE: THE "WINE SNOB" HYPOTHESIS

Part of why I hesitantly use the word *charge* to describe what separates kinky from vanilla interactions that ostensibly look the same is that the Scene heavily socialized me to its norms and ways. When I first arrived there, I would probably unhesitatingly have described that "charge" as erotic, but I learned from all my formal and informal interactions in the Scene over time to question whether that difference really is erotic or something else. As kinksters become more involved in the Scene, they learn to dissect, analyze, and savor their BDSM experiences, and they learn from other kinksters to do so in ways that deemphasize the sexualization and eroticism of their experiences in favor of . . . other things. (Kinksters themselves have never named these things.) Simultaneously, people who view BDSM in entirely sexual ways often self-select out of greater involvement, since they find a lot fewer opportunities for sex than they were hoping for—and some even complain that they feel shamed in the Scene for wanting to combine sex with their kink.

The combined results of this selection and education process are impressive and very statistically significant. When asked to check every box on my survey from a long list of reasons they engaged in BDSM lifestyle and activities, 93 percent of low-involvement kinksters and 94 percent of medium-involvement kinksters checked the (most popular) box for "sexual arousal and pleasure," but only 88 percent of high-involvement folks did. Scene involvement was also inversely related to kinksters' likelihood of describing their BDSM lifestyle and activities as sexual in general, with 32 percent of highly involved folks saying that BDSM was mostly not sexual for them, compared with 14 percent of low-involvement folks. Regardless of level of involvement, almost no one says that "BDSM is not sexual for me," with only 2, 3, and 4 percent of respondents saying this for low-, medium-, and high-involvement kinksters, respectively.

I also asked respondents to rate their level of agreement with the statement, "I prefer for my BDSM play to include sex," and the differences remain statistically significant for levels of involvement even after controlling for several other significant factors. In a multivariate regression that takes multiple factors into account simultaneously, older kinksters were more likely to prefer sexual BDSM than younger kinksters; men were more likely to prefer sexual BDSM than women; women Tops and men bottoms were much less likely to prefer sex with their BDSM than others in their gender; and through all that, with the exception of being a woman Top, by far the strongest predictor of someone's preference for sexualizing their BDSM was their level of Scene involvement, with greater involvement predicting less sexual BDSM.

This effect is extremely robust against a wide variety of controls. My friend Alex coined the term "'wine snob' hypothesis" to refer to the way kinksters learn to distinguish between and highlight "flavors" of experiences and sensations as sexual versus nonsexual that are utterly indistinguishable to people who haven't been taught to notice/believe in them. The idea is that as kinksters interact with more and more sexual and BDSM partners, they learn to focus on subtle differences that would probably be undetectable to them otherwise (and likewise undetectable to outsiders). I decided to test that hypothesis directly by adding two more controls for people's preferences for BDSM: their number of BDSM partners in the last six months, and their number of sex partners in the last six months. Both of these factors are significant, albeit in opposite directions: people with more sexual partners have a greater preference for sexual BDSM, while people with more BDSM partners have a greater preference for nonsexual BDSM. The findings support the idea that *some* of the effect of Scene involvement comes from this increased exposure, since the effects of Scene involvement are reduced by controlling for these partnerships. The effect of Scene involvement, however, remains the most important factor in the equation.

The effects of Scene involvement are even more dramatic if we look at actual behavior and not just preferences. I also used my survey data to predict the odds that someone would have had sex with their most recent new play date, and found very similar results. *By far* the biggest predictor of whether people had sex was whether they met at a BDSM event, party, or social gathering versus some sort of non-BDSM setting such as online or a vanilla setting. Controlling for several other factors, people who met their partner at a non-BDSM venue were at least six times as likely to have sex as those who met at a BDSM venue. Indeed, there was no real statistical difference in the odds of having sex if people met at a BDSM event that allowed sex versus one that didn't, which was the most dramatic evidence of how much Scene norms discourage sexual play. All the same basic factors (age, gender, BDSM role) remained significantly different, but where the respondents met actually had about twice as great an influence on whether they had sex as their own individual preferences for sexual BDSM. Thus, regardless of other factors, including their own desires, the Scene's norms against sex strongly encourage nonsexual BDSM play.

WHY ARE WOMEN TOPS/MEN BOTTOMS DIFFERENT?

I'll talk a lot more generally about BDSM roles and gender in chapter 4, but I'll briefly explain here why women Tops and men bottoms are different than everyone else with regard to their preference for sexual BDSM. The Scene generally describes the dynamics of feminine Tops with masculine bottoms as fem Dom (or sometimes Femme Domme). The fem Dom sub-subculture overlaps heavily with—yet remains strategically distinct from—professional (pro) Doms/Dommes/Dominatrixes. (In case you're wondering, there are also, much more rarely, pro subs as well. One of my interviewees, Pat, had worked as one). In the Scene, fem Doms often pointedly distinguish themselves from their professional sisters, but the distinction tends to break down quickly because so many of them dabble in professional domination, or, like my fem Dom interviewee Lily, train with pro Doms to learn their Topping skills. Lindemann (2010) has explained how pro Doms themselves draw lines between "dungeon doms" who "just do this for the money," versus "real" pro Doms who Dom for both money and pleasure.

This overlap is important in developing the sexuality of the fem Dom sub-subculture because pro doms usually make a point of not having sex with their clients so they can maintain their gray-legal status and a certain personal dignity from not being "prostitutes" (Lindemann, 2012). Thus the women who engage in pro Domming get used to not including sex with their BDSM, and the clients who come to them get used to it, too. Moreover, separate interviews that I've done with producers of BDSM pornography taught me that most fem Dom porn producers recruit most of their Doms from the ranks of pro Doms, and most of those women refuse to have sex on camera. So the cumulative cultural and personal effect of visiting pro Doms and watching fem Dom porn is that the men and women who participate in this kink tend to learn to separate it from sex. And of course, added to all those other influences is the way fem Doms and their subs run up against the mainstream cultural idea that the Scene does little to undo, which is that penetration equals power. Thus, for a fem Dom to be penetrated sexually potentially means symbolically or actually giving up her power. At this point, my impression from having taught classes on fem Dom in the Scene is that a preference for sex actually becomes a major sorting factor for people into these labels. Rather than identifying as subs and Doms, repsectively, bottom-leaning men and Top-leaning women who like sex with their BDSM learn to identify as switches largely *because* they like sexual kink.

WE AREN'T REALLY SURE ABOUT
THE SEXUALNESS OF THIS EITHER

The confusing scholarly argument about the sexualness of kink stems from two long-ignored facts. First, kinksters *themselves* don't agree about whether BDSM is mostly about sex, so if you wanted to resolve the argument, it doesn't help much to ask them. As Sprott and colleagues (2020) found with an intentionally diverse sample of "people who identified as kinky" (who were not necessarily involved in the public Scene) in Northern California, many people struggled to explain the relationship between sex and BDSM for themselves, let alone in broad terms. Second, BDSM is much too broad and complicated to have a single motivation. I asked all my interviewees for their responses to the statement, "Kink (or BDSM) is not inherently sexual." Although the statement intentionally framed the idea in objective rather than personal terms, many people chose to respond to it purely based on personal experience; for those who didn't, I always asked them to clarify their own personal experiences. Their opinions were pretty clearly divided between "That's bullshit," "That's true for some, but not for me," "That's both true and not true at the same time for me, so I guess it's sort-of true," and "That's definitely true."

In the "bullshit" camp was Lorelai's succinct response: "I think everything is inherently sexual." Others seemed to treat it as just fundamentally obvious, with little to add. Much longer and more passionate was Josh, a BDSM organizer who had struggled for years to create more "sex-positive" events (the term that kinksters themselves use to refer to BDSM events that allow sex), who said:

> I call bullshit. . . . There is something fundamentally ridiculous about the idea of having a room full of people performing sadomasochistic acts without sex [or at least] an acknowledgment that it's titillating and exciting and enjoyable, but over and above that, I have a problem with it in terms of how it represents us in the broader community. I think when people see sadomasochism and the way it's portrayed in the media, and it's like this big sort-of scary thing, the easiest way that we can disburse that fear in the vanilla community is just to be like, "It's just kinky sex games. People like to dress up as doctor and nurse, or schoolgirl and headmaster, or slave and slave owner, or whatever. We're just role playing, like, sexual fantasies, and we're having a good time." When you take the sex out, and you go, "No, it's not about sex!" then you're just a fucking sadist! You're just somebody that likes inflicting pain on someone, and it's not about sex. It's just about you being an asshole who likes to torture people. What the fuck is that? How do you sell that to vanilla people? It's patent fucking nonsense.

Josh's response was interesting because he seemed less interested in the truth of the statement and more interested in the public perception of it. Ironically, many organizers arrived at the opposite conclusion, determining that desexualizing BDSM would make it *more* palatable to outsiders. Even when they're not organizers, kinksters are often extremely self-conscious of the ethical implications and perceptions of their BDSM. Thus someone like Duncan, who wasn't an organizer, echoed Josh when he said that kink was always sexual for him, adding, "I would put that [nonsexual BDSM] in the domain of the DSM and neurotic and psychotic people, antisocial behavior. Because, I mean, even if you're not going to fuck, you should be getting aroused." As many kinksters had wrestled with the feeling that their desires were morally wrong or at least problematic at some point in their lives, the fear that they actually were, or at least might be, labeled by others as a "crazy bad person" was never far outside of their collective and individual consciousness. But in all my years in the Scene, I've never heard anyone provide a straightforward answer to Josh's basic question: if sex isn't the motivation here, what is?

Unsurprisingly, folks in the "yes for some, but not for me" camp were usually more moderate in their responses. Mark said, somewhat doubtfully, "I guess that under some circumstances it might not be [sexual]. But that's probably not the way I would say it. For me, it is inherently sexual. But I can see how for other people it could be inherently nonsexual." Connor, who was a BDSM educator and trans man, was less doubtful but explained his own response carefully:

> *Connor:* I think that that is a profoundly personal statement. I have met some people that kink is so separated from their sexuality that I get confused, and I know other people that kink cannot be separated from their sex life because there wouldn't be anything left. So I think that it is a statement that is really useful for some people, but I think it's not valid as a global statement.
> *Me:* How does it feel to you about yourself?
> *Connor:* I can't think of a kink experience that I've had that has not gotten my dick hard at some point, and therefore for me, it counts as sexual.

Olivia, meanwhile, described the bewildering experience of being someone who was totally turned on by kink while her partner wasn't. Her boyfriend had asked her to start beating and flogging him, and while initially a bit reluctant, she found she really got into it pretty fast:

> I'm really wet and I'm really hot and I really need to get laid now and he's, like—it's not sexual for him. He likes the sensation. It's not sexual at all. I'm like, is this going to be a problem? Because if you want me to do this, that's fine. I'm okay with it because I get really turned on, but I need to have some release afterwards. And he's, like, okay.

Olivia's story highlights the truth of Connor's observation that the sexuality of kink is profoundly personal: she and her partner were both really into what they were doing *together*, but they still had entirely different sexual experiences from it.

People who were in the "yes and no" camp sometimes just sounded straight-up confused. When I posed the statement to Amy, she initially responded, "I disagree wholeheartedly," then immediately began questioning herself: "Well, maybe not. Now that I think about it, no, kink [hesitating] I think it's possible to be kinky without sex, but there's still an undertone of sex to it. So maybe [hesitating] I disagree." She said that kink was always sexual for her, but her ambivalence was striking. Natalie, on the other hand, didn't sound confused about her response, although it certainly confused me:

> I agree; I think that it can be [nonsexual]. I am a pain slut. I come [orgasm] from pain. I come from Topping, which is not as common. But it is a very energetic thing for me, and I'm able to channel that. Historically, I'm stone, and the only people I really have sex with are my owners, if I have sex with them. And part of it is because I don't have sex a whole lot. Out of five Owners, I've had sex with three of them.

Natalie fit the profile of people for whom Connor said, "Kink cannot be separated from their sex life because there wouldn't be anything left." On the other hand, at the point where someone is talking about orgasming from a variety of different stimuli, is that really "nonsexual" in any conventional sense of the term? Is sex defined by genital contact, sexual pleasure, or just "feeling" like you've had sex with the other person? Responses like Natalie's raise more questions than they answer.

Others in the "yes and no" camp, like Elise, said that some kinks were sexual for her while others weren't. She said that "service kinks" like doing her Owner's laundry, "ironing his work clothes for him, and cooking dinner for him" weren't sexual—"just enjoyment and pleasure from doing something for somebody else." Then she added, "Of course, something like flogging is inherently sexy. I expect to be fucked afterwards, right. But not all kink is inherently sexual." Like Elise, most kinksters I've spoken with or interviewed who have described "service" kinks typically describe them in nonsexual terms. As we'll see later, there is a joy that submissives described in doing chores for their Dominants that almost no one described in sexual or even erotic terms (nor did the Dominants who received that kind of service describe it as erotic). Kinksters were much more likely to describe physical kinks like flogging or whips as sexual, but as we saw in Olivia's story, there was no universal response to that either.

Liz, who said that she was initially bored by the less-sexual BDSM of the Scene, had completely changed her perspective through her involvement:

> *Liz:* I had the experience of it being entirely sexual for me while I initially explored it [privately], and then I came out in the Scene and found out that so many other people use it to explore so many other things. There are people that use it to strengthen their pain tolerance, there are people

that use it to work through past issues. There are people that use it to try to see what's coming in the future. There are so many dynamic ways to use this tool to explore things that sexuality is a fairly narrow focus. But it is a useful one, very applicable.

Me: Would you say that's most of why you do it—is it's related to sex?

Liz: Yeah, that's how it was introduced to me and that's how I've used it. Although I have been interested in exploring whatever paths it takes me on.

Liz describes BDSM—especially nonsexual BDSM—as an acquired taste that people learn through exposure to the Scene and other kinksters. Although she had still mostly done BDSM for sexual reasons, she was interested in exploring many other options.

People who were just in the "it's not sexual" camp often had radically different interpretations of what BDSM means. Harriet, for example, defined BDSM in terms of emotional intimacy rather than anything sexual. Her response to my statement was, "[Kink is], at least from what I see, it's about an emotional connection that you have with a person and being able to trust them to put you in that [vulnerable] position, trust them not to go past your limits, and to know your limits." The Scene emphasizes the importance of intimacy and trust in BDSM relationships and dynamics, but most kinksters I interviewed didn't define it in terms of emotional intimacy to the exclusion of sexual arousal.

Damon was hard-pressed to explain what he got from BDSM, but was pretty sure that whatever it was wasn't really sexual:

It's hard to draw the line between "sexually arousing" and "satisfying urges that feel too primal to be intimate and sexual." . . . I'm not saying that I never go there, but yeah, giving and receiving intense stimulation that isn't inherently sexual on its own—targeting erogenous zones [for pain and intense stimulation] and things like that, I feel like that's a place that's just even more primal than sex.

The term *primal* floats around the Scene as a word that intentionally conjures kinksters trying to get in touch with "animal instincts" and abandon some of the limitations and constraints of modern society. Many kinksters who say that BDSM isn't sexual for them use this term to describe their motivations for violent play (although they more rarely describe it as their motivation for nonphysical power play like Dominance and submission).

Damon's explanation echoed those of others, who even framed scenes involving nipple clamps and fucking machines (machines designed to provide intense penetration and/or vibration) as at most incidentally sexual. In Damon's explanation, pain and intense stimulation targeting genitals isn't necessarily inherently sexual—just a means to a primal end.

Any scholar, kinkster, or person who's just plain curious looking for a straightforward answer to the question, "Is BDSM sexual?" is going to be inevitably disappointed. The best I can say is that it is sexual for most people in the Scene, most of the time. *But* the more people do it, the more often they come to say that it has the possibility to be about many things they struggle to name other than sex. We'll see some of those things later in this chapter, but I want to leave you with my absolute favorite quote from any of my interviewees. Nate, who was mostly in the "it's-not-sexual" camp, emphasized the subjective experience of BDSM, saying,

> It's like saying, "Is baseball sexual?" No. No, baseball is not sexual. Are there people who go there and get turned on by both watching and playing the sport? Yes, of course. I get turned on by math sometimes. That doesn't mean math is sexual. Maybe it is for me a little bit, but . . .

. . . BUT THE SEX GETS KINKIER

Although Scene involvement is strongly associated with less sexual BDSM, it's also paradoxically associated with much kinkier sex. Just as highly involved kinksters are about twice as likely as low-involvement kinksters to say most of their BDSM isn't sexual, highly involved kinksters are about twice as likely as low-involvement kinksters to say that all or almost all of their sex "involves aspects of BDSM." Scene involvement is also, ironically, significantly positively associated with wanting to allow sex at BDSM events: as kinksters become more involved in the Scene, they're considerably more likely to disagree with the statement "I wish more BDSM events would ban sex." Only about 5 percent of people at every level of involvement agreed or strongly agreed with that statement, but 54 percent of highly involved kinksters strongly disagreed, versus 29 percent of low-involvement folks.

The most interesting differences in sexuality by level of Scene involvement were in response to my survey question, "Are you primarily or only interested in sexual activity in the context of a BDSM encounter? That is, do you feel that your interest in BDSM essentially defines your sexuality?" Among high-involvement kinksters, 42 percent said yes and 9 percent said they were unsure, meaning that a majority thought it possible that BDSM was fundamental to their sexuality (versus 26 percent and 16 percent among low-involvement folks). Several of my interviewees described what this experience of kink as sexual orientation (Moser, 2016) was like for them, which I generally refer to as being "kinksexual." Grace said,

> I think sex isn't the center of my "sexuality." At least, like socially, I'm more interested in playing with people and sadomasochistic activities then I am in sexual activities unless I know somebody really well. [. . .] I think I could enjoy sex without kink involved, but either my past experiences with sex, or just the way I am, I certainly don't find it interesting to think about it without kink.

Nate, who had never had intercourse and described himself as "virgin," had very similar experiences as Grace. He said, "If there is not rope involved or some type of psychological or physical torture, I'm just not having any of it [arousal]." Nate added that he thought he had developed these attitudes in part because of a botched childhood circumcision that meant full erections and orgasms were always physically painful for him until recently, when he had the problem fixed surgically.

Others kinksters (all male among my interviewees) fit the more classical profile of a "fetishist" (someone who is aroused by a very specific thing). For example, Owen explained that he is a true exhibitionist in the sense that even if he does sexual things without other people watching, he always imagines that he has an audience, and that desire has always been part of him. His experience was completely the opposite of Doyle, who said that he hadn't started his sexual life as kinksexual but laughingly complained that his many years of involvement in the Scene had *caused* him to develop a sexuality defined by kink; he said he used to be able to have good vanilla sex in the past, but "I have noticed that a few times in the past couple of years I have tried having good old-fashioned egalitarian vanilla sex, and it's been immensely unsatisfying, immensely. [. . .] I think I was kinky, but I think at this point I may be kinksexual. Dammit." These stories suggest that, unsurprisingly, being "born" kinksexual tends to be highly motivating for people to become highly involved in the Scene; however, some people who stay highly involved may also find themselves drifting in the direction of sexuality defined by BDSM as well.

OTHER THAN SEX, WHY DO THIS?

As people get more involved in the Scene, they steadily pick up more motivations for doing BDSM. On my survey, I gave people a list of 12 reasons to choose from for "engaging in BDSM lifestyle and activities" other than sexual pleasure and arousal. As people's level of Scene involvement increased, their mean number of reasons for engaging in BDSM statistically significantly increased from about 6 for low-involvement people to 7 for medium-involvement people to 8 for high-involvement people. Interestingly, results were also highly statistically significantly different by level of Scene involvement for all the specific reasons except a couple that I'll note below, and as you'll see, people with higher levels of involvement are almost always more likely to choose the motive. As I review each of the reasons, I'll give the percentage of people with each level of involvement who listed the reason in the format "low/medium/high involvement." Then I'll draw from my interviews to show how people discussed that particular motivation playing out in their own lives when I asked them to describe "awesome scenes" they had done.

Physical Nonsexual Pleasure (Including Sensual Pleasure and Nonsexual Masochism): 70% (low)/80% (medium)/86% (high)

The term "sensual" is very popular in the Scene, and 15 of my interviewees used it to describe things they enjoyed. Ryan explained that he was mostly into the sensuality of kink, specifically sadomasochism,

> because the sadism and masochism doesn't necessarily have to do with pain; it has to do with the sensations. I am very sensation oriented. I'm what they sometimes call a touch slut. I like to feel things and be felt. It's very sensual and sexual for me. It doesn't always turn into sex, but—sitting on the couch, watching TV, rubbing someone's foot—it's very sensual. It may not be sexual, but it could be.

Will, who said that kink is not inherently sexual, immediately explained, "There are a lot of sensual [aspects] to it and I think people, in general, have a difficult time differentiating things that are sensual and feel good and make you feel good from sexual [things that] make you feel good and want to fuck." He added that he used to flog a girl who always orgasmed from it, but said, "It wasn't as sexual for me. I was helping her have a good time and enjoying it myself."

Hearkening back to the "wine snob" hypothesis, both Ryan and Will went out of their way to emphasize the idea that they could distinguish between two physical experiences (sexuality and sensuality) that most people couldn't. However, like them, most of my interviewees didn't exactly frame sensuality as being in *opposition* to sexuality, but rather as more of a complementary and distinct experience.

Altered Mental State (Including Subspace and Domspace): 62% (low)/78% (medium)/83% (high)

Kink culture is pretty obsessed with subspace (Simula, 2019b), which is a mental state generally associated with a kind of blissful mental emptiness and/or a desire to just do what the other person wants. During our interviews, 13 of my interviewees spontaneously mentioned subspace, and tens of thousands of people list it as something they're into on FetLife. Tom described one of his great thrills in kink as "the look of a bottom's eyes when just hitting into subspace, into that area, that whole total control." "That look" usually has glazed eyes and a slightly open-mouthed expression. As a bottom, Mila described the pleasures of letting go into subspace:

> I had a really hard week the other week. I was really tired, I was really stressed out. I went to a party, and I looked at Miles, and I said, "Do you need a foot massage?" He said, "Why yes, yes I do." I literally sat and got completely lost in the foot massage, and falling into that subspace, and falling into a place where nothing else is going on around me, and I felt so much better afterwards.

On the other side, kinksters don't actually mention Domspace or Topspace very much (Newmahr, 2011). In contrast to subspace, only a few hundred people on FetLife have Topspace or Domspace as fetishes, and none of my interviewees spontaneously used the terms "Topspace" or "Domspace," although the ideas definitely exist in the community. Tops were statistically significantly less likely than bottoms or switches to say that "space" was one of their motivations for doing BDSM for both medium- and high-involvement kinksters (64 percent Top/82 percent bottom or switch for medium; 75 percent Top/86 percent bottom or switch for high), but the great majority of Tops still said that spacing mattered to them.

Although kinksters don't talk about it much, experienced kinksters automatically know what you're talking about if you say "Domspace" or

"Topspace," and I'm pretty sure most of them can identify people in those headspaces. Thus, for example, when I talked to my interviewee and friend Grace about her relationship with her partner George, I commented that the two rarely seemed to space in their interactions. She agreed, saying, "I mean, I don't think either of us really goes into Topspace or subspace or whatever. It's just, like, the way we are all the time. It comes out in silly ways, but it also comes out in the basis of our relationship." If kinksters didn't know what subspace and Topspace are, Grace and I couldn't have had this kind of conversation. Even though kinksters rarely articulate it, experienced kinksters seem to at least semiconsciously understand that there are typical visible signs of Topspace—an obviously heightened pulse and an eye glint—that complement the open-mouthed glazed-eye looks of subspace. However, as we'll see in chapter 7, the Scene usually values concrete Topping *skills* from Tops more than their ability to space, while it places a high value on bottoms' ability to space and almost no value on any concrete bottoming skills.

Connection/Feelings of Emotional Closeness (Including Love): 80% (low)/86% (medium)/90% (high)

It's worth noting here that for highly involved kinksters, "connection" was actually slightly more popular than "sexual arousal and pleasure" (88 percent). More than half of my interviewees (38) spontaneously talked about the importance of connection/connecting with their partners in their play and sex. In the Scene, the term is almost comically vague and has come to encompass everything from sexual to Dom/sub to emotional to spiritual/ metaphysical chemistry between individuals, between individuals and their communities, and between individuals and the divine. Given the breathtaking span and vagueness of the concept, it's not surprising that so many highly involved folks say they're into it. And yet, kinksters have a habit of framing their interest in "connection" as special or unusual, in spite of the fact that almost all of them are into it. For example, Bill explained that he needed connection to Top someone, saying, "There has to be more of a connection than just, 'I spank you, I boink you.' There have to be some feelings in it." Josh likewise highlighted the importance of connection for him in deciding whether to play with someone:

> If somebody comes up and is like, "Oh, I really want to do a caning scene. And I hear you do caning"—and it's somebody that I have a connection with, and there is some chemistry there that I want to do, that might be a

reasonable excuse to explore playing with them. But the fact that it's like, "You like caning, I like caning, therefore, let's go do caning"—no. It's all about the connection.

David explained connection in reference to the BDSM role that he took on in a dynamic, saying, "There's not a day I say, 'I'm a switch today.' I mean, I crave connection, and whatever way that takes place. At this point, I tend to carry myself in more of a Topspace, because I'm more confident, mature. But I'll bottom to a very select few people." For David, like for a number of switches I know, connection was much more important than any other factor in establishing whether they Topped, bottomed, or switched with a person.

When I teach classes for kinksters on communication, I usually tell them to try to stop using the word "connection," because everyone wants it and the term doesn't communicate much—but someone almost invariably does within less than five minutes of me saying that. On my more cynical days, I think that kinksters began emphasizing connection because the Scene was determined to elide the sexuality of BDSM, and saying, "I just felt so connected to him" sounds much less explicitly erotic than, "I wanted to jump his bones." I can say confidently from all my interactions with them that kinksters are generally *vastly* more willing to tell each other, "I want to tie you up" than "I want to fuck your brains out" (which is a fascinating inversion of traditional vanilla dynamics, where the tying part might be much scarier to voice than the sex part). I suspect that eliding sexual attraction and dynamics is part of why the term "connection" became so popular. But another reason is simple lack of vocabulary. As a group, kinksters struggle to articulate the difference between "I want to tie *someone* up" and "I want to tie *you* up" and settle for explaining the difference as resulting from connection. Since even kinksters never invented a word for BDSM-related "lust" (e.g., "I want him to tie me" or "I want to kick him until he cries"), they substituted the much-overused term "connection." I've also argued to my fellow kinksters that part of the reason we frequently fall back on the weak concept of connection is that most of our BDSM activities were named by Tops to talk about the things that matter to them (often technical, aesthetic, and safety things), whereas if bottoms had named our BDSM activities, they'd mostly be named according to emotions and feelings. Sensing that something amazing and barely articulated happens when they magically Top "just right," Tops too fell back on the mystical idea of "connection" to explain experiences that still have no name.

Adrenaline/Physical Excitement: 62% (low)/68% (medium)/ 74% (high)

As I mentioned in the introduction, kinksters often compare the thrill of many BDSM activities to sports and allude to the same sorts of endorphin rushes. I've also heard kinksters talk about kink as a "drug" that they get "high" off of (like a runner's high) and even sometimes "addicted" to. Ellie described the intense endorphin high she experienced from her first needle scene, when heavy gauge needles were inserted into her:

> I ended up doing four needles [in me the first time] and being like, "Okay, that was nice. I liked it, but I think I'm good." It was a lot of endorphins; I wasn't prepared for the insane endorphin rush that came with it. The most I've ever done is 25, and I could barely do 25. I was a crying mess by the end of it. It was just such an insane endorphin cathartic pain kind of thing that I couldn't even walk. It was amazing.

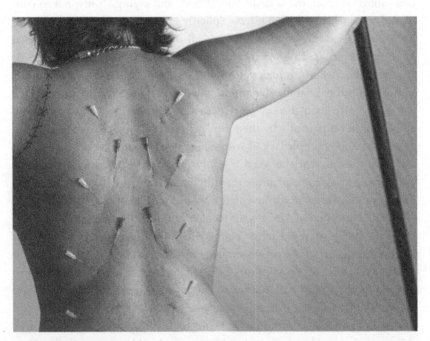

Classic needleplay tends to put needles in the back (although needles can go almost anywhere bottoms can tolerate them). Accomplished needle Tops often take great pride in the aesthetics of their designs. *Photo: Daniel Cardoso; Model: Alex Pryn*

More elaborate needle play designs use thread or fishing wire to create patterns and sometimes to physically challenge bottoms. *Photo: Wintersong; Needles and model: Thista Minai; Model: TasteofOxblood*

Vera described the combined joys of "spacing" (in this case, as a bottom) and endorphin rushes together:

> Going into space, it feels good—amazing. Sometimes when I get beat, I will see endorphin sunbursts in my head, like, colored lights in my head, and I'll be like, "Okay, there goes, my brain just caught up with my body. You can do more now because I just saw the endorphin release." It physically feels good. I have a really high level of, this intense sensation would hurt on you, on somebody else, but on me that feels like a great big massage. It feels really yummy.

Although all my interviewees who talked about endorphin and adrenaline rushes did so with reference to bottoming, I have often heard Tops talk about adrenaline rushes from scenes that are extremely technically difficult (particularly very complicated rope suspensions) or physically draining (especially extensive "impact play" scenes that involve lots of punching or kicking and require heavy exertion). As with headspace, I think the Scene mostly talks about endorphin rushes with regard to bottoming, but Tops frequently experience them, too. Indeed, on my survey, exactly as many highly involved Tops as bottoms said they did BDSM for this adrenaline rush (although medium-involvement Tops were slightly less likely to say so). At all levels of involvement, switches were the most likely to say that they did BDSM for adrenaline (73 percent for medium and 77 percent for high).

Physical or Emotional Challenge: 50% (low)/56% (medium)/ 67% (high)

Despite being obviously related to an adrenaline rush, BDSM for physical or emotional challenge purposes looks and feels slightly different. Newmahr (2011) coined the term "badass bottoming" to refer to bottoming people did for the sake of doing something hard (I also call it "stunt bottoming"). In essence, these acts of bottoming prove that someone is capable of doing something that they or others generally perceive as very difficult. For example, Luke didn't describe any profound emotional or sensual motivations behind his plans to try set a world record for needle bottoming with more than 1,000 needles in him at one time. Although he did mention an "endorphin rush," the only other motivation he mentioned was the prospect of having a picture taken. He explained that he liked to challenge himself during scenes, saying that in a particularly difficult scene,

> Being pushed to the verge of panicking or desperation and being able to control it, or being able to control it until you're able to get out—it's a lot about mindfuck. I like to put a challenge in my mind, and although this is physical, it actually has much more effect on your psyche sometimes.

For Tops, there can be a complementary physical or emotional challenge to these exact same kinds of feats. For example, a friend who's an accomplished needle Top told me how thrilling it is to have to try to stay focused on doing many complex needles for hours at a time to pull off a complex pattern. For both medium- and high-involvement folks, the majority of people in all BDSM roles said that challenge was one of their reasons for doing BDSM, but switches were again by far the most likely (63 percent of medium-involvement switches and 70 percent of high-involvement switches).

Emotional Pleasure and Satisfaction (Including Nonsexual Sadism): 68% (low)/78% (medium)/86% (high)

The vast breadth of emotional experiences that seem to motivate kinksters defies easy characterization. As Simula (2019a) pointed out, kinksters often talk much more about the emotional aspects of BDSM (particularly Dominance and submission) than they do about the physical aspects of BDSM (particularly sadomasochism). Of the people I've talked to and interviewed, the vast majority of bottoms say they're not "true" masochists in the sense that they derive sexual pleasure from pain; rather, they enjoy hurting to please another person and show their submission to them (which my friends and I call "submissochism"). Alternatively, like Vera, above, they say they experience sensations other people find painful as enjoyable. Thus, two bottoms receiving exactly the same physical BDSM activity might have completely different physical and emotional responses—as might their Tops. Some Tops say they're "true" sadists in the sense that they derive sexual pleasure from causing other people pain; others say they really like to Dominate people and hurting someone is just a handy means to an end.

As you read the following descriptions from Derek, Jackson, and Carter imagine each of these Tops caning someone and how different their emotional reactions would probably be. We'll start with Derek, who said he wasn't a classical sadist:

> If you look at the definition of "sadist," it's people who like to inflict pain. I'm not really about the pain—I'm more about the suffering. So if I could just put a clothespin on you, and you cry like a little baby, I'm good with that. I don't really have to hurt you. If I can make you cry, I'm good. I think that suffering is really one of the most pure emotions that you have, and I take it very personal that somebody would want to suffer for me.

Jackson, on the other hand, described himself more frankly as someone who really did like to cause pain:

> He can take a lot of pain, and I love to dish out a lot of pain. Last time, I had him up on a stake and stripped down to essentially his boxers, and it was just a whipping scene. I observe little details, like, how somebody's back ripples when they're in pain. And I'm like, ah!—like a child, you're giving me bright colors, movements, sounds, I clap very excitedly, and it was just that.

I essentially just kept whaling on him over and over, and every now and then I'd stop and I'd put my hands on him, just try to calm him down, and it was just really wonderful. It was a great connection, I found it to be very intense.

And then there were the "service Tops" like Carter, who said they liked hurting other people to make those people happy: "I don't really have sadist in me. I'm into a lot of sensual stuff. But watching somebody that enjoys getting something painful done to them because it takes them to their happy place and being able to do that for them, that excites me, too." As Carter himself noted, kinksters often deride the idea of "service Topping" as somehow less authentic, but when pushed to describe their motivations, many Tops I've met said they really enjoy making their bottoms happy.

Although bottoms and Tops were almost equally likely to say they engaged in BDSM for emotional pleasure on my survey, the quotes of my interviewees here heavily slant toward Tops because bottoms mostly didn't articulate their emotional responses with much depth. For example, Theresa described a memorable scene in which her (female) Master ordered her to be naked in public for the first time: "She said, 'Drop the dress now.' I went, 'Eee!' And I dropped it, and it was sooooo scary, and so wonderful, and so freeing, and so scary. And then it [felt like it] was just her and me [feeling] floaty, and her flogging me with rice paddles and canes and floggers." While the "floaty" feeling Theresa mentioned was almost certainly "subspace," she listed a variety of other emotions (scary, wonderful, freeing) that were obviously also satisfying to her, but not elaborated. Melissa explained that subs become extremely conscious of what their Doms feel and want, saying, "As a sub, sometimes you can really feed off of the Dom really liking what he's doing, so I will do more for them because they were enjoying it." I think one of the characteristics of Topping pleasures can be a hyperattention to certain details that allows Tops to be relatively articulate about describing what they enjoy. But one of the major characteristics of bottoming pleasures is becoming lost in a physical and/or emotional sensation of being with another person that doesn't really lend itself to articulate emotional description.

Service (Giving or Receiving): 65% (low)/65% (medium)/ 69% (high)

The concept of "service" in the Scene generally means doing things for someone else to make them feel comfortable. While it can include things like the aforementioned "service Topping," the generic term *service* usually implies bottoming and/or submission. Lucy described herself as "naturally extremely service oriented" with a focus on "anticipatory service." She explained the concept thus:

> If I'm watching somebody do something, like fix something, and I know that they're going to need a screwdriver, I'll go over and hand it to them. And if [as a service sub] you're given the leeway of being able to use initiative, it's really fun to do that and then have things there for them so they don't even have to ask. For the most part, Doms who really enjoy service don't want to have to sit there and micromanage.

Indeed, as Josh explained from the other side, being a Dom receiving service was all about not having to ask for the things he needed. He described his relationship with his "slave girl" as nonsexual and entirely focused on her serving him, saying, "She takes care of me, which is great." He explained that earlier that day, when someone else had mentioned that their packed living quarters at the BDSM event they were all at had become "trashed,"

> nobody else made a move to clean it. And Jackie just quietly went about making that whole area clean and tidy again. So when she woke me up this morning with breakfast and a cup of coffee, it was all done. Stuff like that really contributes to my life's mission by taking a lot of things off my plate and just helping and supporting me in a number of tactical ways.

Service dynamics are all about one person getting joy from making another feel good, and many people do service work for people they have sexual relationships with (sometimes in an intentionally service-y way). But kinksters who say they have a "service relationship" with someone generally mean they have a nonsexual or barely sexual relationship with someone that emphasizes service rather than sex or BDSM play. Ironically, my survey results suggest that more people enjoy doing service than receiving it. Among those with high Scene involvement, 80 percent of bottoms said they enjoyed service, but only 64 percent of Tops and 63 percent of switches said they did.

Roleplay: 41% (low)/38% (medium)/33% (high)

Roleplay stands out as the only motivation other than sex that low-involvement kinksters were statistically significantly more likely to list than high-involvement kinksters. I think that most of this difference comes from the fact that, as we'll see in chapter 5, the Scene puts such a strong emphasis on "authenticity" that roleplay—where someone intentionally takes on a role that isn't their "true self"—is less popular. Highly involved kinksters tend to take the attitude that "playing doctor" or "playing boss" is something silly that vanilla people do. When kinksters do roleplay, they're often extremely earnest about it or go completely the other direction and become self-consciously ridiculous about it. The descriptions of puppy and pony play in chapter 1 give you a sense of the heavily staged, earnest types of roleplay that highly involved kinksters sometimes engage in. Roleplay in the Scene can take the form of these highly costumed and elaborate kinks, or they can become fundamental kinky relationship dynamics, such as Dominant/submissive dynamics founded on one partner pretending to be the "Daddy" of his "little girl" (an adult).

Satisfying Primal Urges: 54% (low)/52% (medium)/55% (high)

Primal desires stand out for being the only reason for BDSM that didn't differ by level of Scene involvement. We saw Damon earlier explaining how primal urges were something that felt dark and not-quite-sexual to him—a desire drawing on instinct. On the other hand, Tops were much more likely to list this motivation (62 percent high involvement/57 percent medium involvement) than bottoms (48 percent high involvement/43 percent medium involvement); switches were somewhere in between (54 percent high involvement/58 percent medium involvement), which was a little surprising because most primal play classes I've seen in the Scene emphasize animalistic styles of wrestling and grappling, which are strongly associated with switches. Kinksters will occasionally use the expression "to go primal on" someone, meaning that they feel taken over by some sort of barely controlled/controllable violent impulses. Zoe, who was brand-new to the Scene, was the only person I interviewed other than Damon who highlighted the significance of primal desires, and her description emphasized a violent dynamic that involved "letting go of all of your brain and just going with your body," adding that she has "a lot of catlike tendencies" that she was interested in exploring with someone.

Spiritual Fulfillment (Including Meditation, Ordeal, and Catharsis): 21% (low)/37% (medium)/45% (high)

Religion in the Scene generally doesn't look much like it does in mainstream culture. While it's true that the vast majority of kinksters don't literally make

74

a religion out of their BDSM practices, several very prominent kinksters do (particularly Lee Harrington [2016] and Raven Kaldera [2009]), increasing the impression that spiritual kink is a big deal. Even most kinksters who do BDSM for spiritual purposes mostly dabble in it, but those brief experiments often leave profound impressions. When I asked my interviewees to tell me about an "awesome scene" they had done, 12 people spontaneously told me about a scene with spiritual undertones or overtones; 12 more had stories of powerful spiritual BDSM experiences when I asked about them specifically. Most kinksters focus their BDSM spirituality on meditation (especially through bondage), ordeals (meaning experiences that are intentionally consensually hard in order to gain wisdom, knowledge, experience, etc.), and catharsis (meaning spiritual and emotional release). Sometimes, spiritual BDSM takes on a quality of a classical-style *revel*, meaning that the focus is on pleasures for the sake of honoring higher spirits (especially particular gods). My survey results showed that Pagans, (American) Buddhists and Taoists, and people who labeled themselves "spiritual" were much more likely to engage in spiritual BDSM. Among highly involved kinksters, 58 percent of spiritual Pagans/Buddhists/Taoists said they engaged in BDSM for spiritual reasons and 69 percent of people who were spiritual did (versus 39 percent of Christians and Jews and 31 percent of atheists and agnostics).

In keeping with Carlström's (2021) findings with Swedish kinksters, many American kinksters I spoke to understood their experience of spacing (either in subspace or Domspace) as having a spiritual dimension to it. When I asked Ashley, who was raised Christian and now identified as deist, if she felt there was anything spiritual about her BDSM practices, she said that subspace was spiritual for her because

> when you're at the mercy of this one person, and you're giving them all the power, there's something wonderful and spiritual about that. Like, here's my control: I understand and trust you completely to do whatever you want with it—just make sure that I am safe.

The intense vulnerability of submissives giving up control to another resembles many religious experiences, in which people trust themselves to god/s. But spiritually minded Tops also described nearly identical experiences of giving themselves over to what they were doing. Pat, who had been a practicing Pagan kink spiritualist for many years, described one of his most profound experiences as a Top, saying,

I prayed at the beginning of the scene, and said, like, "Let this be the thing that we both want. Whatever it is that we want, help me manifest it since we don't have words for it." And I think I shredded her abdomen, like I just cut her, and put needles through her, and you know I drew runes on her in blood. And to this day, I don't think I have a really clear conception of, "I did this, and then this, and this." I just remember these images of parts of the scene as they manifested. At the pinnacle of the scene, there was this sort of giant bright light that emanated from all of the wounds on her stomach, and it kind of went up through the roof into the atmosphere or whatever, and there was this sort of holy moment. We both sat there and breathed and just bore witness to what was happening, and that was when it was like, not only was she putting all of her trust in me to bring her to where she needed to go, but I was putting all my trust in my spirits. They would bring us to where we wanted to go, and we ended up exactly where we needed to be.

Pat's spacey uncertainty about exactly what he did during his scene closely mirrors the spacey uncertainty of many bottoms in subspace, who often were very unclear about the details of what they had done during their scenes. I've heard several spiritual Tops like Pat describe themselves as "vessels" for divine energy in these encounters, saying that they both Top the person they're working with and bottom to the divine energy they're channeling.

Sofia had also practiced and taught BDSM spirituality for many years. Years before, she had flogged a man to a profoundly cathartic state, and then afterward had analyzed the component parts of the scene to design a ritual she could repeat and teach. While she was exceptionally skilled at what she did, the type of cathartic ritual she created was extremely popular among kinksters who engage in spiritual BDSM. She recounted the original scene she did that inspired her to create her flogging ritual:

[It's] a catharsis thing—getting yourself to an open emotional and energetic state. And the person who is on the giving and receiving ends, I don't necessarily refer to them as Tops and bottoms, it's giving and receiving because it's not a D/s thing, just who's facilitating the experience. So [the first time I did this], I as a facilitator invite him to draw [spiritual] energies up into his person. And using the floggers, I am using these tools sort of like the cosmic eggbeater to mix all of the [energetic] stuff around inside the container that is your skin. My intention, my will, pushes this [flogger], through the surface of this person's skin. I was just talking and as the words came, "I don't know what it is but there's something you clearly want to let go of and it is stuck." So he is sort of crying and suffering and mostly gasping for breath. He is just wracked with sobs (and there's something truly beautiful about a crying man sobbing, just contextually). But besides this, it wasn't even like a divine suffering thing. It was for whatever—I never knew what it was he was working on, and it didn't really matter.

In Sofia's BDSM spirituality, the role of Top and bottom became irrelevant and the idea of pain itself almost seemed incidental—a flogger became a ritual tool, just like a vessel of holy water, to help another person transform.

Connor, who had also been a spiritual BDSM leader for many years, described his most profound spiritual BDSM experience. He was working in a space that had been spiritually consecrated for spiritually focused BDSM, which was specifically labeled the Temple of Atonement. Although many people who came through were making joking confessions, one man who came through very much was not:

He'd been a serial rapist, and he'd gone to prison for 10 years. He'd just gotten out of prison three months earlier and came to [this event]. And I remember him looking up at me, because he was down on his knees, and he said, "I have paid my time, but my soul is still heavy, because I know that I have done wrong." And I beat him within an inch of his life, and made him, out loud, list the names of every woman he'd ever raped. The next day, he brought an offering to me, and said, "Thank you so much. I don't know if I'll ever fully forgive myself, but at least I can now go out into the world," and gave me a necklace that he'd handmade out of clay. And he's like, "It's all I have right now. I don't have any money after getting out. I would have bought you . . . ." But, it was that scene that really anchored in for me that there is no real line for me between kink and spirit, and that even the scenes I do for just fun-play have ripple effects, because I'm a big believer that when we touch someone's life, we leave a thumbprint in their clay.

These kinds of BDSM-based catharsis and ordeal rituals anchor a profound mystical streak among many kinksters.

Although most of the stories I've shared here came from Tops, there is no statistically significant difference in how likely kinksters were to engage in spiritual BDSM by their BDSM role, controlling for spirituality. All my most profound personal experiences of spiritual BDSM have happened while bottoming, and I think it was mostly a coincidence that some of the deepest spiritual BDSM stories I heard came from people who had been Topping.

Aesthetics (Including Aesthetic Objectification, Artistry, and Visual Pleasure): 40% (low)/49% (medium)/56% (high)

Interviewees didn't talk much about artistry in kink, but the interest in kink as art is clear in how people interact online and in person. At events where photography is only allowed by staff photographers (see chapter 6), it's common for people to start yelling for a photographer (or to get friends nearby to try to get them a photographer) while they're in the middle of visually compelling scenes. Kinksters often post pictures on FetLife for their friends to see, and participants and viewers comment on how "beautiful" a scene was or felt. The term "aesthetic objectification," which I rarely hear used but some idea of which floats around in the Scene, refers to the idea that bottoms' bodies become artistic objects, a canvas for their Tops to work with. The idea is a popular one, especially among bondage enthusiasts, who often craft elaborate works of human + rope art. (If you search online for

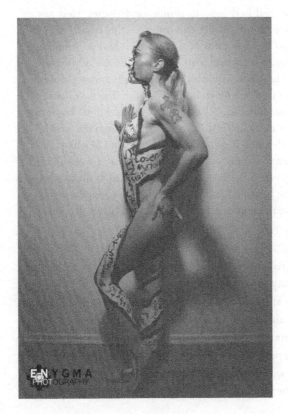

Graphoerotica is usually done for aesthetics or degradation, most often on feminine gendered people.
Photo: Enygma Photography

FKA Twigs' "Pendulum" video, you can see one of the most mainstream of these works of bondage art, created by one of the most famous bondage artists in the world, the British rigger Wykd Dave.) Tops sometimes graffiti bottoms with written words (which is called "graphoerotica"); kinksters paint each other, admire each other's bruises, and even make paddles that are designed to bruise words or images into someone else's body. My partner James taught a well-attended class for a BDSM organization on "sacred body modification," which explained how to do tattoos, body piercings, brandings, and cuttings with spiritual intentions; when, for the sake of seeing people's reactions, I asked what any of this had to do with BDSM, everyone looked at me with a "duh, why are you even asking this?" expression. I never got a satisfactory answer to my question, even though I dated James for years. Clearly, asking why intentional body modification is BDSM is as pointless as asking why anything else is BDSM—it's BDSM if kinksters say it is.

CONCLUSION: "KINKSTERS" AND "KINK" JUST AREN'T THE SAME THING

Asking why *people* do BDSM and asking why *kinksters* do BDSM isn't the same question. BDSM is a subjective, intensely personal experience mediated by social context. For the people who do it the most, that mediating social context is *probably* the Scene (even when they do BDSM privately), but there's no way to know if that's true. The Scene has an investment in giving its members lots of reasons to do BDSM, because kinksters who have lots of reasons for enjoying BDSM are (statistically) much more likely to stay involved in the Scene than are people who "just" want to do it for sex. In addition to finding meaning in a variety of ways from BDSM, another major factor that keeps kinksters involved in the public Scene is the desire to do BDSM with a lot of people; the subcultural institution that best supports that is what we'll explore in the next chapter: polyamory.

"WHY WOULD WE STILL FOLLOW THEIR BULLSHIT RULES?"

Practicing Polyamory in the Scene

Many years ago, at the first Pagan event I ever attended (the same one that would, not coincidentally, eventually introduce me to the BDSM subculture), I was somewhat nonplussed when several people asked if I was mono or poly. I had never been asked such a question before, but I was subculturally aware enough to understand the difference: monogamous people have sexual and romantic relationships with only one person, while polyamorous people have sexual and romantic relationships openly and honestly with more than one person. Despite my awareness, I felt like my hesitant response at the time was rather inadequate: "Theoretically poly, but a long way from figuring out how to practice it." Just as surprising to me was that my noncommittal answer seemed to make perfect sense to the people I was talking to. As I would come to learn from hanging out in more consensually nonmonogamous social worlds, despite the simplicity of the question—"mono or poly?"—there's an entire universe of gray area in between those two points. I would come to learn the phrase "practicing polyamory/ polyamorist" as a formal way to distinguish people who were currently in or actively seeking poly relationships from hypothetical polys—people who, like me at that stage, hadn't yet quite decided if they wanted to commit to this complex lifestyle. Especially in mainstream culture, hypothetical polys are almost certainly the most common kind, as polyamory is a demanding and time-consuming lifestyle that requires knowing the right kinds of people in order to successfully practice (Sheff, 2013).

What really struck me when I arrived in the BDSM Scene in the DC area a few years after that initial Pagan event is that no one there asked if I was mono or poly. By the time I arrived in the Scene, I was a fledgling "practicing poly" myself, and one of the main reasons I joined the Scene was that I wanted to network with other polys (much more than I wanted to network with other kinksters). But unlike many polys, I hadn't gotten a tattoo of the poly heart symbol (a heart with an infinity sign across it), and my lack of any other identifiable marks branding me as a poly person made kinksters' failure to ask pretty telling. Virtually all the kinksters I encountered just assumed that I and everyone else around us were poly—and most of the time, they were correct. I refer to these types of subcultural expectations as *polynormativity*, meaning a social context that expects people to be in polyamorous relationships and treats those relationships as normal; it also expects people, even those who aren't poly, to subscribe to many poly-related values about open communication in relationships. Throughout this chapter, I'll be circling around the question: Are poly people just attracted to the Scene, or does the Scene convert people to poly? (The answer is clearly "both.")

THE SCOPE OF POLY IN THE SCENE

The reason so many Pagans were asking me if I was mono or poly is a residual effect of the fact that the concepts and practices of polyamory were originally developed in Pagan communities. A prominent Pagan family, the Zell-Ravenhearts, coined and popularized the term *polyamory* (Blumberg, 2014). They were a large poly family who lived together in a large house led by a woman named Morning Glory and her husband Oberon. In their media profiles, their family consisted of three bi women who were in relationships with each other as well as in relationships with three other straight men (Daum, 2001). As far as I can tell, the prevalence of poly among bi women in relationships with straight men seems to have trickled down from the Zell-Ravenhearts. Numerous Pagans I have spoken to over the years, including my interviewee Olivia, who was friends with the Zell-Ravenhearts, explained how this family cultivated poly support groups in Pagan communities, creating a lasting tie between the poly lifestyle and Paganism. None of the kinksters I talked to could recount how poly and kink had come to be so closely associated, so I e-mailed Oberon Zell for an answer (Morning Glory is deceased). He told me that Morning Glory's "most significant paramour was seriously into BDSM," and once the two became involved,

> We all started showing up at various BDSM events at the same time we were doing the earliest workshops on polyamory at Pagan festivals as well as the early [conventions for poly people]. As our family structure shifted,

the newer members of the Family were also into BDSM. So polyamory just naturally spread into both the Pagan and Kink communities through our Family and lovers. Morning Glory even guest edited an entire issue of *Green Egg* [their newsletter] specifically devoted to BDSM.

In short, through the Zell-Ravenhearts, poly simultaneously spread through the three closely interconnected subcultures of Paganism, pansexual BDSM, and a new fledgling separate poly community. Nowadays, I'm certain from observation that most polys are not Pagan (though lots are) and most Pagans aren't poly (though lots are). I'm slightly less certain that most polys aren't at least peripherally in the BDSM Scene; even as far away as Paris, Bennion (2022) found that polys were highly involved in BDSM. Polys who have settled family lives with houses and children, and are content with the partners they have, have much less motivation and leisure to participate in debaucherous weekend parties with whips and chains. However, polys who are actively pursuing new partners have few social spaces outside the BDSM Scene to readily meet these potential mates.

My first impression of the Scene as defaulting to poly was never really contradicted. Monogamous people in the DC Scene were so uncommon that someone actually tried to start a special meetup group for them that almost instantly failed. I actively sought monogamous people for my interviews, but when I asked kinksters, they struggled to think of any monogamous people they knew in the Scene. After concluding my interviews, I attended a workshop on monogamy at a large BDSM event; that workshop turned into a support group for the monogamous people in it, validating their lifestyle choices and providing cheerleading-style reassurances that monogamy was a good relationship model. (It's pretty hard to imagine many other social contexts where monogamous people would feel like they needed support and validation.) I later met a monogamous friend-of-a-friend in the Scene who told me that when he and his now-wife met at a BDSM munch, they had "come out to each as monogamous"—because of course poly was the default relationship model among kinksters. More recently, a late-twenties queer genderqueer friend in the Scene noted with frustration that "it doesn't matter how (un)comfortable I am with it; if I want to date in the Scene, I have to date nonmonogamously." In short, monogamous people and monogamy as a concept were pretty foreign to life in the mid-Atlantic Scene.

Kink culture seems pretty certain that it's antimonogamy, but it's often unclear what its enthusiasm for poly really means. The Scene generally fails to distinguish between the desire for multiple intimate relationships (polyamory) and the desire for multiple sexual partners (polysexuality). On the whole, Western culture isn't very good at differentiating between romantic and sexual (which is part of why the label *bisexual* is often so confusing, since many bisexual people are hetero- or homoromantic), and the Scene is no exception to this problem. Kinksters themselves almost always only use the prefix of the word ("poly"), so there's less room for subcultural attention to the similarities and differences between polyamorous folks and polysexuals. Cast together into a single subculture that makes little effort to differentiate them, it's easy for polysexuals and polyamorous folks to end up in conflict with each other over the meaning of intimate interactions.

TABLE 3.1. Simplified Actual and Current Relationship Dynamics by Level of Scene Involvement (US & Canada)

Scene Involvement	%	N	%	N	%	N	%	N
Current Relationship	Mono		Poly		Open/Swinger		(Other/None)	
Low	43%	46	44%	47	14%	15	(32%)	(50)
Medium	28%	164	54%	311	18%	104	(20%)	(146)
High	20%	77	64%	251	17%	65	(15%)	(70)
Ideal Relationship								
Low	33%	52	43%	69	24%	38	—	—
Medium	22%	153	58%	409	21%	149	—	—
High	16%	72	70%	318	15%	66	—	—

TABLE 3.2. Detailed Actual and Ideal Relationship Dynamics by Level of Scene Involvement (US & Canada)

	Comp Mono	Sex Mono	Poly, seeking	Hier Poly	Other Poly	Swing	Open	Reg Part	Looking	Not Looking
Actual Relationship Dynamics										
Low	22%	7%	1%	9%	19%	3%	10%	12%	16%	3%
Med	9%	14%	2%	14%	26%	4%	11%	5%	11%	4%
High	2%	15%	3%	21%	30%	2%	12%	6%	7%	2%
Ideal Relationship Dynamics										
Low	19%	14%	—	24%	19%	7%	18%	—	—	—
Med	7%	14%	—	27%	30%	7%	15%	—	—	—
High	4%	12%	—	36%	33%	2%	14%	—	—	—

Polynormativity in the Scene turns out to have some geographic variability to it, so unlike most of the statistics in this book, the ones in this chapter are only for American and Canadian kinksters. Among American and Canadian kinksters (hereafter for this chapter only, just "kinksters"), only 16 percent of those who were highly involved in the Scene said their "ideal relationship" is "monogamous," and 20 percent said they were currently in a "monogamous" relationship. These numbers were significantly lower than their counterparts with low involvement, with medium-involvement people about halfway in between. Most of the difference was taken up with polyamory, with a steady increase in both preference for and actually being in poly relationships as Scene involvement increased. The preference for swinging or open relationships (more on those shortly) also declined with increasing Scene involvement, but there was no effect on actual relationships.

Around the world, highly involved kinksters had virtually identical rates of monogamy (about 16 percent) for their current relationships, but medium-involvement kinksters in Europe were statistically significantly more likely to be monogamous than their American counterparts (33 percent versus 23 percent). There was also some variation within the United States and Canada: although my samples for narrow geographic areas tended to be small, my respondents from Georgia and Florida confirmed my observations that kinksters there were significantly more monogamous than they were elsewhere, so much that they were mono and poly in about equal numbers.

There was also some demographic variation beyond level of Scene involvement in these preferences and practices. Among people with medium or high Scene involvement, the people who were the most likely to be in (43 percent) or prefer (32 percent) monogamous relationships were straight or heteroflexible women, while gender-nonconforming folks of all orientations were the most likely to be in (66 percent) and prefer (70 percent) polyamorous relationships. Religion was highly significantly ($p < .0001$) related to relationship ideals and practices, with spiritual Christians and Jews with medium/high Scene involvement more than twice as likely as other groups to prefer monogamy (34 percent versus 16 percent). As you'll see in chapter 5, current Christians and Jews are only 19 percent of the Scene. Notably, there is no demographic group by age, gender, sexual orientation, or spirituality with medium/high Scene involvement in which the preference for monogamy even comes close to the majority preference.

The Scene tends to treat an interest in open relationships as an automatic consequence of the other things that draw people to the Scene, such as a desire for new experiences and an emphasis on open communication. Previous researchers (Bauer, 2010; Sheff and Hammers, 2011) have mostly treated this poly/kinky community overlap as normal and expected, but the geographic variation in poly prevalence among BDSM microcultures highlights the fact that this overlap isn't automatic. It's possible that part of why kink and poly so often go together is because of what sociologists call "secondary deviance" (Akers, 1977). In simplistic terms, the theory of secondary deviance argues that once you engage in some form of deviant behavior and accept a label as a deviant, from both a societal and identity perspective, you get subsequent deviance for free. Using this principle, once you've gone to the deviant relationship identity "kinky," theoretically you don't gain much additional stigma by adding the deviant relationship identity "poly." Does society really think you're *that* much weirder if you have one Master than if you have a Master *and* a slave? I personally think that it does, and most kinksters I know say that trying to explain the poly-ness of their lives to vanillas is much harder than trying to explain the kinkiness. After all, there are popular movies, books, and images of BDSM all over the place, but as of this writing, there aren't any very popular poly stories. I don't think conventional theories of secondary deviance do justice to what happens in the Scene, where kinksters usually come for a wild party and then mostly end up with a curio cabinet full of eccentric relationships with titles that don't even make sense to outsiders.

Even accounting for the idea of secondary deviance, we're still left with the fact that there's no inherent relationship between, say, wanting to hit someone with a cane and wanting to be able to have relationships with multiple people. (Notably, there's also no intrinsic relationship between kink and Paganism, and yet, as we'll see in chapter 5, kinksters are *vastly* more likely to be Pagan than the rest of the population.) As tempting as it might be to mistakenly think all those things are somehow innately connected, I think it's much more likely that these adjacent social worlds attract and circuitously recruit the same types of people and then encourage them to take on each other's values. There's a more logical overlap between kinksters and swingers, but kink culture rejects "swinging" in favor of "poly." That rejection largely happens because kinksters don't perceive swingers as sharing most of the values I'll explain in chapter 5, like queer-friendliness and personal and bodily acceptance, that they often frame as important in the Scene.

On the other hand, kinksters and poly folks get along well because they share many of the same core values. In particular, both groups highly value open and frank communication, because it is, by definition, difficult to consensually hurt or control someone without openly communicating with them. It's likewise very difficult to maintain multiple consensually nonmonogamous relationships without communicating about what one is doing with all partners. However, there's another important value that kinksters and poly folks share, which is the idea that individuals have sexual and relationship needs, and that they deserve to have these needs met—even if that requires several people to do so. Lucy, who was Queer, had been involved with the LGBTQ+ community, and had some experience with poly relationships long before entering the BDSM Scene, explained how her enculturation to the Scene changed her perspective:

> The more I learned about things being in the Scene, there's just so many different variations—I mean, I could have a romantic sexual relationship with one person, but they might not be able to play the way I want to play, so then I could play with somebody else and do those things with them. And maybe there's somebody else that I can do these cool [BDSM] things with. So [poly] really seems to fit and work and make a lot more sense. If I could find one person that we wanted to settle down and play house together, I'm open to that also. I just think it's unrealistic to think that one person could fulfill all my needs.

Not only does the Scene attract people interested in poly, it teaches them to articulate and emphasize a value concept that many of them already had, which is that they're entitled to have a wide range of sexual and relationship needs met. The Scene's perspective on poly relationships deliberately expands to encompass nonsexual (and even sometimes nonkinky) relationships as well.

But the Scene isn't equally attractive to *all* poly people: it targets a specific group of poly folks, namely those who are currently seeking less settled, less family-focused lives. In contrast to, say, the poly people studied by Sheff (2013) who all had children, less than half of people involved in the Scene say they want children (and of all the relationship orientations, people who preferred poly relationships were the least likely to say they want children). Among people who are highly involved in the Scene, only 20 percent currently have a minor child living in their household. Only 27 percent of people involved in the Scene who prefer poly relationships are legally married, and about half are currently not living with a romantic partner. Most important, regardless of gender, using their own definition of the term, 42 percent of people who prefer poly relationships in the Scene self-identify as "sluts" (as compared with 21 percent of monogamous people and 44 percent of swinger/open relationship folks), suggesting that the Scene sorts for poly people (and nonmonogamous people in general) who are especially interested in the things the Scene tends to associate with sluts—namely, sexual variety and openness.

That kind of interest in sexual and relationship variety and openness is not easily compatible with "conventional" family values and mores, which emphasize monogamy, the importance of the nuclear family, and the need for parenthood (Broad, Crawley, and Foley, 2004). The Scene generally attracts people who are less interested in all these things, and while it assumes that family is very important to kinksters, it has a very different vision of what "family" means. Like much of white Queer culture (Mitchell, 2008), the Scene often emphasizes the idea of families of choice and sorts for the kinds of people who desire such a family. The general concept of "family of choice" is that our biological families may have little respect or understanding for us, but we can choose people to make a life with who will show us respect and understanding. The Scene's concept of a "Leather family" embodies this ideal; as the name implies, it came to the pansexual Scene by way of the gay/lesbian Leather culture in a convoluted fashion (Rambukkana, 2007). Leather family ties vary greatly in their intensity, but there's usually an assumption that people will provide assistance when needed to other members of their Leather families.

RELATIONSHIPS IDEALS AND PRACTICES: MONOGAMY

Kinksters' general vision of "family" tends to look a bit different than it does in mainstream culture, so perhaps it's not surprising that it has a pretty quirky vision of "monogamy," too. In all my time in the Scene, I only ever personally met one couple who were very active in it but only engaged in BDSM play and sex with each other, and I never interviewed anyone who was keeping to such rules. My failure to find more people in this kind of relationship isn't really surprising, because only 2 percent of highly involved people on my survey were currently in a conventionally monogamous relationship (and only 4 percent of them wanted to be). When kinksters talk about monogamy, they almost universally mean *sexual* monogamy: members of the couple are allowed to engage in BDSM play with others, but not have sex with them. The Scene almost exclusively selects for people who want to do BDSM play with a wide variety of people, which makes kink monogamy nearly impossible. Fifteen percent of highly involved kinksters said that this was the kind of relationship they were in and 12 percent said it was the kind they wanted. All told, 83 percent of highly involved kinksters who were in monogamous relationships said they preferred monogamy.

Unsurprisingly, kinksters who didn't view BDSM as sexual were generally much more comfortable with monogamy than those who did. Highly (but not medium) involved kinksters who preferred for their BDSM play not to include sex were significantly more likely to prefer monogamous relationships (25 percent) than those who preferred or were neutral about sexual BDSM (13 percent). On the other hand, kinksters who viewed BDSM more sexually tended to be annoyed by the sexual limitations of monogamous relationships. For example, Liz was part of the 17 percent of highly involved kinksters who said they were in a sexually monogamous relationship, but their ideal relationship was nonmonogamous. She said she who was only monogamous because her current boyfriend, who was new to the Scene, was uncomfortable with anything else. She explained the rules of their dynamic as him permitting her to play with other people if he "is absolutely sure that my bra and panties are [staying] on. And actually I did an electricity scene like that, and it was hot in its own way. . . . But I try not to do anything that would piss him off if he knew." Her comment "hot in its own way" strongly suggested that Liz thought something was lacking from the scene in its nonsexual version, and her comments in our interview about "pissing him off if he knew," among others, suggested to me that she subscribed to a common view about what she felt were relatively arbitrary lines between sexual and nonsexual BDSM play.

I also interviewed three older men who were currently cheating on their female partners. Two were married and hadn't had sex with their wives in years (one was initiating a divorce, while the other remained married for the sake of a disabled child), and the other hadn't disclosed his bisexual activities, swinging, or BDSM to his serious girlfriend. The one with a disabled child also had a serious long-term girlfriend and two other, more casual girlfriends (all of whom knew about each other and were aware that he was married), so for all intents and purposes, he was behaving as a polyamorous person except for being legally married to someone who knew nothing about any of his sexual or BDSM relationships. Infidelity is extremely frowned upon in the polynormative world of the Scene (possibly even more than it is in mainstream culture), and I was a bit surprised that these men were willing to admit they were cheating. I don't know how people in similar relationship dynamics showed up on my survey; a couple of people wrote in for "other" that they were cheating on their partners or being cheated on by their partners, and this handful of folks are discounted from my overall statistical totals here. Among people with medium or high Scene involvement who said that they were married, living with their spouse, and in a sexually monogamous relationship, 35 percent (17 people) said they'd had two or more sex partners (by their own definition of "sex") in the last year. Among unmarried, cohabiting, monogamous folks, 29 percent (16 people) said the same. These numbers strongly suggest that even by their own definitions of "sex," kinksters tend to get a bit creative with the idea of "monogamy."

I'm not sure how two of the other older men that I interviewed would have described their relationships on a survey. Both men were married to monogamous vanilla wives who permitted them to indulge their kinks (while apparently having no other partners themselves), but within a fairly strict set of sexual limitations. Charles said, "When I go out to parties, this is what [my wife and I] say to each other: no kissing, no fucking, no rimming. That's our rule." Similarly, Owen explained,

> I have a Mistress [Dominant] that I—[my wife] kind of lets me do this, and my bargain was that I wasn't going to actually fully do contact sex, full sex. And there's a lot of gray area. To me, it means intercourse and real, wet and gushy oral sex. They're off the table.

He went on to explain that he'd initially told his wife all about his various exploits, but she finally said she didn't want to hear any more details, telling him to "just abide by our agreements." He said, "The downside of that is it's sort of my own judgment what I feel guilty about," adding, "with women, I've been pretty good, but with men maybe I've crossed the line a little bit—she would be quite surprised that I've become a little bisexual—my oral sex limits are different with men, because I don't feel guilty about it." Kinksters tend to label these intentionally broad visions of monogamy "monogamish," and I assume that these were the kinds of people who were checking the "monogamy" box on my survey while still having sex with other people. Since all the people I happened to interview in these kinds of dynamics were men, I checked my survey data to see if monogamous men and women were about equally likely to have had multiple sexual partners in the last year; my survey sample for monogamous people is very, very small, but the answer appeared to be that they were.

RELATIONSHIP IDEALS AND PRACTICES: OPEN AND SWINGING

In that large gray area between monogamy and poly, "open relationships" and "swinging" are usually more clearly nonmonogamous than "monogamish" relationships are. On my survey, I used relatively formal definitions for these relationship dynamics, defining "swinger, nonpoly" as "primary partners are romantically exclusive but sexually open," and "open" as "primary partners may engage in limited romantic and sexual partnerships outside the primary partnership." These definitions more or less align with the way kinksters use these labels, but the Scene stigmatizes the "swinger" label and subculture so much that it's rare to meet kinksters who label themselves as swingers without also labeling themselves poly. (The most popular group for swingers on FetLife is called "'Swingers' is not a dirty word.") On my survey, 2 percent of highly involved kinksters said they were currently in swinger relationships, and 2 percent said that was their ideal relationship. Open relationships were much more popular, with 12 percent of current relationships being open and 14 percent of highly involved kinksters saying that was their ideal relationship. Although many people in open relationships in the Scene are basically indistinguishable from swingers, the term "open" has far less stigma, so I suspect many people end up labeling themselves "open" when they better fit the profile of "swinger."

Given their small numbers in the Scene, I never interviewed anyone who identified as a swinger who didn't also identify as poly. There was considerable variation among people I interviewed in open relationships. Some people in open relationships expected that most sex or play that occurred outside the relationship would happen together. For example, Ellie and her boyfriend had been together for eight months, and she was clear in her interview that they were theoretically okay with having sex with other people together, but hadn't yet done so. She said, "We have a general attitude of we only play [with other people] together. We've flogged people, we've done electrical play with people, but we've never had a sexual relationship with someone else. We're both really picky about who we sleep with." Similarly, Luther and his wife, who were only very casually involved in the public Scene, had a cuckolding relationship where she would have sex with other men in front of him to humiliate him (which, for all intents and purposes, is still a form of having sex with other people together). Luther seemed to actively support the idea that his wife and her lover might develop a more romantic type of relationship, but it hadn't happened. He said he was also fine with her having sex with other people as well without him, as long she told him. He said, "Harry or Pete or Suzie, I don't care, just let me know. Let me meet the person so I feel that you're safe. And if they want me involved, fine, if you don't, that's fine." But when I asked if she had had sex with other people, he immediately responded, "No, we're not swingers. We're not into that. I would not want that. I mean if she decided 'I want a different guy every week,' I'd say, 'That's too dangerous.' I'm not into that. It's like pain: a little pain can go a long way—a little cuckolding can go a long way."

At one end, "open" relationships were nearly monogamous (partners like Ellie and her boyfriend, who were only interested in having sex with other people together). At the other end, they sometimes started to look like very cautious poly relationships. Carter said that he and his girlfriend had been together for two years, and

> as far as [BDSM] play goes, we have the understanding that we pretty much play with whoever we want. You know, like initial play at a party, it's not a problem, it's, "Hey, I'll be over here"; that's it. And basically unless we get romantically or emotionally involved with someone long-term—I mean as long as you're not screwing each other then there's no worrying about it.

He said that his girlfriend had had a "booty call" the previous summer, but otherwise neither of them had had much sex with other people. He didn't seem particularly opposed to the prospect, but he expected some real checking in before it happened. On the other hand, he also didn't seem to expect that he or his girlfriend would be developing other serious romantic relationships. In that respect, the relationship looked more like the profile of a swinger relationship—one where people had sex with other people without expecting serious romantic attachments. But, as Luther's comment earlier suggested, kinksters tend to assume that swingers want to have sex with *lots* of people, whereas people in open relationships are just open to the possibility of sex with other people.

RELATIONSHIP IDEALS AND PRACTICES:
HIERARCHICAL POLYAMORY

As open relationship dyads become more accepting of romantic relationships with other people, they start to look more like strict hierarchical poly, which can be difficult to distinguish from a relationship like Carter's, but hierarchical poly is a very broad category. On my survey, I defined "hierarchical polyamory" as "a primary relationship (or 2) and other sexual, romantic, and/or kinky partnerships." Twenty-one percent of highly involved kinksters said they were currently in a hierarchical poly relationship, with a further 3 percent saying they were currently in a poly relationship and were seeking a primary; 36 percent said it was their ideal relationship. Hierarchical poly is the type of poly that Sheff (2011, 2013) critiqued as the norm among the poly families she studied, arguing that it tends to be more heteronormative than the people participating in it often want to admit. Many kinksters have picked up on the same critique, and the term "hierarchical poly" has acquired increasing stigma in the Scene. Even kinksters who seem to be participating in hierarchical poly—for example, people who are legally married and only live with their spouse—are often reluctant to label what they're doing as hierarchical poly. For example, Vicky tried to explain her living situation with her husband and her other "poly partner." She said,

> One of the problems that I have is that, especially with things like polyamory and the kinky world, definitions don't necessarily always match. One person uses a word in one way and another person is using it in a completely different way. So I don't like to use the word "secondary" because it doesn't really explain the situation necessarily, depending on what other people think. There's people who are hierarchical, there's people who are like, "It's a puppy pile!"—that's not me.

Indeed, none of my interviewees spontaneously described themselves as hierarchically poly—although one did say that he wasn't. This ambivalence around the term "hierarchical" was also apparent in my survey findings. Among medium- and highly involved folks who were married and living with their partner, 26 percent described their relationships as hierarchical poly, but 25 percent said they were in "other poly" relationships (see below). There are definitely a lot of kinksters who are in relationships that other people would probably describe as "hierarchical" even though they themselves wouldn't.

In hierarchical poly, people usually aim to have a "primary," who is often a marital partner and almost always someone the person lives with. Then people form "secondary" relationships with others. In keeping with the stigma of hierarchical poly, kinksters rarely use "secondary" as a relationship identifier (and when they do, it's usually a sign that they're pretty new to the community). People will often acknowledge *a relationship* as secondary, but they rarely refer to *a person* as secondary. Kinksters don't usually introduce someone as, "Joe, my secondary." But in conversation (usually without Joe present), they might say, "Joe and I have a secondary relationship." Far more frequently, during personal introductions, they'll say things like, "This is John, my husband. And this is Joe, my boyfriend." However, in the Scene, a D/s relationship status takes precedence over all other titles except marital ones. Thus, the introduction might be, "This is John, my husband. And this is Joe, my Dom"—even if John is also the person's Dom. Despite the subcultural ambivalence around the terms "hierarchical poly" and "secondary," kinksters use the term "primary" easily, with 16 of my interviewees spontaneously talking about their primary partners, their desire for one, or their desire not to have one.

Sometimes people also form "tertiary" relationships (a term that is also almost never used in actual practice); these are often hard to distinguish (even for the participants) from "friends with benefits." Rather than describing these generally amorphous and casual relationships as "tertiaries" or "friends with benefits," kinksters more often label such people "play partners," which implies that the defining aspect of the dynamic is the BDSM and/or sexual dynamic. Many of these relationships are very ambiguously defined. For example, Mila explained her current relationship with her Dominant, saying, "I kind of built whatever it is that I have with Miles, which is to say I'm somewhere between being his play partner and his sub. We're not sure where." (Kinksters also generally consider "sub" or "Dom" to be a more serious relationship than "play partner"). Matthew described his current relationships in similarly vague terms, explaining,

[My friend's] wife is now one of my play partners. We're not like dating, but, you know, occasionally, we have sex and I'll take her out because she is awesome. She is a great chick, but nothing hardcore emotional there. And then, there's one or two play partners. Hey, we do kink stuff, a little fuck sometimes—whatever.

When asked to list their "current partners," polyamorous folks will also occasionally list people with whom they have no sexual or BDSM relationship, but with whom they have an intense friendship or bond. They will also occasionally list people they literally see only once or twice a year. When I asked Pat to describe his relationships, he gave me a long list that included a legal marriage and a deep friendship, as well as "a once in a while, like once-a-year-she'll-come-down-and-spend-some-time-with-me-sort-of-girlfriend."

Stricter hierarchical poly relationships really do tend to closely resemble open ones. Mike was somewhere in the border country between open and hierarchical poly relationships but refused to label himself "poly" because he didn't like the expectations that came with it. He labeled himself "nonmonogamous" and said he wasn't currently in a serious relationship but wanted a primary. He explained that for him personally, "It's a primary and then everyone else. There isn't a secondary or tertiary, there is my primary and then literally everyone else is on that [lower] level." Yet when he talked about other relationships that he had had with people, he conveyed a sense of hierarchy, and he seemed much more comfortable with the prospect of his *partner* having another serious romantic relationship than most people who considered themselves open did. The rules of Vera's marriage, on the other hand, conformed more to kinksters' ideal type of hierarchical polyamory. Her husband had another girlfriend (who didn't live with them), and she said that her husband was very tolerant of her need for BDSM (which he was largely uninterested in). But the rules of their relationship dictated that she was supposed to introduce partners to her husband if she was "going to play with them at home, have sex with them, or [do] something that will exchange bodily fluids [i.e., have sex]," adding, "and if it's a relationship, then he wants to meet them."

Hierarchical poly often doesn't follow the normative relationship trajectory of mainstream culture (meet, date, have sex, develop an exclusive relationship, get engaged and/or move in together, possibly get married), since "an exclusive relationship" isn't really part of the agenda and marriage is often unavailable if the people involved are already married. Hierarchical polys often end up substituting two other relationship signifiers instead. The first is what Vera just described, which polys generally refer to as "veto power." The idea behind "veto power" is that person A gives partner B the right to approve or disapprove of potential partner C. People don't usually grant veto power to just anyone, and it's mostly associated with primary relationship status. Many polys don't do "veto power," but the ones who do tend to identify more with the hierarchical model. Vanessa described two contrasting versions of hierarchical poly relating to relationship approval. She explained that her relationship with her current Master/boyfriend developed "painfully slowly" because "his partner, his primary [who he lives with], is very uncomfortable with things moving too fast. It was a year before he and I were allowed to do anything sexual. It was almost two years before we were allowed to even have sex." These kinds of postponements were unusual among kinksters doing poly, and Vanessa said emphatically that in contrast to him, "My wife knows everything that happened [in Vanessa's poly life]. She knows more details than she ever wanted to know. But I don't want to [omit] the one detail that she really wanted to know and I didn't think was a big deal."

Another important hierarchical poly relationship signifier is "fluid bonding," which refers to negotiated arrangements for various levels of "unprotected sex." Both my observations and survey results confirmed that condom use is deeply normative in the Scene, so partners who don't use condoms get a special label of "fluid bonded," and the concept is strongly associated with relationship commitment. When I asked Olivia, a long-term polyamorous woman who said she never wanted to marry, if the partner she was describing was her "primary," her immediate response was, "Yes, we are fluid bonded." She went on to describe how they had negotiated the fluid-bonding arrangement, not how they had negotiated the relationship itself. Having taught several classes on poly fluid bonding in the Scene, I have become cynically aware of the way many primaries hold on to fluid bonding as a way to restrict access to greater intimacy for other partners in their group. For example, a husband might refuse to let his wife become fluid bonded with her boyfriend to try to force them to stay less intimate or to hold onto his status as primary.

In its looser forms, the rules of hierarchical poly start to thin. Will contrasted his constrained and overly structured poly life with his ex-wife to the less structured poly life he had with his current wife, Ellen. He said, "My ex-wife kind of believed that I couldn't be involved with anyone unless she was involved with them too, because they were a threat, so it went bad in a number of ways." On the other hand, he said that Ellen currently had a girlfriend of her own and "has been really helping me with my confidence—to really kind of get me back out there. One of the fantastic things about my wife is she's all about [telling me], like, 'Get your confidence up!' 'Go talk to that girl!' "Go have sex! Find a girlfriend, go!' God, I love her." I don't know for sure how Will and his wife would have characterized their poly life on a survey, but it seemed to be intentionally far less rule-based than many other hierarchical arrangements I encountered. As I taught classes on polyamory in the Scene for the next few years, I found that married and cohabiting partners might have given the general appearance of hierarchy, but for the people in them, hierarchy often wasn't necessarily very important to them.

RELATIONSHIP IDEALS AND PRACTICES: OTHER POLY

As I interviewed folks and taught classes on polyamory, I found that for many polys, the relationship signifiers often associated with hierarchical poly—veto power, fluid bonding, and sometimes even marriage itself—are comforting. But I've heard many polys, especially younger ones in the Scene, describe these signifiers as superficial, controlling, or even just "gross." These people often gravitate more toward forms of polyamory that are known as "anarchical poly," "relationship anarchy," and a related variation called "solo poly." Folks practicing anarchical poly usually aspire not to constrain their partners or themselves with relationship rules beyond basic physical and sexual safety. Grace explained her self-identified anarchical poly relationship with her live-in partner of two years, saying, "Neither of us needs rules, actually. We don't really need to check in with each other about playing with other people. We don't feel a need to lay down how we are going to treat each other in a series of well thought-out paragraphs. I don't know. We just do it, and it works, I guess." People in anarchical poly relationships usually eschew marriage as too conventional and constraining, and particularly cherish the value that their partners stay with them primarily because they want to be with them, not because they feel obliged to be with them.

Anarchical poly relationships weren't common among the people I interviewed in 2012, but they seemed to become increasingly popular over the years. By the time of my survey in 2017, 30 percent of highly involved kinksters said they were currently in an "other poly" (that is, other than hierarchical poly) type of relationship, and 33 percent said that was their ideal relationship type. Folks with medium or high Scene involvement are *much* more interested in "other poly" than folks with low Scene involvement (although the differences for actual relationship practices are much closer). Whereas more folks with low Scene involvement say their ideal relationship is hierarchical poly, that trend is reversed for folks with medium *or* high Scene involvement. Kinksters put up much more resistance to the labels and expectations of hierarchical poly than kinky folks outside the Scene.

However, "other poly" includes many other variations than poly anarchy. It also includes people who do solo polyamory, which usually means people who choose to live without a partner long-term and who maintain multiple relationships with different people. I often refer to this relationship style as "apartment poly," because unlike hierarchical poly, which is more associated with living together and setting up a house, solo poly folks often aspire to have an apartment complex full of their partners living nearby but not necessarily together. None of the people I interviewed described themselves as solo polyamorists, but over the years I've had many opportunities to discuss solo poly at length with several people, including friends and partners. Solo poly folks often like having clearly defined personal space and time, and they like to have their lives physically and mentally organized around freedom.

Another form of "other poly" is polyfidelity, which is basically just monogamy with more people. In "polyfi" relationships, multiple partners generally live together and form a group family with the expectation that partners will have very limited sexual contact with others outside the family group. These are the poly relationships that disproportionately show up in the media for their novelty value ("four adults sharing a home and raising two kids together!"), and my impression is that they're fairly common among poly folks in general. They are, however, almost nonexistent in the Scene, and in all my travels, I've never met anyone in the Scene who was currently in anything like a polyfi arrangement.

RELATIONSHIP CULTURE AND THE SCENE

As we saw earlier, the Scene tends to sort for particular types of poly folks—particularly ones who identify as sluts and are less inclined to have children—and then teaches them to describe their relationship lives in terms of prioritizing individual needs and wants. Over and over, I've heard kinksters repeat the same basic phrase: "I'm just not likely to find one person to meet all my needs and wants." The Scene teaches kinksters that it's okay to want and have more than what one person alone can provide, and it teaches them that their desire for multiple people and a wide variety of sexual and kink experiences is valid and reasonable. I don't think the Scene has to work too hard to convince people on this point; once people have accepted this premise *and* also identified some rather rare and complicated desires in themselves ("I really want to be a pony trainer!" "I really want to be an expert bondage performance rigger!"), some version of consensual nonmonogamy is usually pretty much required to get their needs and wants met. (For kinksters whose desires are much more generic—e.g., "I'd like a sub"—monogamy is much easier than for people with a panoply of quirky kinks.)

Vilkin and Sprott (2021) found the same pattern among "kink-identified adults" (not just those involved in the Scene) in Northern California, who were very likely to be poly, emphasizing the (poly) opportunity to have diverse kink needs and desires met. However, my statistics and observations strongly indicated that the Scene's polynormative socialization program is very convenient (or, in more sociological terms, *functional*) for it as a subculture, because the Scene depends on people wanting to come out to parties and events for the purpose of meeting and playing with new people. Nonmonogamous people are more motivated to create, organize, and attend parties to meet and play with new people than are monogamous people who are only interested in socializing. Although sexually monogamous couples can still participate as long as their relationship rules permit BDSM play with others, I heard many long-term kinksters complain that monogamous kinksters were rare in the Scene in general because they showed up, found a partner, and then left. That certainly wasn't the pattern I observed in the mid-Atlantic: most of the time the social norms of the Scene pressured or persuaded those people to become nonmonogamous. There just weren't enough monogamous people in the Scene for it to be fertile ground for meeting other monogamous people and forming long-term partnerships.

My initial impression of the Scene was that it encouraged superficial hookups and short-term relationships, and this initial impression is sort of true. Thirty percent of kinksters who are highly involved in the Scene had six or more sex partners in the last year, and those numbers are almost double that of people with low involvement (16 percent). For low, medium, or high levels of involvement, if people had sex with their most recent new "play" date, about 90 percent did so within the first three dates (which is in keeping with a recent OkCupid study of mainstream preferences as well). However, people who did have sex on the first date were a little bit (and statistically significantly) different by level of involvement: whereas 24 percent of people with low involvement said they knew their new sex partner "very well," only 12 percent of people with high involvement said the same. These differences are significant but not enormous, and while they certainly suggest that the Scene encourages casual play and casual sex, they don't suggest that it's wildly different from mainstream dating and sex norms (Twenge, 2017).

However, the evidence much more strongly supports the conclusion that the Scene encourages relationships and romantic attachments. The percentage of people who say they have no "serious, committed relationships" steadily declines with more Scene involvement, with 38 percent of people with low involvement having no relationships but only 19 percent of people with high involvement saying the same (age is constant throughout levels of involvement). And the sheer number of relationships also goes up significantly and considerably with more Scene involvement: 35 percent of highly involved folks have 2 or more serious relationships, but only 15 percent of low-involved people do. Scene involvement even significantly affects how likely kinky folks are to say they have a relationship with "some emotional" attachment, with 20 percent of low-involved folks saying they have no emotional relationship at all but 7 percent of highly involved folks saying the same. Regardless of their level of involvement, most kinky people say they're interested in being in a "serious, committed relationship" if they "met the right person right now," with disagreement with the statement hovering around 15 percent for all levels. In short: the Scene has a much stronger impact on how serious relationships are (what kinksters sometimes call "how much relationship") than on how much sex people have.

Part of this difference likely comes from the polynormative culture of the Scene, which emphasizes relationships as being "deeper" (and often implicitly "better") than casual sexual dynamics. Olivia, a longtime poly person, explained that swingers have sex but are not involved in the "whole gamut" of "sharing" and "community" with their partners the way she felt poly people are. Confusing the issue somewhat is that many poly people (especially in the Scene) *also* have lots of casual sexual encounters in addition to having multiple relationships. These swinging kinksters still tend to follow the Scene's polynormative line on the impact of relationships versus casual sex dynamics. For instance, Amy, who identified as both a swinger and poly, said, "I think of poly as a deeper relationship" than what she has with her swinging "friends." Connor also said that his behaviors confused some kinksters, who would assume, "'Oh, so you identify as poly because you fuck all these people,' and I'm like, 'No, I fuck all these people, and I happen to also have multiple relationships.'" He added that he had partners that people assumed were more serious than they actually were, explaining that he wanted to tell people, "'Actually, I'm not dating him at all, we're just event fuck buddies.' I mean, that is a relationship, called *buddy*, but it's not a capital-R *Relationship* in my lexicon" [emphasis original]. The Scene encourages kinksters to believe that relationships are more important, desirable, and meaningful to them than casual sexual relationships, even though a number of dayslong kink events host orgies almost every night.

LEARNING TO PRACTICE POLY KINKSTER-STYLE

With an almost complete dearth of either fictional or real-life role models, very few people just slip into poly relationships on their own without social support, and even fewer succeed without it. Even the most enthusiastic polys pretty much universally agree that polyamory is tricky and takes a lot of work to be successful (Sheff, 2013; Taormino, 2008). I didn't ask on my survey how people learned to "do poly," but my interviewees overwhelmingly reported that they had learned about CNM—and usually poly—through their interactions in the Scene. There were definitely exceptions, but all those people had learned to do poly in LGBTQ+ communities or from Pagan communities. For example, Olivia, who was an older Pagan, said that she had been poly "pretty much [her] entire life." But for people who don't come from these other communities, the Scene mostly teaches kinksters to do poly, whether they are eager to learn or not. Zoe, a new kinkster, was initially reluctant to accept poly but said that exposure to the Scene changed her mind. The connection between BDSM and poly was so strong that she said when she searched for "BDSM" on the dating website OkCupid, she immediately found a friend who was also poly. Andrew, who was also initially hesitant to do poly when he arrived in the Scene, noted that the overlap between kinky and poly folks was "strange" but pervasive. He explained that a woman that he met at a BDSM party introduced him to poly in a "a more personal" way (i.e., by becoming involved with her) and said he thought the desire for multiple partners might basically be a kink in and of itself. He observed, "'Poly' doesn't necessarily denote 'kinky,' but it's definitely an alternative lifestyle. So I suppose it falls under the category of the BDSM thing—barely, I think. Maybe or maybe not." He said he learned about poly more formally from attending classes at BDSM events as well. Duncan summarized his experiences with relationships in general, and poly in particular, by saying grandly, "From the Scene, I discovered everything!"

Having entered the Scene, novice kinksters' relationship possibilities broaden beyond what many of them had ever imagined. Nate, who was young and still a technical virgin, neatly summarized the relationship world of the Scene versus the vanilla world after having been involved in the Scene for about four months. He explained,

> So far I've been monogamous, mostly because I didn't know that there was any other option. Now that I'm in the Scene, relationships in the Scene are a lot more complicated than anything you'll find in the vanilla world.

He said that he regularly met people in the Scene who would say things like,

> "Well, I have this guy as my boyfriend. This girl is my girlfriend, and then my girlfriend has another boyfriend, but I'm not with him. And then my boyfriend has two other girlfriends, and one of them is my play partner, but not the other. And then I have this guy who is totally separate from all of them, who is my Master. And then I also have a pet. I also have this person who I play with sometimes. This person will Dominate me occasionally, but that's really just a friend thing."

Nate's summary is barely an exaggeration. Thirty-six percent of highly involved kinksters said they had three or more partners they had "some sort of emotional and/or romantic relationship with," and 37 percent said they had four or more people they engaged in BDSM play with at least once every three months. If you're wondering what the reality of these relationships looks like based on that description—Are they emotional but not sexual? Are some of these people all involved with one another? Are some of these relationships sexual but not emotional?—your confusion is completely understandable, because based on that description (which is actually how many people introduce their relationships), you wouldn't know the answers to those questions even as a fellow kinkster. These types of relationship arrangements are incredibly flexible and highly individualistic, and will often be completely different by the time you see the person again a month later. Moreover, the Scene teaches you not to care too much about most of those details. It would be weirdly nonnormative in the Scene to, say, ask to tie someone up and then proceed to ask them about their relationship dynamics; kinksters often have casual sex and even casually *date* without asking these questions, so asking would generally be interpreted as a sign that the questioner was nosy or interested in seriously dating the other person. In contrast to more mainstream poly culture, which usually focuses more on settled long-term relationships with a very few partners, the Scene's poly culture cultivates a chaotic relationship buffet that kinksters pick and choose from at will.

These types of informal interactions and conversations with experienced kinksters expose new ones previously unacquainted with poly to its practice and norms. But kinksters also expect broad educational programming at BDSM events to include classes on poly the same way they do on bondage and D/s relationships, with experienced poly folks leading discussion groups and educational lectures about different poly relationship styles and how to manage them. Yet classes on monogamy, swinging, and what I once saw described as "alternatives to poly" are much rarer (although I have seen all those classes at least once in my travels).

In general, the principles of poly that kinksters mostly subscribe to aren't that different from mainstream poly culture. As with mainstream polys, kinksters tend to operate with the assumption of gender equality and some version of "If I get to have other partners, the other person does, too." Kinksters generally communicate this principle with negative or critical examples of people who aren't following it. For example, most kinksters I know critique a persistent negative stereotype in the Scene of a particular type of male Dominant who has multiple monogamous-with-him female submissives. Elijah described this stereotype as his main previous exposure to "poly" in the Los Angeles BDSM Scene, adding the common critique, "For me, that didn't click. You've got to allow your partner to explore, too." Ironically, counter to Scene stereotype, in the mid-Atlantic region, all three of the people I interviewed who were actually in these types of intentionally unequal arrangements were Dominant women with male submissives. But the subcultural expectation is that this type of arrangement is unfair within the Scene's own visions of poly.

Like other polys, poly kinksters almost always subscribe to the philosophy that it's normal and natural to love more than one person at the same time. For instance, though Liam said he learned how to do poly from the Scene, he said that even as a child he'd been confused about why people could only love one person at a time. He said he'd always thought, "Those two people love each other, right? Okay, so now there's a third girl or guy, whatever, but what's the big deal? Why do they need to choose?" In keeping with this belief, poly culture generally argues that jealousy results more from poor communication than some "natural" feeling. Tony, for example, insisted that a partner's other partners should not inspire jealousy, because "it's not a competition. They're your teammates. If you're doing it right, they are there to help more than anything else." Both of these principles are basic building blocks of poly, in or out of the Scene.

But my impression is that kinksters' poly differs slightly from mainstream poly in its apparently greater emphasis on the idea that partners should only be together because they want to be, not because they're bound by economic, familial, or legal obligations. Lily, for example, said, "I really want the people that I'm with to be independent and be with me because they actually want to be, not out of some sense of obligation or history or anything like that," and others mentioned similar philosophies. These ideas were much more common among kinksters practicing more anarchical styles of poly, but they're widespread throughout the Scene and probably contribute to the ambivalence many kinksters have around the term "hierarchical." My earlier statistics about the reversed preferences for "hierarchical" versus "other poly" for kinky folks who are in versus out of the Scene reinforce the impression that the Scene puts a slightly greater emphasis on these values than mainstream poly culture does.

Poly kinksters also often assume that monogamous people (especially monogamous kinky people) were giving up something deep and fundamental—greater opportunities for pleasure, excitement, and exploration—in exchange for social approbation. They took for granted that these things were superior to the advantages of monogamy (such as seemingly greater relationship security and easier navigation of scheduling, time management, and sexual safety). Lane framed monogamy in terms of unnecessary self-denial, saying,

> I think that human relationship dynamics are way too complex to just have one person. It seems so unnatural to me. Why would you give into this almost Puritanical notion of self-denial? I am not a Puritan. Most of the people I sleep with are not Puritans. So why would we still follow their bullshit rules?

Lily, who was in a serious relationship with one man, laughingly described one of the men she had a more casual relationship with, saying he was so submissive that "he almost can't even have sex traditionally. So he has all of these disastrous [monogamous] relationships with women who are not Dominant. Then they crash and burn and he comes to me. [smugly] I'm poly." Kinksters often tell stories like Lily's to highlight their perception of an association between a desire for social conformity to vanilla and monogamous life and the kind of repression and self-denial that Lane mentioned.

Kinksters' skepticism of monogamy often came from bitter personal experience. Doyle said that after repeatedly meeting people and having brief relationships, he became poly with the woman who became his wife because he wanted "it to last" and viewed poly as a way to help escape a propensity for serial relationships. More commonly, people discussed poly as a great way to keep them from cheating on their partners or from being cheated on. Melissa said, "I'm just very sexually expressive and my appetite needs multiple people, and [poly] really helps me get through that without cheating." Bi/pansexuals were especially likely to frame poly as necessary for them. Audrey, who had mostly been in relationships with women before she met her husband, said the couple had initially attempted to be monogamous but ultimately conceded to poly because, "I really missed being with girls" and because her husband's libido was larger than hers. Other studies have found that adult bisexuals are very likely to identify as poly (although the majority of bisexuals appear to be monogamous; Klesse, 2009, 2011).

Nothing highlights the depths of polynormativity in the Scene as much as the way monogamous people framed *themselves*. I interviewed very few people who identified as monogamous, and all of them were currently unpartnered. However, all three women who described themselves as monogamous described their preference for monogamy in extremely self-deprecating terms. Andrea reported that she tried poly with a man who already had a girlfriend but decided she couldn't do it because she's "too selfish," saying she preferred monogamy because she "realized [she likes] all the attention." Mila, who was ambivalent about whether she wanted to be poly, had dated a couple previously but found that she didn't like it, explaining, "It's a little bit that I'm an attention whore, and I was always going to be second." Ashley said flatly that she would be "pretty uncomfortable" with poly because, "I'm a selfish bitch." Note that the way these women learned to frame their preference for monogamy parallels the way that mainstream culture frames bisexuals and polys (with "greedy" being one of the most common adjectives

[Clarke and Turner, 2007]). Noah, the only man I interviewed with a definite preference for monogamy, explained that he felt like poly forced people to artificially claim to be happy about their partners' other relationships when they weren't. Then he apologized for saying that, and after I assured him it was fine, he said, "I think poly is something which one isn't allowed to, you know, express any doubts about sometimes." In short, polynormativity in the Scene is so strong that people are often uncomfortable expressing doubts about the value of poly and frame their preference for monogamy as a personal failing.

Poly culture in general frames communication as central to relationship success (Sheff, 2006; Taormino, 2008), and the Scene does as well. But the Scene takes this traditional poly value one step further and heavily implies that poly is a relationship goal that anyone can achieve through the panacea of good communication. Whereas the broader poly culture often emphasizes poly as an innate, born-this-way orientation like hetero/homosexuality (Klesse, 2014), these discussions are much rarer in the Scene. Indeed, though many of my interviewees drew on born-this-way language to discuss their kinky identities, they almost never drew on this language to discuss their identities as poly unless they had arrived in the Scene by way of polyamory in the first place. For example, Doyle, who was poly, explained,

> A [kinky] friend of mine, last weekend, we were talking about some difficulties I've had in [poly] relationships with communication and things like that. And he's like, "You need to develop a communication fetish." I said, "I communicate the shit out of this, what do you mean, I communicate all the time!" He's like, "Yeah, but did you like it?" I'm like, "No, I hate it."—Oh, hmm, actually *enjoying* talking about your relationship, that's a new one for me. So, I think that's what I'm going to try to develop.

Echoing Doyle, Will attributed the failure of his and his wife's relationships prior to marrying each other to failed communication: "The thing that really did us in in our last [poly] relationships was communication and not really being respected in the things that we were trying to tell our partners. We really vowed to make that our priority, the communication." Through basically every formal and informal mechanism in it, the Scene pushes the idea that good communication is the key to successful poly relationships. While I did occasionally hear kinksters coming out of disastrous (poly) relationships question whether they were "really poly" themselves, most of the time, they learned to attribute (poly) relationship failures to failures in communication rather than essential identity or preference.

Instead of framing poly as an orientation, the Scene frames polyamory in meritocratic terms: if they achieve a high level of self-awareness and communicate well with their partners, the Scene assures kinksters that they too can overcome the sad limitations of jealousy and live a happy poly life. Note that this strategy is functional for the Scene because it thrives on poly membership. The Scene gets and keeps a lot more members if it can convince them that poly is a skill it can teach them than if they have to be born that way. One of my monogamous kinky acquaintances referred with irritation to the "smug polys" in the Scene, which I think refers to the way that poly kinksters tend to assume that (1) of course *you* want to live this way, (2) they've succeeded at something that is difficult to do but worthwhile, and (3) poly life is obviously cooler.

KINKSTERS' POLY IN BROADER SOCIAL CONTEXT

Although kinksters' experience of poly is deeply grounded in the subcultural life of the Scene, we always have to remember that the Scene is in fact a *sub*culture, and it's strongly affected by broader cultural norms. One of those norms is mainstream racial/ethnic differences in perceptions of CNM. Kinksters, who are frequently oblivious to how deeply polynormative the culture of the Scene is, often lament how few racial minorities are in the Scene. Most (largely white) kinksters are unaware of how much more likely Blacks and Hispanics are than whites to disapprove of CNM (YouGov, 2015), which almost certainly affects racial minorities' involvement in the Scene. As I will explain in chapter 5, there are, of course, a wide array of social and structural factors that limit racial minorities' involvement in the Scene, but I think different attitudes toward CNM are important among them.

However, the most obvious influence of the broader social context on Scene relationships is through the increasing social emphasis on what Giddens (1992) called "pure relationships." Giddens argued that as the meaning of marriage and relationships has drifted further and further from childrearing and sharing economic resources with the family, societies increasingly imagine "relationships" as being more about romantic love and desire than about social ties and obligations. The ideology of anarchical polys in the Scene almost sounds like Giddens wrote it himself: the purest of pure relationships, where partners place no limitations on each other, up to and including having relationships with other people. As more and more people in industrialized societies abandon marriage and even cohabitation in favor of an increasingly individualized existence, the appeal of arrangements like anarchical and solo poly seems almost inevitable.

Larger social forces also create strange bedfellows among polys in the Scene. Strict hierarchical poly and hardcore anarchical poly are about as different from each other as relationship models as monogamy is from the concept of polyamory. Yet mainstream cultural norms about monogamy thrust everyone with deviant relationship tastes into an ill-matched mass and leaves them to try to sort it out for themselves. As Doyle explained from his previous relationship with two women:

> Saying you're "poly" is like saying you're "Christian"—you know, it doesn't necessarily mean that you have compatible things. At the time, Tristan Taormino's book [*Opening Up*, 2008] wasn't out and so we didn't really identify the fact that I was nonhierarchical poly, and one other person was sort of polyfidelitous, and the other person was sort of nonmonogamous at the core with two people. So had we realized that at the time we might have made better communication, but as it was, it just exploded in a wonderful big *POOF*.

CONCLUSION: PEOPLE CHANGE

For the purposes of this chapter, I've given you a snapshot in time of people's relationship perspectives and experiences. Since I became FetLife friends with most of my interviewees, I've watched their relationship statuses and ideals change considerably over time. One of my few monogamous interviewees inevitably caved and became poly, but one of my most ardently and passionately poly interviewees eventually became monogamous, then opened up his relationship, and finally went back to being poly. For many, the decision to become monogamous is sometimes tantamount to a decision to leave, or at least heavily disinvest from, the Scene; several of my interviewees had winding stories of involvement in the Scene where they said they left it for years at a time while they were in mono relationships, only to come back when those relationships dissolved. The polynormativity of the

Scene has stayed very much the same over time, but individuals' experiences of it vary greatly depending on who their partner(s) is/are at any given time. And these individual changes aren't really surprising in a subculture that so heavily deemphasizes the intrinsic, born-this-way arguments of the core poly subculture. As we'll see in the next chapter, the Scene's polynormativity has a profound impact on the way that kinksters do kinky ("power exchange") relationships with each other, since almost everyone expects to have a collection of relationships.

THE LOVE LANGUAGE OF KINK

BDSM Roles and Relationships

On a warm spring day in early May 2010, my then-boyfriend and I were still pretty new to the BDSM Scene and were sitting on a bench at Camp O-Town at one of our first big kink events. We were enjoying the sunshine and people watching when our acquaintances Dan and Antonia came walking up the main pathway. As they walked, Dan was punching his fiancée's upper arm hard enough to bruise, while she protested, "Fuck, Sir!" every time he hit her. They repeated this interaction at least three times as they walked toward us. Being on friendly terms with us, when they saw us, they both smiled and waved at us, saying, "Hi!" and then resumed their punching/"Fuck, Sir!" routine. It was all my boyfriend and I could do to keep from laughing hysterically until they were out of earshot. When they were gone, I leaned over and told him conspiratorially, "Toto, we're not in Kansas anymore." He nodded sagely.

For at least a year, Dan and Antonia (who eventually grew to be friends of mine) remained my metric for what a "weird kinky" relationship looked like. They had a reputation locally for being "hard players" (which is basically kinkster-speak for people who are probably kinkier than you—seriously). Although I rarely met people I would describe as "kinkier," I certainly met plenty of people who were *as* kinky. Over the years, I've observed and participated in a wide array of relationships where pain, control, and affection commingled in extremely complex ways. Eventually, my own metric for "weird" and "normal" shifted pretty far, and I started to understand love and violence very differently. One day two years later, a group of our friends were all sitting at a table having lunch together back at Camp O-Town and my husband punched his girlfriend (very hard) affectionately on the shoulder. When she said, "Fuck!" he smiled at her and said, "That means 'I love you' in Kink." I realized that my partners and I had learned to speak the love language of kink, a language where Dan and Antonia's punching/"Fuck, Sir!" routine really just qualified as public display of affection.

Kinky relationships like my husband and his girlfriend's, or Dan and Antonia's, get the most attention from outsiders because they appear so utterly foreign. My friend Alicia likes to joke, "Sometimes, when a man and a woman love each other very much, she asks him to slap her in the face." Her quip illustrates how much kinky relationships violate vanilla expectations that slapping someone in the face is abuse, rather than kinksters' alternative interpretation that it's a sign of intimacy and pleasure. Although several academic papers have looked at the social construction of BDSM roles (Carlström, 2017; Martinez, 2018; Simula, 2012), to the best of my knowledge none has really looked at BDSM *relationships* and the mental gymnastics they often require to overcome a lifetime of socialization that says hitting your partners is wrong. In the previous chapter, I explained how the Scene basically teaches kinksters to take the poly-ness of kinky relationships for granted. Given that polynormative context, in this chapter I'll talk a little bit more about how the Scene constructs BDSM roles, and then I want to focus more on how kinksters learn to construct and maintain their BDSM relationships—over which the Scene exerts a very strong influence.

FROM IDENTITIES TO PARTNERSHIPS

We saw in chapter 1 that kinksters learn to identify with a BDSM role and that these roles are closely tied to gender. But on some level, the Scene understands that people might have BDSM role identities that differ depending on particular partners (although mostly it tends to assume that, say, submissive-identifying people will be subs in their relationships). The Scene expects many kinksters want to be in a "BDSM relationship" with defined roles, traditionally denoted with a slash (e.g., Dom/sub, Mommy/boy, Master/slave). FetLife allows you to declare your own BDSM role identity and to separately declare your "D/s relationship" status with someone, and the options for both are bewilderingly long, including everything from "kajira" to "cuckquean" to "kitten" to "keyholder." Despite years in the Scene, I only half know what some of these more obscure titles mean. Part of my confusion stems from the fact that kinksters obsessively analyze and argue about the meaning of all these titles and identities among themselves, so it's not like you can go check the definitions in an official Kink Encyclopedia.

Because many people learn to take their identities as Dominants or submissives quite seriously—I once attended a workshop where the presenter and many of the attendees agreed that "real Masters" were "born, not made"—these roles sometimes become *the* defining aspect of sexual relationships for a person. (I hasten to add that many kinksters adamantly do *not* take these roles seriously and mock these essentialists.) However, my personal and sociological observations both strongly suggest that this identity construction is extremely problematic because these roles are relational performances much more than they are fixed characteristics of individuals. People submit to or Dominate a particular person, not the world. Consequently, the relationship someone has with an individual constantly refines, reshapes, and modifies these roles.

The Scene assumes that role identities will affect partnership patterns such that kinksters will seek out partners with complementary BDSM roles; that is, Masters and Mistresses are supposed to find slaves, Dominants are supposed to find submissives, Daddies and Mommies are supposed to find boys and girls, and, subculturally speaking, no one knows what the hell switches are supposed to do. People often end up policing their own identities (and being policed by others) in these contexts, such that people will question whether they're "really" Dominating their partner or whether their partner is "really" submissive to them. People frequently find that their relationship dynamics shift considerably over time, so that, for example, my husband and his girlfriend started their relationship as switches, then agreed that he would be her Dominant, then agreed to go back to being switches. Just like any other relationship dynamic, D/s dynamics are complex and often shift regularly. Consequently, we have to look at BDSM role identities *as well as* the relational context of their performance to really understand their heavily gendered meaning and significance.

THE ELEPHANT IN THE ROOM: GENDER

Although I'm going to ultimately connect BDSM role identities with relationships, I want to start by providing more nuance to the relationship between BDSM roles and gender that we saw in chapter 1. Remember that kinksters really don't like to admit that gender affects BDSM roles, even though it obviously does. On my survey, I allowed people to choose a variety of BDSM roles for their identities, but for the rest of this analysis, I'm collapsing all the Top-side and bottom-side categories because there are no statistically significantly meaningful differences between them. For the rest of this section, when I say "Tops," I mean "Tops, Doms, Masters," and anyone who kinksters describe as "left side of the slash" people; and when I say "bottoms," I mean "bottoms, subs, slaves," and "right side of the slash" people. Many kinksters complained online when I did this because they insisted that Tops and Doms, and bottoms and submissives, were quite different from each other. While that may be true at a qualitative level, it's not really true at a statistical level. (I checked.) Table 4.1 clearly shows that men are very disproportionately Tops, women bottoms, and genderqueers switches. But my data suggest that it would be a massive oversimplification to simply suggest that the Scene propels kinksters into those roles.

If we explore the sexed nuances of genderqueers more closely, we see that at all levels of involvement, gender-nonconforming people with penises (GNC-P; see Methodological Appendix) folks are more than *three times* as likely to identify as bottoms or subs than men are, suggesting a pretty strong

TABLE 4.1. BDSM Roles by Gender and Level of Scene Involvement

Gender	Women		GNC-Vag		GNC-Pen		Men	
	%	N	%	N	%	N	%	N
Level of Scene Involvement								
Low								
Top/Dom/Master	2%	2	10%	2	14%	3	54%	37
Bottom/Sub/Slave	69%	79	48%	10	46%	10	12%	8
Switch	29%	33	43%	9	41%	9	35%	24
Medium								
Top/Dom/Master	7%	29	11%	10	15%	12	61%	167
Bottom/Sub/Slave	61%	253	27%	25	36%	29	10%	27
Switch	33%	136	62%	57	49%	40	29%	80
High								
Top/Dom/Master	12%	31	20%	13	13%	6	63%	110
Bottom/Sub/Slave	51%	132	28%	18	35%	16	6%	11
Switch	37%	95	52%	34	52%	24	31%	53

association between increasing femininity and bottom identities. Even though men vastly outnumber GNC-Ps on my survey overall, this trend is so strong that bottom GNC-Ps numerically outnumber bottom men. The reverse effect is much smaller, however: gender-nonconforming people with vaginas (GNC-V) are only slightly more likely (15 percent) to identify as Tops or Doms than women (9 percent).

If we focus more specifically on the effects of Scene involvement, we see that women Tops quadruple from 2.5 percent among low-involvement kinky folks to 12 percent for highly involved kinksters, and there is a parallel decrease for women bottoms. The same basic trend occurs among men with very different consequences: more Scene involvement also pushes more of them to identify as Tops and fewer to identify as bottoms, resulting in *half* as many highly involved men bottoms. In essence, we see two separate trends happening simultaneously: Scene involvement is almost completely associated with women identifying as Tops and with a strong decrease in women identifying as bottoms; at the same time, less dramatically, it also encourages men to identify as Tops more and discourages them from identifying as bottoms. As these are correlations, there's no way to know for sure how much of this is the result of the Scene filtering out and sorting for specific types of people versus actually teaching people patterns of behavior. The gender ratios here become wildly distorted, with low-involvement men bottoms outnumbering women Tops five to one, and high-involvement women Tops outnumbering men bottoms two to one.

Although reluctant to acknowledge the reality of these gendered trends, many kinksters are still very conscious of the social and political implications of their relationship styles, especially relating to gender; however, my interviewees weren't focused on the feminist implications of what they were doing with anything like the fervor of Carlström's (2017) Swedish kinksters. I briefly looked at gender attitudes on my survey and found a few significant differences by level of Scene involvement. Kinksters with medium or high Scene involvement were statistically significantly more likely to agree that they identified as feminists than were kinky folks outside the Scene, but the differences were small, with 48 percent of people with medium or high Scene involvement strongly agreeing and 39 percent of low-involvement people strongly agreeing. On the other hand, there were no statistically significant differences in their agreement with the underlying core value of feminism ("I believe that it is important for women and men to be socially, economically, and politically equal"). The statement that elicited the largest differences was,

"I think that biologically, men are naturally dominant, and women are naturally submissive." For this statement, disagreement steadily and significantly increased through all three levels of Scene involvement, with 61 percent of highly involved folks strongly disagreeing, compared with only 42 percent of low-involvement folks. In short, I think the trends here are much too contradictory to support a simplistic interpretation that the Scene encourages masculine people to identify as Tops and feminine people as bottoms. Although the Scene often looks like it's confirming stereotypical gender roles through its BDSM roles, my data suggest that the Scene empowers women as Tops but probably disempowers men as bottoms.

FROM ROLE LABELS TO ACTUAL RELATIONSHIP DYNAMICS

People can hypothetically identify their BDSM role however they want, but BDSM roles don't mean very much in the abstract; they're mostly important only in the way they're performed in relations with other people. On my survey, I asked people, "How many people do you currently have a defined BDSM dynamic (e.g., rigger/rope bottom, Dom/sub, switch/switch) with?" Then I asked them, for up to three of those relationships, to write their role/their partner's role. Most of these followed pretty standard BDSM labels (such as the examples above), but a few of them were more elaborate: "submissive princess/Master-DaddyDom," "sub, pet/Owner," "Lord/servant," "brat/Alpha brat (top)," "cow/owner," "fucktoy/Sir," "knight/Queen," "switch–mostly top/switch–mostly bottom," "Editor/book," "hunter/prey," "DominAunty/godchild," "girl/Supreme Unicorn," and my personal favorite, "fish slut/Fish Domme" (yes, seriously).

Table 4.2 shows the percentage of people with each BDSM role identity and gender group for up to three of their defined BDSM role relationships, as well as the role they took in playing with their most recent first playdate. I describe people here as "role concordant" if their role in their defined dynamic matches their overall preferred role. You can see these results in table 4.2, but I want to highlight a few important points. First, women are so likely to identify as bottoms that for all three relationship levels, there are numerically more bottom-identified women who are the Tops in their relationship than there are Top-identified women who are the Tops. Second, Tops and bottoms with penises (GNC-Ps and men) have higher role concordance

TABLE 4.2. BDSM Role Concordance for 1st, 2nd, and 3rd Defined Relationships (Medium/High Scene Involvement)

BDSM Role Identity	Top/Dom/Master		Bottom/Sub/Slave		Switch	
	%	N	%	N	%	N
Women						
Relationship 1						
Top/Dom/Master	82%	41	14%	7	4%	2
Bottom/Sub/Slave	19%	59	80%	244	1%	4
Switch	22%	39	47%	83	32%	56
Relationship 2						
Top/Dom/Master	82%	28	15%	5	3%	1
Bottom/Sub/Slave	23%	31	71%	95	5%	7
Switch	51%	52	34%	35	15%	15
Relationship 3						
Top/Dom/Master	89%	16	11%	2	0%	0
Bottom/Sub/Slave	32%	17	65%	35	4%	2
Switch	44%	24	33%	18	22%	12
New Playdate						
Top/Dom/Master	83%	35	12%	5	5%	2
Bottom/Sub/Slave	12%	31	80%	206	8%	21
Switch	50%	86	42%	71	8%	14
GNC-Vag						
Relationship 1						
Top/Dom/Master	80%	12	20%	3	0%	0
Bottom/Sub/Slave	14%	4	86%	25	0%	0
Switch	36%	22	32%	20	32%	20
Relationship 2						
Top/Dom/Master	80%	4	0%	0	20%	1
Bottom/Sub/Slave	20%	4	75%	15	5%	1
Switch	49%	19	21%	8	31%	12
Relationship 3						
Top/Dom/Master	67%	2	33%	1	0%	0
Bottom/Sub/Slave	20%	2	80%	8	0%	0
Switch	32%	7	36%	8	32%	7
New Playdate						
Top/Dom/Master	77%	13	12%	2	12%	2
Bottom/Sub/Slave	15%	4	69%	18	15%	4
Switch	47%	30	41%	26	13%	8

(continued)

BDSM Role Identity	Top/Dom/Master		Bottom/Sub/Slave		Switch	
	%	N	%	N	%	N
GNC-Pen						
Relationship 1						
Top/Dom/Master	100%	12	0%	0	0%	0
Bottom/Sub/Slave	17%	5	83%	24	0%	0
Switch	56%	22	21%	8	23%	9
Relationship 2						
Top/Dom/Master	100%	7	0%	0	0%	0
Bottom/Sub/Slave	40%	6	60%	9	0%	0
Switch	52%	11	33%	7	14%	3
Relationship 3						
Top/Dom/Master	75%	3	25%	1	0%	0
Bottom/Sub/Slave	14%	1	86%	6	0%	0
Switch	33%	5	33%	5	33%	5
New Playdate						
Top/Dom/Master	90%	9	0%	0	10%	1
Bottom/Sub/Slave	16%	5	81%	25	3%	1
Switch	50%	19	34%	13	16%	6
Men						
Relationship 1						
Top/Dom/Master	92%	204	6%	13	2%	4
Bottom/Sub/Slave	9%	2	82%	18	9%	2
Switch	38%	34	27%	24	35%	31
Relationship 2						
Top/Dom/Master	94%	129	5%	7	1%	1
Bottom/Sub/Slave	8%	1	75%	9	17%	2
Switch	59%	35	17%	10	24%	14
Relationship 3						
Top/Dom/Master	88%	77	8%	7	5%	4
Bottom/Sub/Slave	17%	1	83%	5	0%	0
Switch	46%	16	20%	7	34%	12
New Playdate						
Top/Dom/Master	89%	133	7%	11	3%	5
Bottom/Sub/Slave	8%	2	88%	21	4%	1
Switch	58%	47	30%	24	12%	10

than people with vaginas (GNC-Vs and women). Third, in their first listed relationship, switch women are much more likely to be bottoms, and switch men are somewhat more likely to be Tops; but in both second and third listed relationships, switch women are even more likely to be Tops than men. Finally, GNC-V switches are *very* switchy (about equally likely to be a Top, bottom, or switch at every relationship level), but GNC-P switches are very disproportionately likely to be Tops at both the first and second relationship level. Overall, there's a tentative trend here of femininity being associated with exaggerated submission, as a lot of GNC-Ps who look like Tops label themselves switches, while a lot of feminine women who look like Tops label themselves bottoms.

Most of the same general trends hold if we look at the roles that people took in their last first playdate with a new partner. Because of the nature of relationship dynamics and Scene life in general, in first playdates, my observations and experiences suggest that people tend to heavily default to their comfort zones in terms of their BDSM roles; on the other hand, "switch scenes," in which both partners switch in the course of an encounter, are relatively rare in the Scene, so these results are biased against switches and switching. You can see role concordance for those first dates in table 4.2 for each gender group under "new playdate."

Here again we see that numerically, women bottoms who are Topping are almost numerically equal to women Tops who are Topping, although role concordance for women bottoms is higher here. On the other hand, here, switch women Topping numerically outnumber women Tops Topping and women bottoms Topping *combined*. Role concordance also remains highest for Tops with penises, but otherwise, the gender pattern isn't dramatic. For every gender group, at least half of the switches were Topping. GNC-V switches still stand out as the most evenly divided between Topping and bottoming, and no group has a high prevalence of actual switch scenes. In the Scene, switching happens much more in relationships than it happens during a playdate. Overall, role concordance here looks much less disparate by gender group than it does for defined BDSM dynamics.

When looking at real-world role concordance, it's important to re-member that these dynamics are partly a matter of available (desirable) matched partners, not just personal preference. I know many kinksters who say that ideally, they would like to be in a relationship as a sub, Dom, slave, Master, and so on, but they have great difficulty finding a compat-ible partner, so they settle for what they can find. Moreover, many of the switches I know claim that they lean in one direction or another (and thus will often describe themselves as a "bottom-leaning switch," for example), but for simplicity, that wasn't an option on my survey. However, previous research has suggested that many bi/pansexual women switches say that they prefer to Top women and bottom for men (Simula, 2012). My data allow me to test whether this actually happens on first playdates. Among bi/pansexual women switches, 38 percent playing with men Topped, while 55 percent bottomed. Meanwhile, 78 percent playing with women Topped but only 17 percent bottomed. Those numbers definitely appear to support that preference (there aren't enough bi/pansexual men to provide parallel statistics for them, nor even enough man-man play to provide more general numbers). Although available partners probably skew those numbers (available men are disproportionately Tops and available women disproportionately bottoms), I think the differences here are too large in favor of Topping women (compared with bottoming for men) to think that available partners are the whole of the difference.

THE DIRTY LITTLE SECRET: BDSM ROLES AND SELF-ESTEEM

In the end, I think the Scene's dirtiest secret about BDSM roles isn't really about gender but about self-esteem. Recall that I explained in chapter 1 that increasing Scene involvement is strongly associated with higher self-esteem. However, BDSM role + gender turns out to heavily mediate that relationship. As shown in table 4.3, for three of the four gender groups (men, women, and GNC-Vs), there are stark differences within each gender by BDSM role such that Tops have the highest self-esteem, followed by switches, followed by bottoms—for nearly every level of Scene involvement. GNC-Ps are the exception, with no consistent patterns, although they still have differences in self-esteem by BDSM role and level of Scene involvement. Of all groups whose self-esteem improves the most through Scene involvement, GNC-P bottoms experience the greatest boosts; on the other hand, the only group that really takes a hit on self-esteem from being involved in the Scene are bottom men—reinforcing my earlier point that the Scene isn't always good for them. Top men's self-esteem steadily improves with Scene involvement, and there really aren't enough GNC-P Tops to confidently say what their pattern is.

TABLE 4.3. Mean Self-Esteem by Gender, BDSM Role, and Level of Scene Involvement
(–2 = Strongly Disagree to 2 = Strongly Agree with "On the whole, I feel I have good self-esteem")

Gender	Women		GNC-Vag		GNC-Pen		Men	
	Mean	N	Mean	N	Mean	N	Mean	N
Level of Scene Involvement								
Low								
Top/Dom/Master	—	2	—	2	—	3	.32	37
Bottom/Sub/Slave	.18	79	–.10	10	–.30	10	.57	7
Switch	.59	32	.44	9	.44	9	.62	21
Medium								
Top/Dom/Master	1.10	29	1.30	10	.08	12	.88	161
Bottom/Sub/Slave	.47	253	0	25	.19	26	.15	26
Switch	.74	136	.54	57	.25	40	.56	79
High								
Top/Dom/Master	1.29	31	.46	13	.50	6	1.07	110
Bottom/Sub/Slave	.87	132	.33	18	.87	15	.27	11
Switch	.88	95	.62	34	.25	24	.85	52

All my experience teaching, going to classes, and interacting with people in the Scene has left me with the deep impression that kinksters want to believe that people's BDSM roles are the pure product of individual preferences. On the rare occasions I've heard people mention that bottoms often seem to have lower self-esteem, kinksters tend to look shifty and change the subject. Admitting that people like being degraded *because* they don't feel good about themselves is a grim notion in a culture that so strongly emphasizes consent and "genuine" desires. My numbers can't tell causal directions here—I don't know if people with lower self-esteem choose to be bottoms or if something about being a bottom generally causes lower self-esteem. I strongly suspect that both factors are true, as I'll show more in chapter 7 when I talk about social status in the Scene. But I do cautiously think that part of the reason there are so many fewer women bottoms among more highly involved kinksters is that Scene involvement is strongly associated with their increased self-esteem. On the other hand, since Scene involvement seems to negatively impact men bottoms' self-esteem, this also may be part of the reason there are fewer of them at higher levels of involvement.

CHAPTER FOUR

THE FANTASY: 24/7 RELATIONSHIPS

So how do these relationship dynamics play out? Alas, I never interviewed anyone who claimed to be in a "Supreme Unicorn/girl" or "Fish Domme/ fish slut" relationship, so I can't give you more details about what these truly unusual-sounding (even by the generous standards of the Scene) relationship dynamics look like in practice. We'll have to stick to understanding more conventional kink relationships. Kinksters generically formally refer to these dynamics as Total Power Exchange (TPE) relationships, but informally mostly just call them 24/7 relationships. The desire for these relationships motivates many kinksters' involvement in the Scene (finding partners and supporting their existing relationships), and the ideal of them is part of the central core of Scene culture. Among the folks I interviewed who were currently in relationships, more of them (27) were in some sort of 24/7 relationship than people who weren't (22). BDSM relationships with defined roles (e.g., Dom/sub) often don't meet the subculture's ideal type for a 24/7 relationship, but that ideal type tends to inform most other BDSM relationships. Kinksters will often consciously reflect on how much their defined BDSM relationship conforms or doesn't conform to the ideal of a 24/7 relationship. On my survey, only 17 percent of highly involved kinksters said they weren't currently involved in any defined BDSM relationship (versus 32 percent of medium-involvement folks). In short, BDSM relationships are a common goal for kinksters, especially if they're highly involved.

Although I've been trying for years to fully understand what 24/7 relationships are, I've mostly given up at this point because no one has anything resembling a common definition for them. As much as there is a consensus, it seems to be that 24/7 relationships are ones in which Dominance and submission play out in some way in a relationship "outside the bedroom," which is to say beyond sex and kink contexts. In essence, both partners agree that the Dominant partner is always in charge, at least when they're together. In the words of Mary, who had been married to her Dom for many years, the essence of their D/s dynamic was that "he'll always win every argument. 24/7, I am trying to do the best that I can to make his life happy and easy. My first concern is sort of for him." The ambivalent "sort of" there is telling, as there's a general agreement among a lot of the people who engage in these relationships that slaves and submissives should always take care of themselves first, and then *whenever possible* take care of their Masters and Dominants. Natalie, one of my respondents who was a switch and had been both a "Daddy" (her word) and a slave, was adamant about this rule, saying that in a previous relationship as a slave "[I thought I] needed to be what [my Master] needed, and what he wanted, and screw my needs. And, yeah, that never goes well." Now, she tells everyone, including her "boy," that a slave's "prime directive" is "take care of the property [i.e., themselves] first." She added that "it's kind of like the airplane mask idea. Help yourself first; then you can help everybody else."

Trying to parse the differences between the various relationship dynamics of submission and slavery further adds to the confusion. For the people who participate in these dynamics, many insist that there are crucial differences between submissives and slaves. Theresa, who regularly taught classes on 24/7 dynamics and had been a slave to Thelma, her wife of 16 years, explained that the fundamental difference between a submissive and a slave is that a slave has given up the right to really say no (although not the right to object to a decision). She explained,

> I could say, "I don't like this, I hate this, I dislike it, no no no no no," and she can go, "Thank you for your opinion." And then we go. And she can also say, "This is the end result I want. Make it happen." Whereas with a submissive you kind of have to go, "Take this step and this step and this step. And if you do, I will reward you. If you don't, I will punish you." Whereas a slave goes, "Uh, if I displease my Master, the world is ending." So in her capacity as Master, she can say, "I want my home to look a certain way, I want my children to be cared for in a certain manner." And everything I do, from going to the grocery store to scrubbing the toilet, is for her. And it's all-pervasive.

Although Theresa's description was certainly very articulate and there is no doubt that the distinction between these relationship types is extremely important to many of the people who engage in them, in practice, I'm hard-pressed to imagine any external observer being able to tell the difference between Dominant/submissive versus Master/slave relationships most of the time.

Having acknowledged that many folks in them perceive D/s and M/s relationships as being quite different from each other, I'm going to discuss them as being basically the same because I haven't found enough differences to do otherwise. I'm also going to use the default language most kinksters do for both, which is just "D/s relationships." In chapter 2, I talked about the "wine snob" hypothesis of BDSM—that increased exposure to the Scene teaches people to identify and focus on extremely fine variations of experience that are utterly indistinguishable to most people. I believe that the differences between D/s and M/s relationships fall into this category: differences that are real to the people who can "taste" them, but indistinguishable to almost anyone else.

In addition to the idea that one person has willingly given up control to the other person, these relationships also usually incorporate a sense of belonging and ownership/being owned. There are many symbolic markers and small rituals that people use to help preserve this actuality and/or pretext of control. The most obvious of these are the verbal markers of authority. It's common to hear subs refer to their Dominants as "Sir" or "Ma'am" as a form of address ("Yes, Sir." "Can I get anything for you, Sir?" "Fuck, Sir!"), and more rarely grammatically torturing it into the subjective case ("Sir told me to come find you."). Other common superordinate titles include Master or Mistress and Daddy or Mommy. Subs rarely get special forms of address from their Dominants. Kinksters often emphasize a sense of personal belonging by referring to the person as "my _____" (Dom, sub, slave, Mistress, etc.). But switch relationships get no such verbal designations; kinksters might say, "We switch," but they won't introduce a partner as "My switch" unless they're trying to mess with people or convey some sense of ownership of the switch.

Another important symbolic marker of these types of relationships is what kinksters broadly call "collars." Both submissives and slaves usually wear "collars" to indicate their owned status, and these take a wide variety of forms. There are traditional collars, which are often leather and have a ring or lock attached to them, but since many submissives and slaves prefer to wear them at all times, these collars are impractical. More frequently, people wear contemporary modifications that involve fairly subtle, nearly solid pieces of metal around their necks that can come off only with a key. However, I have also seen "collars" that were rings, bracelets, or even anklets with lock charms on them. The most important subcultural features of collars are usually that they're supposed to be a gift from the Dominant partner to the submissive partner and that ideally only the Dominant takes them off. Some people even acquire body modifications as a symbol of their owned status, with genital piercings being extremely popular. Much more rarely, people get tattooed.

The polynormative culture of the Scene means that highly involved kinksters often expect to maintain multiple relationships simultaneously, so the daily realities of 24/7 D/s dynamics often vary greatly based on the seriousness and intensity of the underlying relationship between the partners, and the 24/7-ness of some of these relationships can look pretty confusing to outsiders, especially when a sub has multiple Doms. There are three basic categories of these types of D/s relationships: relationships with primary partners (i.e., hierarchical-style poly dynamics), sexual and/or romantic relationships with secondary partners, and nonromantic and/or nonsexual relationships with secondary and tertiary partners. The practicalities of multiple relationships can sometimes make the idea of "ownership" look a bit notional, but kinksters generally expect poly D/s relationships to allow subs and Doms a lot of flexibility in their various partnerships. Regardless of whether they're primaries or secondaries, the D/s arrangements tend to follow what I call "terror D/s" (meaning dynamics emphasizing objectification, fear, and degradation) versus "affirmative D/s" dynamics (meaning dynamics emphasizing a sense of uplifting the submissive). Although people in the Scene do sometimes float around the idea of "affirmative D/s," the Scene itself has no labels for these differences, and I've rarely heard people talk about them as different relationship goals (even though they obviously are). I'll start by explaining terror D/s and affirmative D/s in primary relationships, and then explain how these dynamics shift in secondary relationships.

THE REALITY OF TERROR D/s: "I DO THESE THINGS FOR HER BECAUSE SHE'S SPECIAL"

Thirteen people I interviewed were currently in what they described as 24/7 relationships with their primary romantic partners. (Seven of those 13 people also had 24/7 relationships with another, less serious partner as well.) Because primary partners usually live together, they have to constantly deal with the daily realities of life together (paying bills, cleaning house, and sometimes raising children) while simultaneously trying to live out an exotic fantasy of control. In particular, although the fantasy of Master/slave dynamic claims that slaves focus their whole existence on their owners, the reality is that owners still have to acknowledge and care for the personal needs of their slaves, which do exist independently of the owners. As Natalie's earlier comment about the "prime directive" shows, most people who are in these relationships for the long haul recognize there's a fantasy of "my needs are my Master's needs" that is often at odds with the life of a real human being (even one who has been willingly designated as "property"). Having acknowledged that conflict, much of the subsequent negotiations within the D/s dynamic become focused on trying to maintain the illusion that both people are "really" focused on the Dominant's needs.

My observations mostly confirmed that the more people tried to emphasize the exotic fantasy dimension and the less they dealt with the practical realities of living a loving life together and acknowledging that the submissive really did have needs, the more dissatisfied they became with their relationships. Derek's relationship with his long-term live-in girlfriend, who was his slave, was a great example of this complex set of exotic and mundane contradictions. In his interview, he reiterated that he and his slave had had numerous conflicts in their relationship, and their relationship explosively dissolved a few months after I spoke with him. Their relationship was a pretty extreme version of terror D/s, even by Scene standards, and his partner later accused him of having sometimes abused her. His description of their relationship really highlighted the tensions between trying to simultaneously maintain relationship reality and kinky fantasy:

A slave really doesn't get choices. She does what I tell her to do. It's a funny thing if your slave is your girlfriend. The slave doesn't get choices, but the girlfriend does, so it's hard. It's a hard dynamic to keep because she really thrives off intensity. We've definitely had, like I said, some relationship issues through it all. But I feel like we have a lifetime commitment to each other. That's why I can call her my slave, and that's why I can say I own her. I truly believe she derives satisfaction from making me happy. How could you ask for anything more than that? When you have somebody dedicated in life to making you happy—even at their own expense. The tough part is trying not to take advantage of that, and we've had our struggles, but I don't think I could have a better partner. She has needs even though she doesn't necessarily verbalize them. And my job is really to pay attention to those needs. Because you know, even—let's face it, it's *all kind of a fantasy so you've got to really have some balance*. So even though overtly she's good to pleasure me or make sure I'm happy: no. Suddenly I need to make sure her needs are met. If I play with [my other partners], she needs to feel special. So I make sure I make her feel special. I surprised her, like the other Sunday. So I woke her up with kind of this aggressive sex style that she loves. And then after I was done, I put her in the tub, and I pissed on her, which she kind of likes to do. But then I gave her a bath, and I washed her hair, you know. And I took her to brunch, and I spent all day with her. We went to the zoo, and we did special couple stuff that she likes to do. And then here's the fun thing. What she really appreciated was when we got home, I threw her in the basement and locked her in it at 6:00, and I kept her there pretty much all night. And I'd go downstairs and beat her every once in a while and throw her in the cage, and that's the stuff she really gets off on. In other words, I was paying attention to her. And I don't do those things with my other play partners. I do those things *for* her because she's special. [italics mine]

Although Derek's story illustrates many common themes among terror D/s relationships, I must emphasize again that his relationship was pretty extreme even among those who idealized terror D/s dynamics; however, in many respects, it matched the ideal type of that dynamic, as was evinced by Derek's popularity as a Top with a certain type of bottom and his part-time gigs as a BDSM performer online. Terror D/s usually involves some form of what kinksters call "consensual nonconsent," which is the fantasy that the bottom is saying no to whatever is happening. This dynamic also tends to include heavy doses of humiliation and degradation (such as pissing on someone or locking them in a cage) and violence (such as beating someone). Perhaps most importantly, terror D/s derives from the pretense that the submissive has been (willingly) *demoted* and/or *objectified* to "property" (often with accompanying degraded and objectifying slurs such as "cunt," "bitch," "fuck-hole," "sex toy," or my personal favorite, "robot"). The pretense of the sub's demotion in primary relationships is obviously at odds in some very complicated ways with the fact that the Dominant has agreed to be in a *romantic relationship* with the "property," which is why I carefully use the term *pretense*. As Derek explained, in order to continue for any length of time, the Dominants in these *relationships* usually have to regularly do things to make the submissives still feel "special" even though the idea that the submissive is basically less than human is the foundation of their dynamic.

Despite the best efforts of the Dominants, these terror-based D/s dynamics are very difficult to maintain as primary relationships for exactly the reasons that Derek described: although both partners might take really great pleasure in their kink dynamics, those dynamics don't tend to smoothly integrate into the routine aspects of life together. Another reason they often become difficult to maintain is that in long-term dynamics of extreme consensual nonconsent, the notion of consent starts to feel very blurry. I once attended an excellent workshop on "terror play" where a few of the bottoms explained that although they really did love to be "terrorized" and even loved the person who was terrorizing them, over time, it became increasingly difficult to separate their "rapist" from their "boyfriend." These types of D/s dynamics usually become very messy at the point where there are real relationship problems (most frequently about commitment, but also more mundane concerns like money or chores as well). As increasingly actually hostile partners try to maintain a relationship dynamic founded on a pretense of hostility, a pervasive sense of abuse more than pleasure emerges. The result is acrimonious breakups such as what ultimately happened to Derek and his girlfriend.

Despite the problems that often plague these terror-based D/s dynamics, both the Tops and bottoms who engage in them often experience deep feelings of connection and intimacy as a result of their vicious kinks. Derek's comment from the Top's perspective that he does "those things for her because she's special" complemented the comments of Grace, who was the only other person I interviewed who was in a primary terror-based D/s dynamic, in this case as a bottom. Grace explained that she and her live-in partner, George, had no complex D/s arrangements, but their dynamic was simply founded on her "obedience" and his desire to be allowed to do things to her that scared her or made her angry. She said this dynamic increased her feelings of intimacy with him:

> Basically, the thing that comes to mind for me is a stun gun. I have a near phobia of electricity and before I went away for a monthlong trip this summer actually, he took out a stun gun, and he said he was going to zap me with it. I was like, "No, no, I'll do something else." I had to go out of the house for some reason, and I was like, "I'm going to go now." He was like, "No, you are going to stay and use the stun gun." I wouldn't go near him, and then when I was near him, I would cry and I kept saying, "No, just wait a minute, just wait a minute" for a long time. But then he did it. And I was okay, and I don't know, I felt emotionally intimate.

Until their extremely amicable breakup, Grace and George had one of the most entertaining relationship dynamics of anyone I have ever known. George, who was more than twice Grace's size, would occasionally pick her up and use her as a "human flogger" to hit other people. George has an incredibly dry wit, and Grace says that when she once asked him if she "had a safeword," he snarkily responded, "Well, if I was raping you in the ass, and you yelled RED [i.e., safeword], there'd be a conversation." Many people in the extremes of D/s relationships (especially the terror-based varieties) often give up on the idea of safewording as a matter of intimacy and trust. George and Grace's vicious D/s dynamic was founded on George's utter degradation of her (he was known to regularly shake his head and say with mock sadness, "Sometimes she forgets and thinks she's people") as well as his total control over her (she was always required to ask his permission to go to the bathroom when they were together, and for months at a time was allowed to pee only if she had his cock in her mouth or stuck her finger up her own ass). And in spite of—and, as Grace's account would suggest, *because of*—these dynamics, their great affection for one another was always readily apparent. As strange as it might sound, both the stories of Derek and Grace showed that the terror D/s at the heart of their dynamics was central to the feelings of relationship intimacy and affection they shared. In keeping with the research arguing that BDSM is a serious leisure activity (Newmahr, 2010; Williams et al., 2016), exactly like any other shared extreme hobby like rock climbing or jumping from airplanes, extreme kink was a way for couples to build trust, spend time together, and increase their feelings of intimacy.

THE REALITY OF AFFIRMATIVE D/s: "WHEN MY LIFE IS GOOD, HER LIFE IS REEEEALLY GOOD"

Given that I interviewed only two of them, it's obvious that very few people in the Scene enter into—and even fewer successfully maintain—terror D/s primary relationships. In contrast to the porntastic fantasy D/s tropes underlying so much of terror and degradation Domination, the vast majority of long-term primary D/s dynamics are strikingly ordinary and usually center around affirmative D/s. Instead of building trust and intimacy through fear and degradation, affirmative D/s dynamics build trust and intimacy through responsibility and rules. These relationships are founded on the idea that the submissive is now a *better person* for having become the Dominant's property; to show their appreciation for this uplift, the sub's role is to make the Dominant's life more pleasant in every way possible. Although people in these relationships might still occasionally play with violence, fear, and degradation, those things are definitely not the building blocks of the D/s dynamics of these relationships. Perhaps most importantly, the people in these relationships usually described them as being natural or instinctive, rather than emphasizing the feelings of contradiction that Derek described.

When I asked Mary how she and her husband, Marvin (whom she had been married to and engaging in D/s with for decades), negotiated their dynamic, she said it had really evolved naturally, explaining, "I would be sitting on the floor at Marvin's feet any chance I could without a thought about being anywhere else. If he needed a drink, I would just go get it for him. Now [due to chronic illness], I can't do that so much. It's sort of a treat when I get to do that, but yeah. It was instinct." Mary's comments also subtly revealed the way she was obeying Natalie's "prime directive," quoted earlier, to "take care of the property first": since Mary now suffered from physical ailments that prevented her from being able to move around easily, she had mostly stopped getting drinks for her Dom. She described consciously maintaining her D/s relationship, in spite of the organic way she described it developing. She explained that when their kids were young, "It was not an obvious D/s relationship between their dad and I—both of us being feminists and having to sorta temper everything with raising daughters to be feminists. . . . I think, being a feminist and being a submissive, I spoke up for myself a lot. Things were pretty even in our day-to-day life." In Mary's description, the D/s dynamic between her and her husband was simple, direct, automatic, and grounded in a gentle kind of everyday submission.

Like Mary, Theresa described a dynamic with Thelma, her wife and Master (her word) of 16 years, as being natural and easy. Unlike Mary, Theresa and Thelma had a 23-page contract they had written together outlining the details of their dynamic. Theresa said that "she pretty much has control over everything except my career, in which case she can advise and does advise." She said that Thelma would often tell her what to eat or wear, or what time to go to bed, and that "usually I agree to it because it's good for me." She further explained:

> *Theresa:* She can say, "I want you home by X time," or she can say "I am sending you to your lover. You will please him in this, this, and this way. You will make him smile, and I will believe you."
> *Me:* And I guess you have to trust her not to say things like, "You will make him mad."
> *Theresa:* [sounding almost shocked] Oh, gosh, no, that would not be—I do trust her not to say things like that because she wants my life to be good! And I trust her to want my life to be good. Because when my life is good, her life is reeeeally good.

Theresa's M/s dynamic was constructed around the idea that she and her Master were going to make each other happy by building a good life together, and this was the core of what I have come to see as affirmative D/s.

The stories may be less dramatic than Derek's, but the relationship appears to be a much more conventionally happy romantic one.

Another common theme among affirmative D/s dynamics is the idea that both partners take care of each other. Both submissives and Dominants in these dynamics would often describe themselves as "being responsible" for the other partner in certain ways. Chloe's description of her role as a slave of her long-term primary partner (whom she was planning to move in with soon) begins with her taking "care of him":

> I have to take care of him, and make sure he's fed, and has clean underpants. I mean, it is very much like a vanilla relationship. We have little nuances that change it from being a vanilla relationship to a constant thing. It's very subtle things. Like, I have instruction on where to walk when we're in public. I'm either directly to his left or I'm two steps behind him to the right at all times. Or when we go out, he always wants to drive.
>
> If we're shopping, he always wants to be the person to hand the money to the cashier. I have to get his approval before I order something out. Like, I don't have to really ask him what I can eat, but I do have to get his approval over something. Sometimes we'll discuss it, and we'll be like, "Well, maybe we'll just share something" or whatever, which is kind of vanilla. But I do have to actually get his approval. Like, [most] people wouldn't notice but it adds a little bit more to our relationship.

Slaves and submissives like Chloe tended to do practical things for their Dominants like feeding them, washing their clothes, or reminding them to take medications. Although the Dominants usually maintained technical control over many aspects of the submissives' lives (Chloe also mentioned that she sought her Master's approval for any major body modifications or before buying a new style of clothing), submissives frequently functionally managed the daily aspects of life for both themselves and their Dominants.

While the submissive version of taking care of a Dominant tended to emphasize practical tasks, for Dominants, taking care of a submissive tended to be more focused on emotions and security. Will explained this fairly typical division of labor in D/s relationships as he described his dynamic with his collared "little girl" (his legal adult wife, who often interacts with him as her "Daddy"):

> I take responsibility for her health, her safety, and trying to fill the needs that she needs. And she takes responsibility for keeping the house clean, because that's mostly her role, and serving me in the ways that I need. Whether it be,

"Hey, get me a glass of water," or "I really need you to wash the dishes," or something like that. She takes care of the household stuff, and I take care of a lot of the other stuff. Not so much right now since I don't have a job, but a lot of it actually is me taking care of her mentally and emotionally because she has issues sometimes.

Although the majority of D/s dynamics involved female submissives partnered with male Dominants, this practical/emotional division of roles between Dominants and submissives seemed to remain fairly similar even when the gender of the partners changed. Luther, who was the only man I interviewed who was currently in a 24/7 primary D/s relationship as a submissive, explained that to serve his wife, he would "cut her toenails, make dinner, clean the house, serve the food, go get her drinks, pick up her clothes, put away her clothes, run her errands, clean her shoes, do laundry, make the bed, change the sheets, whatever it takes, whatever she wants." In return for his service, she put a chastity belt on him regularly to show that he was "hers" and to assert her "total control of [their] sexuality."

What stands out in the accounts of both terror-based and affirmative-based D/s primary dynamics is the way that they are all first and foremost *relationships*. Despite the trappings of kink, these relationships really focused on the same thing all romantic relationships do—love, emotional intimacy, emotional support, taking care of the other person—or they failed. However, the Dominants and submissives in these relationships choose to interpret their mutual responsibilities for each other in a particular way, emphasizing power inequalities and interpreting specific acts like getting water for someone as signs of power and obedience. Rather than looking for equality (or defaulting to an unacknowledged power imbalance) in the way that they take responsibility for one another, people in primary D/s relationships deliberately use symbols of power to encourage the sense that one partner is more in control than the other and decide that it means something different when the Dominant takes care of the submissive than when the submissive takes care of the Dominant.

NONPRIMARY D/s RELATIONSHIPS: "WHAT COULD BE MORE ROMANTIC?"

As mentioned earlier, 7 of the people who had a primary D/s dynamic with a partner also had at least one nonprimary D/s dynamic with another partner;

another 14 people had a nonprimary 24/7 D/s dynamic but no primary dynamic. Because some people were ambivalent about the sexual/romantic nature of their nonprimary D/s dynamics, I didn't try to count them separately. Given the wide range of relationship possibilities outside of a primary-style relationship, it's no surprise that nonprimary D/s relationships outnumber primary D/s ones considerably.

That said, there are other reasons why nonprimary D/s relationships outnumber primary ones. While some people in the Scene desire primary D/s dynamics, many kinksters are extremely skeptical of those relationships (in general and/or for themselves); thus, many people argue that heavy D/s dynamics are *best* practiced outside a primary relationship. For example, Sofia, who was a self-identified Dominant who had been in the Scene for many years and had had several collared partners with whom she did not have primary relationships, nonetheless said quite emphatically, "I want to be in a primary partnership with someone who's my equal. I don't want to be making decisions for other people. I want people to have their own opinion!" Sofia clearly thrived on her D/s relationships with her nonprimary partners, but she also didn't want to do it every day, all the time. Luke, who was mostly submissive, was less adamant than Sofia about the problems with a hypothetical 24/7 relationship, but he was still very skeptical about the idea, saying, "I would be okay with, like, a total power exchange or something, but I still like taking into account, like, reality of life. You have a job, you have family, you have other obligations. So you have to kind of have somebody who's sane enough to realize that." The professed skepticism from many kinksters toward primary D/s relationships, combined with the yearning for *a* D/s relationship, helped contribute to the proliferation of nonprimary D/s relationships.

Because they are often so loosely defined, nonprimary D/s relationships have far more leeway to focus more on kink and less on emotional support. A 24/7 relationship where you see the person only a couple of times of month is pretty flexible with the idea of "24/7" (although sometimes it just means that in the time the partners spend together, there is a very clear system of control). There also tends to be a lot less emphasis on the day-to-day aspects of control (nonprimary Doms rarely make decisions about what their subs will eat or wear every day, for example). Despite their greater emphasis on kink, these relationships tend to focus more on emotional connection than kink if they last for more than a few "playdates." Natalie explained in detail all the ways that she "checks up on" her "boy" (i.e., submissive), even though they are "secondaries" and he has a primary who is not Natalie: asking for regular text messages from him, calling people to make sure he was safe when a tornado hit, and paying for him to go to kink events where he serves her (which is common in these dynamics). She explained that although D/s was heavily integrated into their relationship, the ultimate foundation of it was caring for each other. Even John, who glibly claimed to have had a six-month relationship with his partner "Megan's tattoos" (as if she were an art object he was dating rather than a person) quipped, "Our relationship is based on (a) Megan doing stuff for me and (b) me hitting Megan." When I asked if the relationship was "romantic" or "just for fun," he said, "Well, what could be more romantic than hitting someone and having them do stuff for you?" In the love language of kink, hitting someone and having them do stuff for you is often the quintessence of true love.

As Natalie's and John's comments would suggest, the same dichotomy of objectification/degradation/terror (John) versus affirmative-based (Natalie) D/s applies to nonprimary D/s dynamics just as it does to primary D/s dynamics. For example, Owen, who was married to a vanilla woman, said that for his D/s Mistress (who his wife knew about), "What I like is to be a good whore," adding, "I'm like a pet. I'm a little pig." Although Owen was not masochistic, he enjoyed feeling degraded in the same way that many people in terror D/s dynamics did. Owen specifically explained that although he sought sexual D/s relationships with other women, because of his wife's preferences he was careful to try to keep those other relationships relatively unromantic. By contrast, Vanessa, who was the Dominant of her wife, and had a Master with whom she had an intense affirmative D/s secondary relationship, explained that "[my Master] just said he deserves the best, and that I'm the best for him. And it's not up to me to decide otherwise. He's taken certain words out of my vocabulary—I'm not allowed to use the words 'fat' or 'ugly' or 'disgusting' or any of those terms [to describe myself]." As with primary D/s dynamics, the vast majority of nonprimary D/s dynamics were grounded more in affirmative than terror-based D/s. However, based on my observations of kinksters, I suspect that terror-based D/s dynamics tend to be more sustainable in more casual relationship dynamics. When people have less of a romantic relationship like Owen and his Mistress, they have less at stake in trying to maintain the illusion that one person is a "whore" or whatever other degraded label they prefer.

NONPRIMARY D/s RELATIONSHIPS: SERVICE

Perhaps one of the most unexpected relationships that the Scene fosters are nonsexual D/s relationships, usually heavily focused around service, many of which include components of mentorship. These service dynamics are almost always a form of nonprimary D/s dynamic. A few people adamantly maintained a nonsexual relationship based on the preference of one of the partners (e.g., based on one partner's asexuality [Sloan, 2015] or another's monogamy). However, the majority of these nonsexual relationships were rather ambiguous, both in terms of sex and in terms of romance. Tellingly, it was often impossible to tell from people's descriptions if they had a sexual relationship without explicitly asking them. For example, Pat, who was a very well-known presenter within the Scene, explained,

> I have a slave of almost four years, and she and I do a lot of traveling together. She goes to events with me very often. And we have a nonsexual relationship, although sometimes we play and that line gets kind of blurry. But for the most part we don't consider ourselves romantic partners. . . . She gets the experience of being around me as I do the things that I do so that she can learn how to do them.

Mila described a similar kind of ambiguity in her evolving relationship with her Dominant, Miles. When I asked if they had a romantic relationship, she responded ambivalently, "Nope, he's got a girlfriend. It's not romantic at all. It's a little romantic. Not really. It's not that kind of romantic. He's had a girlfriend for four years now. She and I are friends. It's all cool." Miles and his girlfriend were poly, and while Mila was initially hesitant to be poly, she eventually began dating him after our interview. Although Miles and Mila were not having sex at the time of our interview, she described how much she enjoyed being his "cup holder," massaging his feet, and having him single-tail her. If anyone else wanted to play with her, they were required to get Miles's permission. These service-based nonromantic (maybe)/nonsexual (maybe) relationships usually did not fit in very well with the terror/affirmative D/s dichotomy described above, since neither play nor sex was really at the heart of them. They were focused on the joy that one person received from serving another and the gratitude the other person could bestow in reward for that service.

CONCLUSION: A DIFFERENT LOVE LANGUAGE

It's tempting to accept at face value the idea that BDSM relationships are unequal, but the supporting evidence for that idea was very ambivalent. Connor described a class taught by a BDSM slave he admired, saying, "She taught a class called 'powerful slavery.' She reminded me of the profound act involved in handing yourself over to another human being, because how can you hand over your power if there's no power to hand over?" Despite the issues of self-esteem I discussed earlier, this philosophy is definitely at the heart of the way the Scene imagines D/s relationships: a strong, independent, competent person makes the conscientious and willing decision to give over control of themselves to another person. At that point, it's pretty difficult to tell if a relationship is really unequal or if people have simply designed a host of complex personal rituals to symbolize inequality between them.

Even Chloe, who was in one of the most conservative D/s arrangements of anyone I interviewed, said that her arrangement with her Master was "kind of like a 1950s household" in that he was in charge and she did most of the chores for him. Then she added, "but not quite, because I'm still expected to get a job and support myself and all that." Moreover, Chloe maintained her own (nonsexual) slave independent of her own relationship with her Master. On average, the power inequities that kinksters celebrated and eroticized in their relationships weren't that unequal by the standards of a society where married women still do an average of about twice as much housework as their husbands. Indeed, I've often half-joked that most D/s relationships I see among kinksters are more power-equal than my parents' (presumably vanilla) relationship. The thing that seems weird to the rest of society is that many kinksters—who are often very upset about this inequality on a social and political level—have nevertheless decided to personally enjoy it in their own lives. From a sociological perspective, the most deviant things about relationships in the Scene are that women can be the ones in charge of them and that partners actually openly negotiate their power inequalities.

Perceptions, much more than actual behaviors, often shape the foundation of D/s relationships. The people in these relationships decide to interpret various actions as signs of Dominance or submission, but there are very few actions that are inherently Dominant or submissive. I know many subs who say an important part of their job is cooking for their Doms, but I also know at least one Dom who says that cooking for his subs is part of his Dominant caretaking. Among the examples we saw in this chapter, Derek, a

Master, washed the hair of his slave; meanwhile, Mila, a submissive, rubbed the feet of her Dominant. Depending on how people do these things, they can be *either* Dominant or submissive (or switchy, but that's kind of a different story). People in the relationships chose to interpret "taking care of each other"—something that both Dominants and submissives try to do— as signs of Dominance or submission. Taking care of each other is something that basically everybody tries to do in relationships, and there's nothing particularly kinky about it, but people in 24/7 relationships learn to emphasize it to highlight their D/s dynamics. However, as most of my interviewees noted, minus the trappings of BDSM (most notably collars), outsiders observing their relationships would probably never know they were doing D/s.

In the end, BDSM relationships survive or fail on the basis of trust much more than rituals of perceived inequality. Mainstream vanilla culture tends to be pretty comfortable with the idea that engaging in risky behavior with other people works well to build trust; organizations spend millions of dollars to send people out to engage in trust-building exercises where they must fall into each arms and climb complex rope courses. Mainstream culture decided that these things aren't kinky, so it's okay for everybody to do them. In reality, of course, there's not a very big difference between a ropes course and many kinds of rope bondage (indeed, the hip harnesses used in both are nearly identical); nor is there a very big difference between being told by a camp counselor to fall into people's arms and many acts of Dominance/ submission. In effect, BDSM is just a very powerful, very stigmatized trust-building exercise, and it's incredibly effective for building trust and intimacy in relationships. Due to its risks and complexities, the Scene tries to be very careful about how it teaches people to manage these relationships, and how it manages partnerships and play. In the next two chapters, we'll move up our scale of analysis from these more individual and intimate personal experiences to the larger subcultural values and rules that shape the way kinksters do BDSM casually and in relationships.

LEARNING THE ROPES

Values and Rules in the Scene

OUR PEOPLE

The BDSM subculture is a voluntary (deviant) social group that very particular kinds of people self-select into, and you can start figuring out which kinds of people select in pretty quickly once you become involved. Even assuming, as the Scene often does, that a taste for kink is an innate characteristic of a person the same way that being gay is, people still have to make a choice to actively participate in the subculture. That said, we'll see that many of the people who show up in the Scene ended up there because they felt unwelcome so many other places, so their "active" choice to participate was definitely limited by other social constraints. In an ideal study, I'd love to be able to compare information about all the people with kinky tastes who did or didn't join and stay in the Scene. But as we saw in chapter 1, a taste for kink is very, very difficult to define and measure, and our pool of potential kinksters might reasonably include almost everyone. Given that large pool of potential kinksters, in this chapter I want to explore how the Scene as a social and cultural entity filters for (i.e., attempts to attract and maintain) the "right" kinds of people and then teaches them how to do kink and relationships "right." As they learn to do BDSM "right," kinksters learn to recite a list of formal rules (some of which I'll explain in this chapter, some in the next), but as we'll see, the degree of conformity with these formal rules varies considerably based on the rule.

The classical sociologist Robert Merton (1938) famously described a typology of deviance based on a continuity of conformity. According to Merton, conformists accept mainstream social goals and actively work toward them in the conventionally accepted way, innovators accept the goals but don't use socially accepted means to achieve them, ritualists don't accept the goals but keep working toward them anyway, retreatists give up on the goals and conventional social participation (and are often associated with drug subcultures), and rebels make new goals and create new routes to achieving them. These are, of course, "ideal types," which means that no one/group perfectly conforms to them. If we follow this typology, I think that the Scene mostly lands in the rebels category, at least for relationships and sexuality. This typology is useful here because it helps clarify why kinksters often don't get along so well with some people in adjacent subcultures. Burners, for example, with their idealism and heavy drug use, in this typology would land squarely between retreatists and rebels; swingers, who subculturally traditionally claim they are "monogamous," would be more like innovators—keeping to a traditional vision of what relationships look like while trying to maintain them through unorthodox means. Kinksters as a group, on the other hand, tend to be highly conforming in their educational and professional lives (that is, they tend to be well educated, and many are very serious about their careers), but rebels in their private family lives. An extremely popular kink on FetLife is for "a white picket fence and a dungeon in the basement." The phrase intentionally conjures an image of conventional middle-class conformity subverted by hidden relationship deviance, and it captures the deviant spirit many kinksters aspire to.

When most kinksters describe the kinds of people who are attracted to the Scene, they generally list: weirdos, geeks/smart people, polyamorous people, and people who are very "open." I'll profile all these qualities in this chapter, but keep in mind that aside from those qualities, kinksters don't tend to be very aware of the actual characteristics of "our people." Kinksters tend to have a basic awareness of their demographics—enough to know that the pansexual Scene largely consists of heterosexual/flexible cis men and bi/pansexual/queer cis women who are almost entirely white and in the 25–45 age range. But they're often unaware of some of their other demographic idiosyncrasies, such as their high levels of formal education, Pagan or no religious affiliation, low rates of marriage, and low desire for children. It's a chicken-or-egg question whether the Scene's demography shapes its values and norms or if its values and norms shape its demography, but I'm pretty sure the final answer is: both.

THE LAND OF MISFIT TOYS

In my considered opinion, the most important value the Scene expects from its members (even more than the desire for BDSM) is a desire to invert a classic high school social order: no more cheerleaders and jocks or "Queen bee" prom queens at the top of the social hierarchy. Instead, the Scene is all about geeks, geek sexy, and geek desire. "Geeks," in the context of the Scene at least, mean people who show unabashed enthusiasm for the things they love, are "smart," and value weirdness. In terms of hobbies and interests, it includes people who love Dungeons & Dragons–style role-playing games, attend Renaissance Faires, enjoy fantasy and science fiction novels, and/or did theatre in high school and college. This particular conception of "geek" has been heavily promoted at massive "alternative lifestyle" events like DragonCon and AwesomeCon (Kington, 2015), which are enormous hotel-based gatherings that draw sci-fi and fantasy fans to do everything from get books signed by their favorite authors to participate in a kilt-blowing contest with a leaf blower. These cons aren't BDSM events per se, but they heavily influence the culture of the Scene. The Scene often treats these alternative lifestyle events as a recruiting ground, with many kink events advertising via programs, flyers, presenters, official promoters, and most importantly social networking to find new attendees.

Geeks in all these adjacent subcultures often frame themselves in opposition to "jocks," so it's probably not surprising that I've rarely met folks in the Scene who mentioned a serious high school or college athletic career (although many men have some background in martial arts) and only a few people who even mentioned enjoying watching sports. Only one of my interviewees spontaneously mentioned involvement in sports (having been a wrestling coach), but 5 spontaneously mentioned theatre, either as a profession or a hobby. Moreover, 11 of my interviewees spontaneously used the word "geek" positively to refer to themselves or other people, suggesting some of the pleasant connotations the word has for kinksters. Geeks are supposed to bring unabashed enthusiasm with them, and enthusiasm is a driving force for how the mostly volunteer-driven world of the Scene functions. And as we'll see in the next chapter, geeks also heavily shape the culture of aesthetic performance in the Scene.

The "geek chic" culture of the Scene also highly values intelligence, both abstractly and as an erotically desirable characteristic of individuals. When kinksters learned that I have a PhD, their first response was often, "That's hot." In interviews, eight men and three women mentioned that intelligence was one of their biggest turn-ons when asked what they looked for in a partner. Moreover, kinksters often believe that as a group they're smarter than the rest of the population. For example, Nathan argued that "people in the Scene are generally a lot more intelligent than the general population," adding, "I think it's more a correlation between the open-minded and the intelligent." Nathan's argument is that the Scene attracts people who are more open-minded and that open-mindedness is highly correlated with intelligence. His argument is well supported by science, which finds that intelligence and what psychologists call "openness to experience" are highly correlated (Kanazawa, 2010). But as we'll see throughout the rest of this chapter, the Scene wants people who are open-minded *in particular ways*.

Despite the geek chic that pervades the culture of the Scene, many kinksters don't self-identify as geeks. However, virtually all kinksters I've met perceive themselves as very weird. In the Scene, these self-identified weirdos find a home because the Scene not only tolerates but actually *values* weirdos—particularly people who are weird and (at least learn to be) proud of it. John, who had been a BDSM party promoter and organizer for many years, explained that his entire business strategy had always focused on creating events for "weird people" that they would enjoy. His business strategy was clearly sound in theory, as Gabe explained that the greatest value of the Scene for him was to be in the company of other weird people. He explained that he loved the Scene because he enjoys

> just hanging out and talking and getting to know people for real. You know, the Lifestyle and the people that are attracted to it—it's the Land of Misfit Toys. And I totally relate to that, because I am a misfit toy. It's just hanging out, and drinking, whatever—but meanwhile people are getting tied up and screaming and all that, like, simultaneously.

"The land of misfit toys" is a reference to the 1964 animated movie *Rudolph the Red-Nosed Reindeer*, which features an island that is home to toys rejected from Santa's workshop because they're weird, disturbing looking, or don't work right—but are harmless and good-hearted. As Gabe's quote suggests, the Scene often imagines itself as a similar collection of harmless and well-meaning social misfits that society lacks the imagination and willingness to embrace and understand.

I've heard many people over the years use the specific phrase "misfit toys" to describe folks in the Scene, evoking the sense that kinksters were rejected from mainstream social worlds but finally found a home in the Scene. For example, Pat was a transgender man who did not yet reliably pass as a man. Yet he said that when I go to a Scene event I don't get stared at for having blue hair, or for being fat, or for being gender nonnormative. Like, people just kind of go, "Oh, that's Pat," and they move along. Whereas in the real world, or in the vanilla world, like, it's perfectly acceptable to stare at someone like me and kind of make judgments of me based on knowing nothing at all. But I think in Scene community there's a lot more acceptance of people who look and act different.

That warm feeling of acceptance often permeates kinksters' social lives inside the Scene, from casual acquaintances to lovers and spouses to deep friendships that people often refer to as "family." Kinky people check out the Scene for all sorts of reasons, but when they stay, it's usually because they feel a deep connection with the types of people they meet there and an almost giddy sense of belonging.

All told, five interviewees referred to the Scene as "home," but many others talked about the feelings of acceptance they found there. Lane, a trans woman, said that in her initial exposure to the Scene, she was instantly taken with "the freewheeling acceptance of diversity of bodies and actions, and it was sort of this feeling of, 'Hi, I'm home. This is awesome.'" Melissa, who was a larger woman, felt celebrated and accepted in the Scene, saying, "They're open to so much more [here]. You're a woman with curves—they love it!" For the people who become loyal members of the Scene, it's a place they feel accepted for who they are, regardless of level of weirdness, gender nonconformity, or body type. And for many, it's the first time in their lives that they've ever felt cool.

HOMOGENEOUS NONCONFORMITY

When reading the glowing accounts of the people who form the core of the Scene, it's easy to get a very rosy and idealistic picture of it. As someone who was enthusiastically courted and embraced by the Scene, and who felt cool for the first time in my life there, it's easy for me to slip into that biased perspective. But the enthusiasm of those who describe the Scene as "home" is entirely the result of self-selection: the people who love the Scene stay in it and are around for a researcher to interview. In addition to that core, I intentionally interviewed people who were on the edges of the Scene and I personally know many others, which gave me more perspective about how people on the periphery often perceive it.

Kinksters loyal to the Scene love to celebrate its differentness and diversity. But to people on the periphery, that "differentness" and "diversity" often starts to appear suspiciously homogeneous. My interviewee Elise stumbled across this truth when she said she had defended the Scene to her Dom/boyfriend from a different country who was reluctant to participate in the public Scene, assuring him that "when we come together in a group, like in our munches, it's just about getting together with people who think the same way." The Scene celebrates certain *types* of nonconformity like those mentioned by Pat, such as Muppet hair colors (i.e., bright Manic Panic–style colors) and gender nonconformity. But these are the types of nonconformity that signify the sorts of people who "think the same way," as opposed to, say, punks or people from the body mod subculture (both of whom very occasionally appear in the BDSM Scene).

We also have to be cautious about characterizing the Scene's acceptance of certain groups. For example, in general, compared to mainstream society, the Scene is very tolerant of larger bodies. However, I know at least one woman in the New York–area Scene who put a toe in and promptly left because people were actively criticizing her for having public sex with her larger body. These kinds of comments are an explicit violation of formal rules in the Scene, but they happen anyway. That said, the Scene varies massively by geography and microculture, and I could never safely generalize about all parts of it, even within the same geographic locale. One of the major variations among those microcultures is tolerance of queerness and fatness, with some very tolerant and others not tolerant at all. I personally attended and even worked at BDSM parties and events in different parts of the country that I would never want to go to again because their attitudes and practices were so far out of line with my own values and ideals.

Even within a single geographic area such as the DC/Baltimore Scene, there are distinct groups that hold their own parties, munches, classes, and get-togethers, and these microcultures vary massively in terms of how tolerant and accepting they are of certain kinds of diversity. In DC, one of my interviewees, Harry, told me, "I sometimes tell the joke that [the] BDSM [Scene] is the last place where fat girls go to get fucked," explaining that since he's "not into that," he often didn't go to many social gatherings in the Scene. His "joke" was notable for several reasons. First, he was the only person among all of my interviewees to make such a blatantly fat-shaming comment. Although I've heard similar whispering comments from good friends over the years, the Scene's norms of "body positivity" strongly discourage people from openly observing the obvious fact that kinksters appear to be considerably heavier on average than other people in their demographic group. Second, most of the time, when I've heard people make those observations, nearly all of them (like Harry) usually talk about larger *women* in the Scene, even though men in the Scene tend to be larger too. People in the Scene (as they do outside it) seem to care a lot more about women's weight than about men's. Third, Harry's attitude helped filter him out of a lot of Scene socializing, even though he was clearly very interested in BDSM personally. Thus, some parts of the Scene do seem to successfully filter for body positivity.

Nonconformity is both a performance and identity, and in the end, I think the Scene filters more for people who *identify* as nonconformists than for people who perform nonconformity. One of my interviewees, Damon, really embodied this point. He was very kinky in his personal practices by pretty much any definition of the word. Nevertheless, he said that he rarely participated in the Scene because it was filled "with those people who didn't quite escape being a nonconformist in high school—the kids with the chip on their shoulder because they can't fit in." His comment surprised me, as he was in his early 30s and was wearing a skull shirt, heavy black pants, and several rings. He also had numerous piercings and black-painted fingernails. He looked like a stereotypical Goth—the usual sort of "nonconformist" one finds in the Scene. When I asked him about the seeming contradiction between his words and his looks, he shrugged and said that he had been a jock in high school and that he always felt comfortable fitting in with virtually every group. He clearly had no interest in identifying as weird, nor in associating with people who did. People like Damon don't fit in well in the Scene because it wants people who want to feel normal by surrounding themselves with people who are "weird like us"—not people who embrace an identity as normal.

In keeping with the "weird like us" mentality is an idea that people should "just be themselves" and engage in BDSM for "authentic" reasons. Kinksters don't tend to define what "authentic" means very well in this context, but the general idea is that the Scene wants passion and desire to drive people's enthusiasm for BDSM, not, say, mental illness or feeling genuinely (as opposed to consensually) coerced or pressured. The Scene also imagines financial gain as a kind of inauthentic pressure and thus officially excludes people from engaging in BDSM for pay at Scene events. Vicky explained that what she enjoys about many BDSM events is that "people are being authentic. They're being themselves. They're searching inward and figuring who they are out, and you don't get that a lot in society in general." The Scene cares a lot about having people who follow their authentic (kinky) desires, and it has pretty strong opinions about what is and isn't *actually* authentic.

It's easier to explain what the Scene considers inauthentic than what it considers authentic, so I'll focus on what it considers fake. In a podcast interview with director Holly Randall (2018), the BDSM porn star Casey Calvert described with a combination of frustration and genuine loss what seemed a bizarre conundrum to her. She had entered the Orlando, Florida, BDSM Scene as a young adult and become an accomplished "fetish model," meaning that she did BDSM photographs, usually posed alone, for pay. While doing those photographs, she had been popular and extremely welcome in the Florida Scene. Eventually she was recruited out of her modest fetish model career by the most successful agent in the porn industry and was persuaded to move to Los Angeles and become a hard-core porn star. She quickly became one of the—probably *the*—most popular and successful female porn stars with a heavy focus on BDSM. But when she attempted to join the Los Angeles BDSM Scene, she found that her success in the porn industry made her unwelcome. She noted that she was still welcome in the Florida Scene where she came from, but in Los Angeles, she was bitterly startled to find that people acted like what she was doing was "sacrilegious. [Now] I'm a professional, so I'm not welcome, because it's my job, so it's not 'genuine.'" To be clear, Calvert wasn't trying to violate the official rules of events that forbid doing BDSM for money at them; she was simply perceived as tainted with inauthenticity because of her career.

It might seem odd that kinksters would be so hostile to someone who was representing many of their passions to a large audience (with many of them probably watching her porn themselves). But in the eyes of the Scene, being weird and being true to yourself isn't supposed to be about *getting paid*. I also think Calvert's choice of words ("sacrilegious") is pretty telling here, since there are some definite spiritual undertones and overtones in the Scene's imagining of authenticity. There are a few BDSM professions the Scene deems acceptable for "real kinksters," but all of them are portrayed as ultimately helping the community: writing and teaching about BDSM, being a BDSM organizer/venue owner, and being a BDSM craftsperson (that is, someone who handcrafts tools such as rope, whips, and floggers). In my time in the Scene, I've never known more than about 10 people at a time to be in each of those categories making anything resembling a sustainable full-time living. Professional Doms (and much more rarely subs), who earn a much more sustainable income and often run BDSM events and parties in many parts of the Scene, are still welcome in the Scene, but are strictly forbidden from recruiting clients at Scene venues.

OPEN AND LIBERAL

In addition to promoting a particular value set of "weirdness" and "authenticity," the Scene sorts for and encourages an interest in open relationships (as we saw in chapter 3), general open-mindedness, sexual openness, and general liberalness. As Nathan's earlier quote indicated, the Scene wants people who are open-minded and willing to explore new mental and physical possibilities, to challenge their boundaries, and to question what they've been taught. In particular, the Scene wants to attract people who will be open-minded and open-mouthed about sexual and erotic experiences that mainstream society tries to hush up (even if they aren't necessarily so open when they initially arrive in the Scene). Alice explained that "[BDSM] events foster this incredible dynamic of openness, like people can just talk freely about anything." By contrast, people who prefer to remain private and reserved about sexual matters usually find life in the Scene hard going, although the ones who stay often say the Scene taught them to open up.

Given the Scene's emphasis on openness to new experiences, it's hardly surprising that kinksters' political orientations tend to be very liberal, and most kinksters take the liberalism of other kinksters for granted. I didn't survey kinksters about their political beliefs, but I have only ever met two open Republicans during my time in the mid-Atlantic Scene. Whoever kinksters might be privately voting for, openly supporting conservative or Republican ideas in the Scene is deeply nonnormative, and kinksters as a whole tend to view conservatives with contempt.

However, the conservative/liberal dichotomy here goes beyond politics and extends into more general attitudes and behaviors. Researchers have shown that conservatives are much more afraid of dirt, much more easily grossed out by horror movies, more susceptible to fear in general, and much more interested in "purity" than are liberals (Inbar et al., 2012; Jost et al., 2003; Oosterhoff, Shook, and Ford, 2018). As the Scene almost never deals with politics directly, I suspect it's ultimately filtering more for these more subtle qualities of liberalism—tolerance, courage, and willingness to stand up to the status quo—than for explicit political beliefs. One of my interviewees, Logan, alluded to this kind of conservative/liberal dichotomy when explaining why he was not more actively involved in the public Scene despite being very interested in BDSM and identifying as kinky. He explained,

> I'm in investments. So I work in a field that's very conservative, very buttoned up, you know, Monday through Friday, 9:00 to 5:00, with the tie and the jacket and everything else. Because of that, I've always been very quiet about [BDSM]. So the munches and some of the public events, that has been a hurdle for me to get over because that's putting my face out there. That's making it public.

Logan didn't mention politics directly when talking about his "conservative" industry, but rather emphasized the fear of being discovered by "putting my face out there" in the public Scene that the "buttoned-up" attitudes of his coworkers created. The public Scene, after all, is *public*— and generally perceived as deviant—so joining it requires a willingness to defy social convention that is much more associated with liberalism than with conservatism.

Conservative attitudes and religiosity are highly correlated in America, but the lack of participation in organized religion among kinksters is still pretty impressive. My survey results showed that only 18 percent of American kinksters say they practice Christianity or Judaism, and my interviews suggest that most of those kinksters still aren't going to church or temple very often. On the other hand, the Scene is so closely aligned with what I often only half-jokingly refer to as the "disorganized religion" of modern Paganism that I have argued elsewhere that Paganism forms the spiritual core of the contemporary Scene (Fennell, 2018). Twenty-four percent of US/Canadian kinksters identify as Pagan, 7.5 percent as Buddhist or Taoist (which in terms of Scene spirituality tends to be extremely Westernized and closely linked to Paganism), and 6.5 percent as other (which in this context mostly means "spiritual," a vague category that tends to be Pagan-influenced in the Scene), for a grand total of about 38 percent of Pagan and Pagan-adjacent folks. The beliefs and practices of modern Paganism are not very well coordinated or clearly defined but often emphasize personal gnosis (meaning personal insight and knowledge about gods/religion/morality/truth/etc.), vaguely defined divinity, and the sacredness of Earth and corporeal experience (Ezzy, 2014). All three groups of Pagans, Buddhist/

Taoists, and spiritualists tend to be oriented toward individualistic religious experiences, antiauthoritarian spirituality, and impatience with the idea that myth is literal truth. Most importantly for the Scene, Paganism is friendly to sexuality and carnality in a way that most conventional organized religions aren't (Kraemer, 2012). It's also worth noting that both atheism and liberalism are highly correlated with intelligence (Kanazawa, 2010), further reinforcing the geek chic of the Scene.

HOT BI BABES

While kinksters tend to be strangely oblivious to their spiritual/religious demographics, they tend to be a lot more aware of a subcultural preference for bisexual women, who sometimes get somewhat sarcastically referred to as "hot bi babes." In general, the Scene is more friendly to ladies (regardless of sexuality) than gentlemen in pretty much every conceivable way. This preference is even institutionalized at some BDSM parties, where there is a "couples" and "single women" entrance fee that's lower than the rate for "single men." Many folks in the pansexual Scene have heavily criticized this practice as both sexist and heterosexist, and it was well on its way out by the time I began studying the Scene in 2012; by 2017, it was almost extinct. The policy is still fairly standard at swinger events that allow single men (which many don't), and as far as I can tell, the Scene inherited the practice from swinger events. Even though most BDSM parties and events have the same admission rate for men and women, my survey data make clear that the Scene likes women more than it does men. Compared to their responses for men, people of all genders preferred being around sexually aroused women, found them more arousing, and thought women were generally more agreeable as well. The vast majority of official policies in the Scene reinforce these perceptions by not-so-subtly directing most regulatory supervision at men. Even though these rules ostensibly apply to everyone, they operate with an implicit assumption that men are the ones most likely to break them. Overall, the Scene generally thinks of men as disagreeable and less attractive, and expects them to cause trouble.

In terms of sexual identity, the Scene doesn't seem to really care much what someone *identifies* as, just what they *do* and what they're comfortable with. Most importantly, the pansexual Scene seems to filter for people who are willing to engage in BDSM play with people of the opposite sex and/or gender and people who are comfortable being watched by all genders while doing so. One of my interviewees, Jackson, identified as a monogamous gay man and was married to a man, but said he was very happy in the pansexual Scene because BDSM wasn't sexual for him and he was happy to engage in it with people of any gender. Likewise, my survey results showed that while there are many Queer and homoromantic folks in the Scene, literally almost everyone in the "pansexual" Scene engages in BDSM play heterosexually at least sometimes. If I were to invent words for what the Scene seems to filter for, I would say it filters for people who are "hetero-play" and "hetero-comfortable," meaning they're interested in BDSM play with the opposite sex/gender and they're comfortable being in a sexually charged environment with people of the opposite sex/gender. In the pansexual Scene, one will almost certainly be flirted with, propositioned by, objectified by, and erotically gazed upon by people of the opposite sex and gender, and people who are uncomfortable with or actively turned off by any of those things generally aren't comfortable there.

Many of my gay male friends and Queer friends of all genders complained that they felt the "pansexual" Scene wasn't welcoming to people like them. But despite those tensions, the pansexual Scene is, at least to my pansexual sociologist's eye, a bisexual paradise—especially compared to any other social spaces. The pansexual Scene remains one of the only social spaces that is organized for, supports, and celebrates bisexuality (Klesse, 2005; Simula, 2012). Bisexuals, pansexuals, and trans folks consistently have, by far, the worst mental health and highest suicide risk among lesbians, gays, and bisexuals in the United States and around the world (Taliaferro et al., 2018; Taylor, 2018), and studies find that bisexuals report weak support for their identity or experiences from either straight or gay communities (Callis, 2013). However, in the pansexual BDSM Scene, I find evidence from both my survey and my observations of social encouragement of and support for bisexual behavior and identities.

Table 5.1 shows my survey results for sexual identity, demonstrating the high prevalence of straight men in the Scene compared with bi/pansexual/queer women. But even straight people in the Scene have often had same-sex experiences: 53 percent of straight-identified women on my survey reported ever having sex with a woman and 19 percent of straight-identified men reported ever having sex with a man. The cumulative numbers of nonstraight people for every gender group mean that a literal majority of people in the

TABLE 5.1. Sexual Identity by Gender-Sex for People with Medium/
High Scene Involvement

Gender	Women		GNC-Vag		GNC-Pen		Men	
	%	N	%	N	%	N	%	N
Straight	13%	86	2%	3	12%	14	48%	211
Heteroflexible	27%	181	9%	14	21%	25	31%	135
Bi/pansexual	42%	284	39%	61	30%	36	11%	48
Homoflexible/gay	5%	35	10%	16	4%	4	4%	19
Queer	10%	70	34%	53	29%	34	4%	18
Asexual	2%	14	7%	11	5%	6	1%	6

Scene are open to same-sex/gender sex, to some degree. Scene norms seem to be much more supportive of women's bisexuality than men's, yet both my survey and interview data suggest that bisexual men possibly receive the greatest benefits from the Scene's bi acceptance. As I mentioned in chapter 1, bisexual men appear to receive the greatest self-esteem boost of any group from Scene involvement. Moreover, several (formerly straight-identified) men I interviewed told me compelling stories about broadening their sexual horizons since entering the Scene, either actually having sex with men or intentionally opening themselves up to the idea of being attracted to a man. And while many bi men I knew in the Scene complained that it wasn't as welcoming to them as they wished, when I asked what social space was more welcoming, they universally said, "Nowhere."

Despite labeling itself the "pansexual" Scene, it doesn't really advertise or promote itself as a bi/pansexual haven. I only occasionally see kinksters wearing Bi Pride paraphernalia, and I almost never see kinksters making a concerted effort to organize socially or politically on behalf of bi/pansexuals. Somewhat ironically, the people I interviewed who were the most likely to mention bisexuality as part of their attraction to the pansexual Scene were the queer people who had arrived in the pansexual Scene because they came to feel excluded from the lesbian Leather communities. As they do outside the Scene, bi/pansexuals in it tend to end up in hetero partnerships, which inevitably influences dating and sexual norms. To a large degree, the Scene is functionally binormative rather than heteronormative, but binormativity isn't really a documented social or academic concept because binormative spaces outside the Scene are basically nonexistent.

CHAPTER FIVE

WHY IS THE SCENE SO WHITE?

The Scene's overwhelmingly white racial demographics make it tempting to assume that insidious factors drive its segregation. Race and racism in the Scene have had sensationalistic appeal to academics and the media, mostly thanks to the *extremely* rare public kink of "race play" (which engages with consensual racial degradation). For example, in her book on race and pornography, Cruz (2016) luridly paints an image of the supposed popularity of race play, citing the 1,500 members of a race play group on FetLife. Even at the time of that study, 1,500 members on FetLife were a *minute* percentage of its several million users. Meanwhile, a Google search for "race and BDSM" almost entirely finds academic and nonacademic hits for race play, not the experiences of kinksters of color. In reality, despite a decade of involvement in the Scene, I have never personally witnessed a single public race play scene (although I have heard of them happening). To say that race play is taboo in the Scene would be an understatement, as I have literally never met a white person who admitted to enjoying it. The only people I have ever personally spoken to who said they enjoyed it were Black.

Others have assumed that the common use of BDSM role words like "Master" and "slave," along with erotic imagery of people in collars and on leashes, disturbs Black people with its evocations of slavery and discourages them from joining the Scene (Erickson et al., 2021; Weiss, 2011). This certainly might be true, but it does not adequately explain why there are even fewer Brown people than Black people in the Scene. Brown people in the Scene are so rare that I knew a man whose scene name (which I assume he chose for himself) was simply "The Mexican." There were so few obviously Mexican people in the Scene that the name seemed entirely reasonable. Although I have known a number of Hispanics in the Scene, nearly all were perceived as white in and out of the Scene.

As I mentioned in the introduction, as a white sociologist thinking about race, one of the first things one learns to do is shut up and listen, both for what is said and what is unsaid. I attended one of the few discussions I saw for people of color in the Scene that was open to white people in New York City, and several Black people attended (a few other white people attended as well, but all of us mostly stayed quiet). I expected to hear impassioned complaints from Black kinksters about the prejudice and discrimination they experienced from white kinksters, but to my surprise, Black people talked more about how being involved in the Scene often felt like a decision to alienate themselves from (often much more religious) Black family and friends. At an informal social gathering at a Black play partner's house that was heavily attended by Black kinksters, I heard more of the complaints I had expected. Black women there complained about how much work they had to do to educate white men they tried to date in the Scene about race and racial problems. By far the most surreal moment for me in all these interracial encounters I witnessed was when (completely coincidentally) two Black men were hitting on me simultaneously at a BDSM event. In the middle of this amiable chatter, they began discussing a happy hour later at the event for people of color, and one of them commented to the other in frustration, "Ugh I just hate white people sometimes," then quickly turned to me and said, "No offense." "None taken," I assured him, "I hate white people a lot of the time, too."

The Scene is a voluntary social group, and there are a lot of reasons that racial and ethnic groups in America tend to "choose" not to mix and mingle in their spare time. The vast majority of Americans' core social groups are of the same race, and this homogeneity is especially true for white people; the trend holds true with almost no variation across age, gender, education level, and even political party (Cox, Navarro-Rivera, and Jones, 2016). To describe this phenomenon as "self-segregation" is only technically true in the sense that adults in a free country have the right to associate as they choose. In reality, research shows that these patterns of adult racial "self-segregation" are heavily influenced by larger social structures—most notably, childhood school integration, which most people did not actually have control over for themselves (Kao, Joyner, and Balistreri, 2019). In other words, adults who attended integrated schools as children are much more likely to maintain interracial friendships and date interracially as adults—but children usually don't have much choice about which schools they go to. From where we live to where we go to school to the voluntary social organizations we participate in as children—like Girl Scouts, religious organizations, or sleepaway camps—the institutionally racist structure of American society works hard to ensure that racial and ethnic groups feel and to some degree *are* qualitatively different from one another (Plummer et al., 2016). Indeed, qualitative analysis of the profiles on the massive dating site OkCupid showed that interracial differences between different racial groups—especially in terms of hobbies, tastes, and interests—were considerable (Rudder, 2014). Voluntary social groups such as the Scene have no meaningful way to compel people to attend the sort of cultural sensitivity training that would help them bridge the divides that an entire social architecture has constructed between them. People show up to the Scene to have a good time, not to listen to lectures from sociologists.

Although my survey results suggested that Asians and Blacks are about equally common in the Scene, I assume that most of the Asians are on the West Coast, where I did not study. In the mid-Atlantic BDSM Scene, "kinksters of color" almost entirely meant "Black people," and so basically all my racial observations of the Scene are about Black/white interactions. The social reality of being a Black kinkster not only means having to constantly interact with white people, often literally being the only Black person in the room, it also means accepting a dating/marriage pool that is almost entirely white as well. These demographic realities have important gendered implications, since in American society as a whole, Black men are twice as likely as Black women to marry a white person (Livingston and Brown, 2017). In keeping with that larger social reality, my observations *strongly* suggest that Black men considerably outnumber Black women in the Scene, and that they are more likely to easily find (white) partners in it. (Unfortunately, the gender imbalance in my survey responses makes it impossible for me to test this observation statistically.) Conversely, I think it likely that the gender disparity in my survey results means that Asians appear overrepresented, since I strongly suspect that Asian women—who are much more likely than Asian men to marry white people in the larger culture (Livingston and Brown, 2017)—considerably outnumber Asian men in the Scene. If my observations are correct, then my survey results, which suffer from women's overresponse compared to men's, are underestimating the presence of Black people in the Scene and overestimating the presence of Asians (although I do not think by a great deal in either case).

However, the challenges of interracial dating are again not sufficient to explain the low numbers of people of color in the Scene, since Hispanics and Asians are very likely to marry interracially but still barely appear in the Scene. Given that a survey of the racial demographics of 2014 attendees at Burning Man (the defining event for the burner subculture) found that Blacks and Hispanics were also wildly underrepresented at that event (1 percent and 6 percent, respectively [BRC, 2014])—I think we must turn to much broader sociological explanations than "racially loaded terminology" or "the stresses of interracial dating" to explain why there are so few people of color in the Scene. In an article about race at Burning Man (Thrasher, 2015), a Latina woman named Favianna Rodriguez described why she thought there were so few people of color attending, saying, "Even as progressives, we [people of color] don't think about how to experience the universe through pleasure. And the problem is that fun and leisure have become the domain of white people. And that's how white supremacy works. It disconnects our selves from our bodies." If she is right, then the idea of hobbies and leisure is inextricably bound to white privilege.

As appealing and well-reasoned as I find that explanation, it cannot account for why the only subculturally adjacent event that I ever observed that was extremely well attended by Black people was a weekend-long porn-focused event. This event intentionally promoted itself as BDSM and swinger friendly, although it was not an event where either activity took place much. The main draw was "meet your favorite [female] porn star." Since the event mostly had the feel of a giant strip club, I had assumed the attendees would mostly look like the usual customers at strip clubs (older, unaccompanied white men), and these certainly were the plurality of the crowd. But it was far more racially integrated than any BDSM- or subculturally adjacent event I have ever been to, and there were many Black women there as well (although still almost no Hispanics or Asians). With many sex and BDSM toy vendors, this event fit the profile of a place where people might "experience the universe through pleasure," and the many Black attendees I saw there seemed eager to do so. So perhaps we must turn to a rather different explanation to understand why so few people of color participate in the BDSM Scene.

The explanation I propose is deviance and, to a lesser degree, geekdom. The BDSM subculture descends directly from the geek/nerd subculture, and as best I can tell (despite being much larger, the geek subculture has been studied much less than the BDSM subculture has), the racial demographics of both are basically the same: almost entirely white, with a very small but prominent presence of Blacks, and extremely few Asians or Hispanics. A quick Google search on Black nerds and geeks finds information on a lively sub-subculture (originally calling themselves "Blerds"), but the same Google search for Asians and Latino/a/x/Hispanics finds almost nothing. In order to really understand the racial composition of the BDSM Scene, someone would first have to satisfactorily explain the racial composition of the geek/nerd subculture—and to the best of my knowledge, no academics have tried. However, the burner and swinger subcultures are much more distantly removed from the geek/nerd subculture than the BDSM subculture is, yet those subcultures seem to maintain fairly similar racial demographics. To my sociologist's eye, a key unifying factor in these disparate subcultures is pleasurable deviance: the willingness and desire to defy mainstream expectations in search of personal satisfaction—a deviant quality conspicuously lacking at the previously mentioned porn-focused convention I attended, which seemed uninterested in defying any conventional social norms. Others have observed that white privilege almost certainly enables people to more readily participate in "deviant leisure" activities (Martinez, 2021; Sheff and Hammers, 2011; Williams, 2009). Not only do racial minorities have to navigate the ignorance (and occasional outright hostility) of the sea of white people in these deviant leisure groups (Erickson et al., 2021), they also have to overcome a truly impressive array of social structural obstacles that discourage interracial interactions (with largely segregated primary schooling being one of the most egregious) just to be there in the first place. Additionally, they may face pressures from their ethnic subcultures not to join deviant subcultures *as well as* skepticism and hostility from members of the subcultures themselves about the legitimacy of their involvement or belonging. The accounts of the aforementioned "Blerds" on blogs (such as Blerds.com) demonstrate that Black nerds feel pressured from every side not to join the geek/nerd subculture: mainstream culture, Black cultures, and the geek/nerd subculture all question their legitimacy and belonging as "geeks."

Conceptualizing racial demographics of subcultures in this complex and nuanced way—as a combination of larger social structures, mainstream cultural pressures, deviant subcultural pressures, and pressures within ethnic subcultures themselves—suggests that explaining the presence or absence of any *specific* racial group in these deviant subcultures may require an explanation specific to that group. For example, despite the fact that Indians represent a fifth of Asian Americans, I have never personally met one in the Scene in any region, and I have only ever met one Filipino (also a fifth of Asian Americans); nearly all the Asians I have met in the Scene are ethnically Chinese or Japanese. And presumably, the reasons that Indian Americans are not really involved in the Scene might be quite different from the reasons why Mexican Americans are so rarely involved. Our explanations for the racial demographics of the Scene and its adjacent subcultures can focus both on why there are *so many* white people in them as well as why there are *so few* people from a particular racial/ethnic group.

I want to conclude this short section on race by emphasizing how nascent my ideas here are. I am fairly confident in the social "facts" that I have provided (the racial demographics of the Scene and its adjacent subcultures), and I am reasonably certain that any theoretical explanation that tries to explain the racial composition of any one of those subcultures without accounting for the others is probably short-sighted and likely incorrect. However, race was not the focus of any aspect of my study, and the extant research on race in the Scene is very, very scant, with only one academic study really talking to kinksters of color themselves (Erickson et al., 2021). As a white person in the Scene, one quickly learns to feel that whatever one says about race in the Scene is "wrong," and no matter how well-intentioned, I do not think any white sociologist is in a good position to explain the social worlds of people of color in general or the Scene in particular. When I discussed my hesitancy to study race in the Scene with Dan, a Black friend, he scoffed, saying he thought I would be fine. I said I thought there were things that Black people would be unlikely to share with me as a white person. Our conversation meandered, and he told me that he had recently seen the movie *Get Out* with his white girlfriend and been so traumatized from watching it that he had immediately gone home and called a Black friend for support. I pointed out that he had precisely illustrated my point, since the most "logical" person for him to share his grief with would have been the person he saw the movie with (his white girlfriend), but instead, he had depended on a Black friend—someone he just expected to understand and appreciate his experience. He said, "Oh, you're totally right."

STRUCTURED CHAOS

The Scene constantly does an uneasy dance between recruiting people with a highly individualistic antiauthoritarian streak and people who will actually be willing to follow its many rules and respect its own (fragile) institutions of authority. The Scene filters for certain types of people and then subjects them to an intensive socialization process. As a deviant subculture, the Scene teeters on the cliff's edge of criminality and respectability, but its well-educated members are often middle- and upper-class professionals who tend to be heavily invested in keeping it from tumbling over that edge. For a deviant subculture, the Scene has a remarkably rigorous education system for teaching Scene norms and values, as well as specific techniques for any particular kink. Most large-scale BDSM organizations nowadays host regular BDSM 101 nights where newbies usually get a general introductory lecture and then can choose from a variety of stations where people will demonstrate different kinks on them, such as tying them up (or showing someone else the basics of how to tie) or dragging (without cutting) knives across their flesh (or showing someone else the basics of how to do that). Most groups regularly offer in-depth classes on everything from flogging techniques to advice on how to have Dominant/submissive relationships to how to talk to your partner about kink. Volunteers mostly teach these classes for free or a nominal fee, and their low cost keeps them widely accessible to almost everyone who participates in the Scene. On the occasions when people show up to parties or events without exposure to this formal educational curriculum, more experienced kinksters around them will usually informally recite rules to them; formal greeters are sometimes officially tasked with providing introductory tours and information for newbies.

Sociologists refer to these official lessons and rules as *formal norms*, whereas the unofficial norms of practice are *informal norms*. Most of the time, informal norms follow formal norms, but occasionally they contradict each other (one of the classic examples being speed limits in America, which formal norms say should be the top speed but informal norms say should be the minimum speed). In most cultures, there are many more informal norms than formal ones to guide our lives because it's impractical and unnecessary to try to codify every rule of behavior. The Scene is the same as everywhere else in that it has many unwritten rules guiding behavior that the vast majority of people are unaware of, and when I talk about informal norms in it, I have to rely heavily on my observations and experiences much more than on my interviews or survey data. This problem is especially difficult in the Scene because many of the informal norms differ from the formal norms, but kinksters don't like to admit that contradiction.

In the Scene, as in most cultures, when you break the kinds of formal norms that these BDSM classes teach, there are officials to reprimand you. The most conspicuous of these are dungeon monitors (almost always called DMs), who are the volunteer security guards of kinky playspaces. But—again, as in most cultures—when you break the informal norms, the consequences (or what sociologists usually refer to as *sanctions*) tend to be much hazier. Negative sanctions for breaking informal norms might include people giggling, looking at you awkwardly, avoiding you, glaring at you, or much more rarely, actually calling you out. However, most of the time, positive sanctions of praise and encouragement for desirable behavior promote informal norms in the Scene (as elsewhere) far more than negative sanctions for undesirable behavior. In the Scene, the most conspicuous positive sanctions are good reputation (see chapter 7) and eager playdates (meaning it's easy to find many people to play with). In my observations, the Scene has three main goals for its members: self-actualization and exploration, pleasure, and the development of a wide range of relationships. All of its structures, from education to socials to big events, are intended to further those goals. But there's a constant tension in the Scene between pleasure and self-exploration versus the need for community and individual safety, continuity, organization, and shared values. Simply put, if people aren't having fun, they don't have much incentive to keep paying to attend these voluntary social events, but if behaviors aren't regulated at all, people start feeling unsafe and thus also aren't likely to come.

OFFICIAL LESSONS

Whereas most of the filters I've been discussing so far in this chapter are relatively subtle, there's nothing subtle about the official lessons of the Scene, which tend to be posted everywhere for everyone to see at classes, events, and parties. Since you, too, can read about most of these rules with a quick internet search (if you're curious, start with the impressive *Wikipedia* article on BDSM) or in a detailed academic analysis by Galilee-Belfer (2020), I'm not going to dwell on them for too long. The first and most important rule of BDSM is that the difference between BDSM and abuse is consent: with BDSM, people knowingly consent to what they're doing, but in abusive relationships, people don't agree to what's happening to them. Consent is so fundamental to kink culture that 21 of my interviewees spontaneously mentioned it even though I asked no direct questions about it. The importance of consent usually gets folded into a classic Scene initialism: safe, sane, and consensual (SSC). Safe things are allowed to "hurt but not harm" someone. In practice, this generally means not doing anything that would be likely to necessitate a hospital visit. No matter how black the bruises on someone's ass from a paddle, the Scene looks very askance at someone, say, intentionally breaking another person's arm. Although many things that kinksters do *look* very dangerous, in fact, most of those things are designed to look and feel dangerous without actually *being* dangerous. Virtually all the serious kink injuries I know of resulted from the most sportlike of kink activities: wrestling (which isn't that different than in the vanilla world; there are just fewer rules and no official point system), any kind of "struggle play" (in which the bottom puts up physical resistance to their Top[s] and thus minimizes the Top's ability to protect the bottom), and rope suspension. The concept of "safety" is often generally broadened to include "psychological safety" as well, although this concept is obviously much less concrete and much harder to clearly define.

An important related rule is, "Don't drink and kink," and virtually all BDSM parties and events explicitly forbid people from engaging in BDSM play while intoxicated and include it on the list of rules participants have to sign when they enter. Many parties and even daysling events are officially "dry" (meaning alcohol isn't even allowed on the premises). Kinksters certainly drink at many events and parties, but people often comment to their friends, "I'm too drunk to play," or laughingly tell friends that they're going to drink instead of playing. Most kinksters internalize this rule so completely that I've rarely heard stories of authorities at mainstream BDSM events having to aggressively enforce it: most heavily involved kinksters *really* don't want to get in trouble for intoxication or get a reputation as someone who "plays drunk." The Scene's anti-intoxication bias is so strong that people actually come to the Scene to get sober. Even at the few "BDSM" events or parties I've attended where heavy drinking was normal or expected, the general rule of don't-drink-and-kink was still so well obeyed that people almost never actually engaged in BDSM play there. Most of these types of parties label themselves "fetish" parties, and they vary wildly in their proximity to and overlap with mainstream BDSM events. Mainstream kinksters often sneeringly refer to them as "S&M parties"—"Stand & Model," since people usually just stand around drinking and chatting while dressed in fancy kinky clothes.

Part of the reason for the "don't drink and kink" rule is that kinksters assume intoxication leads to compromises with both safety and consent: the Scene assumes that a drunk Top is more likely to injure their bottom and a drunk bottom is more likely to compromise their own standards of consent and be unaware of physical injury. The "safe and sane" combination in the first rule emphasizes that people should be aware that just because something is physically safe doesn't mean that it will be mentally safe for a person. People have to remain conscious of triggers for them and their partners—things that will trigger trauma responses based on past experiences or that will take them out of a headspace they want to be in and into one they don't enjoy.

In order to promote enjoyment and safety, Scene culture teaches members to figure out their "limits," meaning the things that they're willing and not willing to do. "Hard limits" are generally things someone is unwilling to do under any circumstance, while "soft limits" are things someone might be willing to do under certain circumstances but require a lot of prior negotiation. Then the Scene teaches everyone to communicate those limits before they play. This communication process, in which people also are supposed to get some idea of what people are going to do together as they play, is called a "negotiation." During those negotiations, "no" is supposed to mean "no," but the Scene often assumes that once play commences, "no" might lose its conventional meaning and be replaced with a safeword. Thus I knew a girl who used to half-joke that "'fire truck' means 'no'; 'no' means 'make me.'" Whatever the safeword is, using it is supposed to mean that play stops. In almost all public playspaces, "house safewords" are defined so that "yellow" means "pause or check in," while "red" means "stop." At many public spaces, "red" means that the entire play is supposed to stop, but there are several variations on these rules.

Another formal rule of the Scene is privacy. Events often specifically forbid anyone from attending who is not doing so purely for personal pleasure. They also explicitly forbid photography by anyone who isn't authorized by the event to take photos, and even those people are only allowed to take pictures of people wearing specific wristbands or with explicit permission. People often surreptitiously break this rule by taking photos of themselves, but the real spirit of it is you aren't supposed to take pictures of anyone else or post any pictures online (and these rules are almost never broken). Events also explicitly forbid outing another person, meaning that if you see someone at an event, you aren't allowed to, say, tell their mother or their employer. Thus, there's an understanding that people may not always use their real names in Scene spaces. Instead of using their legal names, people typically adopt "Scene names," and it's bizarrely common to have fairly intimate relationships with people for months or longer without knowing their actual names. This kind of privacy is such a big deal in the Scene that many kinksters complained when Facebook started "suggesting" friends to you based on places you had both been together, because now people were learning the full legal names of their Scene friends. It's actually pretty normal to casually date people in the Scene who only know your first name. Moreover, the Scene operates with a bizarre related semiformal norm about what to do if you happen to bump into casual Scene acquaintances in vanilla contexts: ignore them. As far as I can tell, conformity to this norm is pretty high, as most kinksters I know have a story about running into a fellow kinkster they don't know well in an unexpected place (especially at work or in work-related contexts) and carefully ignoring them. The guiding principle is "never make someone explain how they know you." The Scene is full of cautionary tales of people who got outed and lost their jobs and/ or custody of their children, and privacy norms are always emphasized with a reminder that these risks are real and that "kinky" isn't a legally protected status the way religion is.

Another aspect of formal Scene learning is the idea that BDSM can have therapeutic properties (Lindemann, 2011) and become a powerful tool for working through and managing past trauma experiences (Hammers, 2014). Like the "gang rape" scene described in chapter 1, the Scene teaches that the potential healing properties of BDSM are one of its most exalted features and should be respected at all reasonable costs. Scene culture teaches respect for individual BDSM "journeys" and special respect for the possibility that those journeys will include spiritual and personal growth. The respect for that powerful potential of the Scene feeds another rule, which is, "Your kink is not my kink, but your kink is okay." This phrase is meant to capture a spirit of neutrality and nonjudgment: as long as your kink appears reasonably safe, sane, and consensual, people aren't supposed to judge or criticize you for it. Kink culture reminds us that we all find things hot that someone else might find objectionable, and we shouldn't make ethical judgments based on an instinctive "eww" response. However, this rule often comes into conflict with a less commonly quoted rule: "Audiences have to consent, too." Basically, the principle is that if the whole point of your kink is making other people uncomfortable, it's probably not going to be welcome at most public play events. Thus emerges a sort of corollary halfway point where the Scene claims not to be judging you for your kink but nonetheless asks you to do it at home or with carefully selected audiences if you know it is likely to be poorly received.

The last formal rule of the Scene that I'll discuss here is both explicit and implicit, which is that the Scene is the best authority for doing BDSM "right." Whenever people inquire about learning to do most BDSM activities, the usual response in the Scene is, "Come to a class! Come to BDSM 101 night! Learn hands-on from a teacher!" The Scene believes that it is the best teacher of BDSM and that kinky people who try to get by without it are likely to fail, get hurt, and/or feel alienated. The Scene teaches kinksters that the rules are good ones, set up for good reasons, and that following them is to everyone's advantage. The Scene believes that its authority matters and has a pretty low tolerance for people who try to question it. Although the Scene lacks the clear authority to allow or disallow people (since there is so little organizational unity, even among parties or groups within the same region), people who have little respect for the Scene's rules and authority tend to get permanently disinvited from groups or places or mocked to their faces or behind their backs; many simply leave on their own in frustration.

OFFICIALLY SANCTIONED LESSONS YOU LEARN MOSTLY FROM TALKING TO PEOPLE

The last section briefly described some of the broad rules that most Scene events introduce participants to quickly, and I'll talk more about some of the specific formal and informal rules of behavior in the next chapter. But for now I want to move on to slightly less formal rules of the Scene that kinksters learn mostly by interacting with each other. Most of these rules don't have classes taught *about* them; rather, classes tend to take these rules for granted and proceed as though they're obvious facts. Indeed, most moderately experienced kinksters treat all the norms I'm about to describe as so basic they become invisible, and I'm forced to rely disproportionately on the quotes of highly experienced key informant organizers and educators in order to explain them.

The first of these informal norms is that even though formal Scene norms say that *everyone* is responsible for ensuring safe, sane, and consensual interactions, in practice, the Scene mostly expects *Tops* to be responsible for these things. All the pre-play negotiation techniques the Scene traditionally teaches emphasize Tops trying to extract information and "consent" from bottoms. This division of consent labor/power is so well known that many experienced kinksters argue that bottoms are the ones with "real power" in a Scene. For example, Dylan, who had been a kink educator for years, explained BDSM roles to me thus: "A Top is a person who makes most of the decisions while playing. The bottom is the person with all the control. They say, 'Yes, you can do it. No, you can't.'" The classic negotiating techniques taught in the Scene involve Tops asking bottoms questions like, "Where am I allowed to touch you?" and "Do you have any injuries I should know about?"—but the Scene doesn't traditionally teach bottoms to ask those questions back. There's been a lot of pushback against these norms since about 2015 as bottoms started fighting for more respect, recognition, and legitimacy, and the norms have shifted slightly.

Partly because of the way the Scene values Tops, the idea that Tops are the ones who are responsible if "something goes wrong" during a play session is deeply embedded in Scene culture. Even if it's pretty obvious that, say, a bottom didn't communicate at all clearly during a scene, Tops tend to hold themselves responsible for problems—and others generally hold them responsible as well. Doyle, who was a well-known BDSM educator, was one of the only people I interviewed to openly critique this norm:

> While I think that consent is a wonderful thing to have, I think it has been narrowly defined [in the Scene]. I have known bottoms who will say, "Well, once I'm in scene I can't make any decisions, and so anything that goes wrong is your fault." I know Tops who have things go wrong in a scene [with those bottoms], or things not go according to plan, and they think, "Oh my God, I'm a bad Top, I'm horrible, I can't believe I did it!"—that's owning shit that isn't theirs when it was a mutual situation.

As Doyle noted, I have also heard Tops take responsibility for scenes gone wrong that seemed much more mutual to me. On the other hand, unsurprisingly, people often have a habit of assigning blame to *other* Tops for scenes gone wrong but then abnegating responsibility when *their own* scenes go wrong. But on the whole, I think people tend to mostly take this norm of Top responsibility to heart. Alice, who mostly bottomed, said that when she Tops people, "I always want to get to know [bottoms] very well, and what their limits are, as well as what their fun buttons for me to push are." She added that as a result, Topping for her is "far more conscious and deliberative" than bottoming.

This assignment of responsibility sometimes creates serious problems in the Scene. Because Tops learn to take so much responsibility for consent and safety, especially among hard-core players, Tops often end up caring more about consent than bottoms do. For example, I've been propositioned for play at least twice by drunk female bottoms I didn't know well (and I have several friends with the same story). When I turned them down because they were drunk, they responded, "Why does that matter? I'm bottoming." Much more grimly, multiple people independently described the worst public consent violation I ever heard of in all my travels; it occurred not long before I entered the Scene, and part of why it happened was that it went against expectations. A male slave (a title for arguably the most consensually abject form of bottom) was playing with his female Mistress (a title for arguably the most consensually powerful form of Top) in a public dungeon. It was fairly common knowledge that she had recently had a hysterectomy, and her slave certainly knew it. Yet he insisted on having penis-in-vagina sex with her anyway—and even though she said, "Red," no one in the dungeon stopped it because (1) as we'll see in the next chapter, safewords have a very different social function than what kinksters generally believe and (2) the idea of a slave raping his Mistress was so incomprehensible to everyone that no one could make sense of what was happening. Indeed, several of the people who told me this story shook their heads in confusion and made a comment like, "What kind of slave would rape his Mistress?!" In recent years, several Dominant women confessed that they had been raped in the Scene, but they hadn't publicly reported their experiences because they were afraid that admitting they had "lost control" of their submissive would taint their image as Doms.

Another important lesson kinksters mostly learn by talking to others (but that, again, is officially sanctioned) is the idea that reputation is meaningful social capital. I'll explore this in depth in chapter 7, but for now, I just want to outline the norm that people expect their reputations to matter. Lacking much in the way of formal mechanisms or objective criteria (such as credentials) to determine if people are actually safe, sane, and consensual players, the Scene is left with the dubious alternative of reputation. Most experienced kinksters take this principle for granted, so that Lucy, who was an experienced kink educator, expressed dismay that many people didn't seem aware of it. She said that when she was teaching at an introductory event recently, "We were just talking basic BDSM 101 stuff and somebody said, 'Ask for references.' And someone else was like, 'What do you mean, ask for references?' Like, if you meet someone and you want to get involved with them, or play with them, or do something with them, ask other people about them!" She pronounced this last with a sort of "duh!" tone to her voice, as if it was just an obvious fact of how people logically interact in the Scene.

Though often treated as an obvious fact of kink life, basic logic should explain why this semiformal norm is extremely difficult to implement in practice. First, only people who have been around for a while and played with a fairly large number of people can have meaningful reputations. So if you're playing with someone who's rather inexperienced, it can be very difficult to get useful information about them. Second, social interactions in the Scene often encourage spontaneous play interactions. Although formal norms tell people to get information about people before playing with them, in reality, it's pretty normal to see total strangers standing around (in public parts of kink events and parties) holding a fun looking "toy" (Scene jargon for anything you can use for sex or BDSM, such as floggers, whips, carpet beaters, dildos, etc.) and either have them ask if they can use it on you or wander up to them and ask them to do so. Those types of brief interactions don't really meet classic Scene ideas about a playdate, but even full-scale playdates often emerge almost entirely spontaneously, with full-on scenes sometimes happening on the spot. Since these interactions are usually very public, people often don't ask for references; the public (or at least semi-public) nature of their play interactions provides a sense of safety. Fourth, people trust their own judgment much more willingly and readily than that of strangers or even acquaintances. If they do ask for references about Person X, they're usually only going to trust information from someone *they* trust. And related to both of the last two points, the small size and air of intimacy in the Scene cultivates a sense that everyone already knows each other even when they don't, which heightens the feeling that "my friends" know and trust Person X even if they don't.

We should also notice that although the semiformal norm claims that everyone should ask about references, in reality, when people do ask, they're almost always bottoms asking about Tops. These interactions are only occasionally useful, since the tiny social world of the Scene ends up creating strong informal norms against talking badly about someone. Thus the only people who are usually willing to definitively recommend against playing with someone else are *very* good friends or partners of the asker. Through interacting with others, kinksters usually learn a pretty different variation on the semiformal norm that shows up in classes, although one that's still more or less in keeping with the theory of the original.

Another lesson kinksters learn largely through social interaction is to awkwardly balance the tension between two simultaneously completely contradictory norms: one that says BDSM is more intimate and powerful than vanilla sex, and the other, which says BDSM is a nonsexual, nonthreatening, low-intimacy interaction that it's perfectly reasonable to engage in with nearly total strangers. The peaceful coexistence of these norms has never ceased to boggle my mind, especially since I've almost never met anyone who even commented on the contradiction. Most kinksters seem to reconcile the contradiction for themselves by explaining it away in terms of situation and personal preference. In this vein, kinksters will say that certain BDSM activities (like playing with rope or boots) are generally not especially intimate for them, but that they reserve other activities (like sex or needle play) for people they have a "real connection with." Or they'll say that sometimes BDSM is very intimate and powerful (and/or sexual) for them, and sometimes it isn't.

The basic structure of teaching BDSM almost forces the awkward coexistence of these intimate/not-very-intimate norms. In order to learn whether you enjoy most types of sadomasochistic activities, you have to experience them, and for most of those activities, you're much better off experiencing them from someone who knows what they're doing. That simple fact creates a potentially awkward educational necessity: a Top who's willing to do something to an inexperienced bottom they don't know very well, and vice versa. When new kinksters first enter the Scene, they're encouraged to play with a (supposedly well-vetted) variety of strangers who will introduce them to new experiences and sensations. There are a few Tops who specialize in this type of initiation, usually for a particular type of kink. Most of them burn out quickly (usually within a year), and many of them primarily identify as submissives and say they enjoy "service Topping," meaning that they get pleasure from providing a desirable experience for the other person through their Topping. Inevitably, the intimacy of these types of interactions is not usually very deep.

And yet, alongside these extremely superficial demonstrations and interactions with strangers are repeated subcultural assurances that BDSM is deep and intimate. Lisa defined BDSM in terms of intimacy, saying, "For me, it's not inherently sexual but intimate. . . . I like the intimate connection." Harry also emphasized the intimacy of BDSM, saying that it was a much more "intense experience" for him than "regular sex." He said that compared with regular sex, "I think the connection one can have with another person doing [BDSM] is more intense in a way, can build stronger bonds or relationships." Lucy also said BDSM could be more intimate than sex: "One of my favorite forms of Topping is with needles, which is a really, really intimate act. In some ways, it's more intimate than sex, depending on how you do it, because you're piercing someone's skin. I mean, you're playing with their life force, their blood and their body."

Even though these competing norms of intimate BDSM and nonintimate BDSM cause conflict when experienced kinksters complain that they feel pressured to do BDSM with "newbs" they have "no connection with," I've never heard anyone frame this conflict broadly or ideologically. Kinksters always frame it in individual terms, as a matter of individual preference (and sometimes even as a personal failing), rather than observing the way that the culture pushes two completely contradictory attitudes toward BDSM simultaneously. The formal norm says clearly that BDSM is very intimate, but from the moment a person walks into a BDSM 101 night and starts casually engaging in BDSM with a total stranger, the Scene begins implicitly defying its own formal norms. The myriad other incredibly casual BDSM interactions kinksters have—from "trying out" new "toys" on total strangers to going to BDSM technique classes and finding a (likely stranger) practice bottom once they get there—reinforce a very different informal norm that BDSM isn't necessarily intimate at all.

UNOFFICIAL LESSONS YOU LEARN
BY INTERACTING WITH PEOPLE

The previous section progressed through norms that increasingly emerge out of officially sanctioned norms toward ones that emerge more from social interaction. In this section, I'm going to focus even more on the way some informal norms in the Scene explicitly contradict (or at least appear to contradict) the formal SSC norms of the Scene. Despite the fact that the Scene encourages kinksters to teach and believe in the virtues of safe, sane, and consensual play, even moderately experienced kinksters start becoming rather dismissive of the "safe and sane" parts of the equation as long as they think their play is consensual. Bauer's (2014) dyke and trans kinky interviewees specifically sometimes argued that they thought their play was neither objectively safe nor sane, but because it was consensual felt that it was still acceptable (p. 77). While I have only occasionally encountered people in the pansexual Scene who stated the point so bluntly, I'm certainly accustomed to debates about where the lines really are. For example, I had friends who were seriously discussing a scene in which one of them would consensually break the other one's rib (although they never did). They argued that rib breaking wasn't seriously harmful, and that as long as the bottom was prepared for the consequences, it seemed acceptable.

Many kinksters have formally pushed for a change to the SSC language, arguing that it lacks nuance. People have proposed other acronyms such as RACK (risk-aware consensual kink) and PRICK (personal responsibility in consensual kink), arguing that rather than emphasizing "safe or not," responsible kink education should involve making intentional decisions about psychological and physical risks with the best available knowledge. Over time, my observations and interactions with very experienced kinksters led me to believe that even these acronyms reflect an idealized version of what many kinksters want and do. Contrary to the suggestion of these acronyms, my experiences indicate that the kink culture actually *admires* dangerous, violent, and risky kinks, and on some level encourages people to engage in them. As this encouragement is very subtle, it took an extreme example during my fieldwork to be able to find evidence of it. So please indulge me as I tell you a detailed story about my experience doing literally the stupidest thing of my life: getting suspended outside in rope during a tornado at Camp O-Town.

The vast majority of rope suspensions are done by white men tying white women, but I actively sought more diverse photo representations. Bondage in general, and rope suspensions in particular, are by far the most popular kink for artistic photography, with a large-scale rope photography contest happening annually on FetLife. Unless they are anonymous, rope photos usually contain credits for the person who did the tying as "rigger" or "rope," the person being tied as "bottom" or "model," and the photographer. *Rigger/model: Daniel Cox; Model: Miiko Rose; Photo: Candice Anne*

Rigger/model: Mae; Model: Kai; Photo: Jon Gunnar

*Rigger/model: Lexa Grace;
Model: Shakti Bliss; Photo:
Jake Wing*

It is relatively uncommon for rope photos to show the rigger. Much more frequently, they only show the person being tied. *Photo: Jon Gunnar*

Rope suspensions are difficult to describe, but they're basically exactly what they sound like: typically one person (the Top) ties up another person (the bottom) with rope, connecting the rope to a secure point above, until the bottom's entire body weight is off the ground. Looking at the pictures here, you might reasonably think that rope suspensions are quite comfortable. In fact, they usually vary from being "a little uncomfortable" to "extremely painful" to "actually quite dangerous." In my case, my friend Damien, with a little help from my husband Jonny, was trying to rapidly suspend five women, including me, outside. We were in an area where cell phones didn't work especially well in a time before all cell phones started beeping at you whenever there are severe weather alerts. Consequently, none of us knew that a mini tornado (called a microburst) was on its way. When we set out to start, it looked like it might rain within the hour. In reality, after maybe 20 minutes, the five of us bottoms unexpectedly found ourselves naked, tied in the air to tire swings with no quick escape, with hail pounding painfully on our exposed flesh, giant trees threatening to fall upon us, and the temperature plummeting so fast that hypothermia quickly became a real concern. Although I don't think the person who was suspended the longest hung for more than 10 minutes, we were pretty thoroughly stuck because the jute rope that we were tied in, which becomes nearly impossible to untie when it's wet, became drenched in moments. Fortunately, we all got out fine, no one got sick, and I think even the filthy and soaked rope eventually recovered.

As we stumbled back to the main part of camp in the aftermath of the storm, we learned that 30 cars had been severely damaged, the roof of a cabin at camp had been destroyed, and a tree with a trunk the size of my kitchen had fallen over in the middle of camp. Miraculously, no one was injured—which was great, because we had a cool picture to prove to everyone what we'd done! Because in our arrogant stupidity, with rain pouring, wind howling, hail pounding, and trees threatening to fall upon us, we'd still paused long enough to grab a couple of good shots of our adventure. Now, I think it's pretty obvious that if the Scene actually subscribed to the "safe and sane" part of its principles, we should have been publicly shamed for what we'd done. Although we had no idea a tornado was coming, we knew the wind was picking up, we could tell rain was coming, and we didn't stop when we heard the first rumblings of thunder. We even joked that the lightning would be a great background for our photo. But people didn't treat us like the fools we were. Instead, they seemed awed by our daredevil stunt to the point that by the next weekend, when I went to a different kink event in another state, several people responded almost reverentially when they heard I had been part of the "Tornado Suspension." People's general admiration was sufficiently great that no one ever even reprimanded us for taking a picture at the event (which was technically against the rules) or posting it online later (which was an even greater violation of the rules).

All over the Scene, I've consistently found people praised far more for being "badasses" and "hard-core players" than for being "meticulous and knowing their own limits well." The desire for harsh and vicious play runs strong enough through the Scene that a few people I've met have half-joked that they prefer the acronym BORK—balls-out reckless kink—to SSC. My friend Evan, an experienced kinkster who introduced the term to me, described it as "a mostly joking embrace of the absurd in response to the risk-averse illusion of safety and control" that pervades much of the Scene.

Part of the joke is that smart, conscientious adults should be allowed to do objectively stupid things if they want to without having to subscribe to the Scene's usual pretensions of safety. However, Evan followed up his explanation with a rather profound point, which was, "I don't really get up to much of anything that I would actually consider reckless these days because there's frequently little connection between how risky something feels and how risky it is, and I'm more interested in the feels." In general, Scene norms about safety, sanity, and consent have *very* little recognition of this distinction, and many experienced players become increasingly frustrated with attempts to create the illusion of safety, sometimes at the expense of making things actually safer.

These issues of safety, sanity, and even consent often become blurry in practice because they're predicated on dubious assumptions about what people actually want. For instance, the whole principle of SSC is based on the idea that people want to be in a safe and consensual interaction, but as Evan's comment suggests, many people want to *feel* like something is reckless, and they often *don't* want to feel like they're in a consensual or safe interaction. Despite the fact that FetLife constantly deletes any "rape"-related kinks on the site, as of this writing, 176,000 people on the site nonetheless say they're into consensual nonconsent. Given that rape, or something like it, is a pretty serious turn-on for a large segment of the general population (Lehmiller, 2018), the Scene generally has to try to find ways to manifest those fantasies. Rape play and CNC scenes are somewhat normalized within large sections of Scene culture (although heavily debated and loathed in other parts of it) because so many bottoms want to *feel* violated without actually *being* violated.

Another problematic assumption underlying formal norms about consent is that consent should be based on (1) knowing one's limits and (2) communicating them to another person. Even assuming a new kinkster knows their limits, learning to communicate them to another person is a complex process often riddled with errors and trouble. Formal Scene norms tend to frame limits as concrete, constant, simplistic, and knowable things, but in actual practice, limits are often inconsistent and situationally specific. While many bottoms care deeply that their limits are respected, I've encountered many others who actively seek out and prefer Tops who "push" their limits—a phrase that means very different things to different people. For example, Mila spoke glowingly of one of her favorite Tops, saying, "She's one of the three people that exist that can really kind of push my limits in terms of pain, and I can take it and tolerate it. And I, you know, yeah, I kind of love her, she's kind of amazing." For Mila, part of what made the Top so good is that the Top "pushed her limits" for pain. I've had similar conversations with many bottoms who say that the deepest intimacy for them emerges from finding people who they'll make exceptions for. The fantasy of the Dom Who Is the Exception, the Special Person the sub does forbidden things for, is so common in the Scene that it often creates a world of trouble for people trying to create standardized communication around consent and safety. Thus a contradiction emerges between a formal norm of knowing, communicating, and respecting limits and a desire from many hard-core bottoms to basically throw all their limits away for someone who is desirable enough.

Yet even setting aside the complication that many bottoms actively *want* to have their limits pushed is the complex reality that, for everyone, finding limits is an ongoing process. Like many people in the Scene, Oliver framed exploring his limits as one of the basic joys of life in the Scene, and part of the journey toward personal authenticity described earlier, saying, "Kink is just having people, friends, learning new things and just all about personal growth within myself—finding my limits, finding more things that I'm interested in that I enjoy doing." While formal Scene norms emphasize the importance of staying within limits, informal Scene norms heavily emphasize this process of exploration. Vera explained that she had come back to the Scene after about a decade's absence and had made a point of relearning what she liked and hated, challenging herself to remember that the things she likes might have changed. She said she made a point of experimenting with things that she used to like and hate to see if her feelings had changed—and some had, while others remained the same.

While people usually frame this process of exploration in a positive light, it almost inevitably takes people to places they didn't really want to go at some point. Melissa explained that she had learned through experience that she was more interested in submission (giving herself to the control of another) than masochism (experiencing pain), saying she had experienced too much pain in a lengthy scene:

> That much pain was just too much. It was a good experience and it was a bad experience melded into one. I found out what I liked, what I didn't like. I wasn't clear about some things, because I had never experienced any of it, and it's so important to be extremely clear. But if you don't know what you like, you have to experience it before [you can know], so it was a good experience for me to know what I like and what I don't like.

Scene culture encourages people like Melissa to frame their experiences in the best possible light—to see a "learning experience" rather than a moment of "violation," "abuse," or "trauma." This framing is mostly successful, although one person's "learning experience" can be another person's "trauma," and Scene culture is unprepared for that variation. In spite of the fact that most bottoms experience a moment when "finding a limit" turns into "a really bad experience," the Scene has basically no system for dealing with this reality.

It's important to notice that throughout these accounts, *bottoms* are the ones the Scene encourages to push and learn their limits. The concept of Tops having limits or needing to push their limits barely enters into Scene norms. Instead, the Scene teaches Tops to learn skills (e.g., to tie rope, to flog, to do knife play) and teaches bottoms to learn their limits and communicate them. These are very different lessons, and one of the critiques of traditional BDSM education that has appeared in recent years is that bottoms and Tops have been taught so differently that they sometimes have difficulty communicating across their different experiences and expectations.

CONCLUSION: DEMOGRAPHICS OR VALUES?

At the start of the chapter, I posed the chicken-or-egg question of whether the Scene's demographics shape its values or if its values shape its demographics. That question is, of course, impossible to definitively answer, but I can say that when I have visited BDSM microcultures with different demographics (especially those in the American South), their values were also a bit different as well. I know that most kinksters tend to be oblivious to the links between their demographics and their values. For example, as I mentioned in chapter 3, I've often heard white kinksters wonder why there are so few Black people in the Scene. In addition to Black people's lower tolerance for nonmonogamy, another reason is that Black people in America are much more devoutly Christian than white people; the Scene isn't very friendly to Christianity, and most forms of traditional Christianity aren't very friendly to BDSM. However, we can't know if the Scene is so unfriendly to Christianity because it's so full of white people or if it's so full of white people because it's so unfriendly to Christianity. The same general idea holds for many of the values I've described in this chapter: despite being a collection of self-identified weird people, kinksters tend to be weird in rather similar ways, and people who aren't "weird like us" mostly stay away or leave quickly. However the trend started, it becomes self-reinforcing as people who feel out of place self-select out, or never knew the kinds of people who would guide or bring them to the parties and events in the first place.

The Scene constantly worries about attracting the "wrong" kinds of people—namely, people who are attracted to the Scene without being "authentically" interested in BDSM and people who would be inclined to violate its myriad rules. It has many mechanisms for discouraging those people from becoming involved in the first place, making them unwelcome if they arrive, or just flatly kicking them out if they try to stay. As a self-policing entity, the Scene aspires to be a reasonably well-ordered and regulated place, and it's looking for people who want to rebel against an existing normative relationship system, not completely retreat from the basic social order. Consequently, it wants to attract people who like order and rules but use order and rules to facilitate very unconventional relationship, kinky, and sexual goals. Thus the Scene perpetually does an uneasy dance to maintain this weird balance between rebellious deviance and rule-based conformity. It wants people who question authority, but not so much that they'll question the very bossy authority of the Scene itself. And, as we'll see in the next chapter, there are *still more* rules.

WELCOME TO THE DUNGEON

Performing Kink

So let's say you've made the leap. You've been curious for a while about kink, you've read the basic rules of how it's done, and you show up for your first dungeon party. You get the address through a sometimes elaborate series of networking contacts (or sometimes with an efficient Google search), and then you inevitably drive through some very poor neighborhoods until you arrive at something that looks vaguely like a beat-up warehouse. The buildings in the neighborhood are often deserted, because zoning regulators (if the venue is truly legal, which many of them aren't) don't want to bother neighbors with the sounds of loud music, cracking whips, and screaming patrons. The dungeon itself doesn't even have a sign on the door, because most dungeons don't want you there unless you already know where you're going. To make it worse, it's usually already totally dark, since most parties don't really start until 9:00 at night. You check the address at least three more times before you get out of your car because you look conspicuous around here: you're not dressed like everyone else, you look confused, and you and your car almost always look richer than the people around you because the people around you are generally *poor*. Even worse, everyone in the neighborhood knows why you're here, and they're mostly annoyed that people like you are jamming up the parking on their street and doing apparently shady and dubious things until late at night every weekend. And you temporarily become overly self-conscious of the judgment of these "outsiders." If you're a woman, you're likely to be perceived as a hard-core slut; if you're a man, you're likely to be perceived as a criminal who hurts people for fun.

In a subculture of people who pride themselves on not giving a shit what vanillas think about them, I'm well known for being one of the proudest and out-est. But I've never gotten out of my car to walk into a dungeon without having to take a nervous breath while all those thoughts run through my head. And when you're brand-new, you have no idea if the thing you're about to walk into is more or less scary than walking on these dark city streets late at night. In this chapter, I'll tell you more about what happens when you walk through that often literally hidden entrance. I'll start by describing and explaining yet more formal and informal rules of interaction, then briefly explain the systems for enforcing them, and finally analyze what sociologists call the *material* and *nonmaterial culture* of dungeons and the scenes that happen in them. Throughout, I want to try to maintain a lens of performance (Fahs, 2011): in the Scene, kink gets done in very particular ways. Kinksters call it "the Scene" because it's a place of perpetual performance, and they refer to what they do as "scenes" and even sometimes verb it. An actual exchange might go something like this:

> *Friend 1:* Did you play with anyone last night?
> *Friend 2:* Yeah, I scened with John.

Kinksters learn the "right" ways to do BDSM by observing and socializing with each other in these places of public performance. And on some level, they remain aware that dungeons are places where people are performing something (usually BDSM and occasionally sex) that mainstream society says should happen only in intimate settings—if it happens at all. But remember that trying to order and regulate the performance of BDSM requires kinksters to validate and normalize it. Inside the doors of the dungeon, kinksters declare ourselves to be normal, but the moment we leave, we're back to being stigmatized sexual deviants.

So how do you get into this haven? In many of these warehouse dungeons, there isn't even a door handle outside and you have to ring a bell or knock to get in. There's generally (again, intentionally) no indication of what you're supposed to do. All these measures reinforce the impression that you're about to enter a super-secret special club. Once you finally do manage to get inside (often having to wait until someone else comes along), you're usually in a dimly lit or glaringly fluorescent entry room, you pay someone money, and then you finally go through a door or a curtain and get to see the things you came to see. (And if you're a true newb, many parties will have someone working as a host to take you on a guided tour.)

The term "dungeon" conjures up images of the dark basements of gothic medieval castles with cold, damp stones, few windows, and medieval torture devices. Despite the name, most modern BDSM dungeons aren't in castles (although people do occasionally throw BDSM parties in gothic-style

St. Andrew's crosses (the wooden X's here), rigs, and spanking benches are the most popular types of dungeon furniture. *Photo: Nightowls1206*

buildings to add flair). I've only been in one BDSM dungeon that had actual stone walls and flooring, and like most modern BDSM dungeons, it didn't contain many classic torture devices. BDSM dungeons are usually large, dimly lit rooms containing a variety of furniture that people can creatively use to hurt one another, with few or no windows to maximize privacy. At some point in the 2000s, most kink event and party promoters started using the term "playspace" as the official label for these spaces in an attempt to move away from connotations of nonconsensual torture and toward connotations of consensual fun. Despite being the official term in print, "playspace" mostly hasn't sunk into the spoken kink cultural lexicon among the people I hang out with or interviewed. Everyone in the mid-Atlantic still generally calls them "dungeons" unless they're event organizers or staff consciously trying to change their language.

Standing public dungeons (as opposed to parties that temporarily "take over" a venue like an art warehouse) are almost always the central hub of their local public BDSM Scenes. Typically, they only host kink parties at night; by day, they're often (fetish/erotic) photography or film studios or house professional dominatrixes who entertain clients there. Whether permanent or temporary, most large public dungeons tend to feel a little like a cross between a goth dance club and a kinky indoor jungle gym. Some of them are dimly lit with colored lights, while others are just dimly lit. In volume, they tend to vary from rather loud to very loud, with a combination of music (especially industrial dance music like that of VNV Nation) and chatter, punctuated by screams, squeals, grunts, and moans.

For kinksters, the most important distinguishing characteristic of dungeons is their equipment. Although there is no standard set of required BDSM furniture, some of the most common pieces are: St. Andrew's crosses (large wooden *X*s that have metal rings at each end of to allow bottoms to be cuffed to them), suspension rigs (large wooden or metal structures that support most people's weight and are tall enough to keep them off the ground while tied up), cages (from large pet crates up to very elaborate creations clearly meant for humans), bondage tables (which look rather like massage tables with attachments all along the sides for rope), spanking benches, cock-and-ball-torture chairs, wrestling mats, and a strange wooden ladder-like thing that no one seems to know what to do with. There's also often a corner or room set aside for "medical play" (which is the grown-up version of "playing doctor" and usually includes a gynecologist's exam chair) and a massage table set aside for "fire play" or "needle play." And lastly, most dungeons include a boot-blacking stand for people to get their shoes polished (which is sometimes as innocent and straightforward as it sounds but can sometimes involve, say, getting your boots licked).

Despite being geared toward kink, most large public dungeons rarely only contain space for people to engage in BDSM play. Confusingly, kinksters often refer to their local dungeon or club in reference to the whole building, but once you arrive, you find that only the room/s with BDSM equipment in them are *really* called the "dungeon" or "playspace." Most public dungeons actually contain multiple rooms or try to divide their spaces to encourage different types of activities in particular places. They often have an area with couches primarily intended for socializing (although people do sometimes engage in very loose or casual play in those areas, some dungeons have rules against it). In the DC/Baltimore area, large dungeons often include a room (or sometimes a set of private rooms) more oriented toward sex, with mattresses or large, cushioned sex furniture. Elsewhere, I've rarely seen dedicated sex furniture in dungeons, even in dungeons that allow all forms of sex. Even though these different rooms are all part of a single space, people's behavior is often very different in each of them, in accordance with posted rules and informal expectations.

Technically speaking, in the lexicon of the Scene, a dungeon can be any room that has BDSM furniture in it and is intended for play (typically as opposed to education), and the majority of the dungeons kinksters use aren't standing locations. Many private homes have dungeons (some wealthy people dedicate an entire floor to them), and the owners of these dungeons sometimes host semipublic or private parties. Additionally, many public dungeons are temporarily erected at campgrounds and hotels for large days-long BDSM events or for a night's party at a particular warehouse or club. I have been to standing and temporary dungeons in many places, from Canada to Iceland to Florida to Colorado, and most of them are so similar to one another in spirit, appearance, and social structure that they're almost interchangeable.

THE RULES

The rules in these dungeons, which are related to the larger Scene norms I've explained previously, are so universal that most veteran kinksters can recite them by heart. Many formal dungeon rules and norms are an attempt to manifest the broader rule-based principles described earlier. But there are also many informal norms in dungeons that almost no one is consciously aware of. I'm going to talk about both the formal and informal norms together here because they're too entangled to reasonably separate.

Rule #1: Consent, Safewords, and Bodily Autonomy

The first formal rule in most dungeons is: "All play is consensual," which isn't surprising, since consent is the foundational rule of BDSM for kinksters. Most dungeons go further and also formally instruct people to obtain consent for any physical touch. Kinksters mostly follow these rules pretty well. It's normal in the Scene for people to ask permission before hugging, and people generally try to ensure they have consent for anything from kissing to sex to whipping. In practice, my observations and data suggest that these rules apply much more to people with penises than people with vaginas. Everyone, regardless of sex or gender, seems more concerned about people with penises nonconsensually touching people with vaginas than any about other gender/sex interaction. People with penises are often very conscious about asking people with vaginas if they can touch them, but I've rarely witnessed such caution in any other interaction configuration. On my survey, people with penises were much more concerned than people with vaginas about being perceived as rule violators. This trend is in keeping with larger cultural trends that often perceive penises as more threatening than vaginas in exposed spaces like bathrooms (Schilt and Westbrook, 2015)—or, in this case, the relatively sexually open environment of the Scene. The Scene seems to be fairly successful at promoting a sense of consensual safety, as there was a lot of agreement from all genders on my survey that they felt safer in the Scene than in many public vanilla settings, and the strongest agreement was from people with vaginas.

The related consent rule of most dungeons is: "The house safeword is RED." This rule sounds beautifully simple in theory but in practice is a mess. "Safeword" and "red" are actually verbed in the informal kink lexicon, as in, "I safeworded out of that," "He redded," or, "He tried to get her to red." Perversely, the Scene's emphasis on the importance of safewords ends up creating a lot of pressure *against* using them publicly and sometimes privately as well. Ellie described her surprise after seeing a scene in a public dungeon where someone actually said "red." As we discussed it further, she said,

> I think with public play people tend to keep it a little more tame and a little more calm, just because I think there's almost a little bit of embarrassment that goes along with safewording in public. I don't know if I necessarily agree with that. I mean, if you need to safeword, you need to safeword. But I think there's a little bit of a stigma. [After I commented that it was on both sides, she agreed.] Definitely, because the Top is like, "Oh, I did something I shouldn't have," and the bottom is like, "Oh, I'm not a good bottom; I couldn't take it." Yeah, but I think the bottom has a responsibility to keep the sensibility to be like, "I need to safeword," at the same time as the Top needs to be aware of the bottom to the point where [the Top] can say, "This is getting to be too much."

Ellie's comments hearken back to another point from the previous chapter about the Scene holding Tops more responsible than it holds bottoms for bottoms' well-being. Her description of the archetypal responses of each is in keeping with what people often say about scenes that "went wrong" in which the bottom had to safeword. (Note that hypothetically Tops can also safeword, but there's very little understanding or context for it.)

The Scene cultivates a stubborn pride among bottoms that encourages them not to safeword even when they're in private. Melissa explained that she endured a lengthy private scene that she hadn't entirely loved, saying,

"We went to his house, and I was dressed way up. I got collared and leashed, and this was my really first big BDSM Scene, and it was so intense. And we had set up safewords, but I don't like saying safewords, so I went through the whole goddamn thing." While many bottoms I know don't share attitudes like Melissa's, the perspective is so common that there is a pervasive fantasy among bottoms of a Top who will push the bottom right to the edge of wanting to safeword but never quite crossing that line. Indeed, in a caning class I attended, the teacher taught us a strategy to help bottoms not feel like they needed to safeword. The instructor suggested that when Tops realized that bottoms were getting to the edge of their endurance, they should start counting down from a number so that the bottom will know when the scene will be over and not need to safeword, and "everyone will leave the scene satisfied." The sense that safewords are a sign of failure is pervasive in the Scene. In general, bottoms often reserve safewording in public for situations in which something has gone seriously wrong (such as being on the verge of fainting or throwing up, both of which I've seen scenes stop for).

But people often don't safeword even when something *has* gone seriously wrong—thus, note that in my story about the tornado suspension, of five terrified bottoms, not one of us safeworded out of what was literally a life-threatening situation. Admittedly, safewording probably wouldn't have helped us much in that scenario. (I don't think the weather gods usually listen to safewords.) Yet we had created a situation in which none of us wanted to use our safeword for fear of spoiling the experience for the others, which is a common consent problem in group play/sex situations. Furthermore, experienced rope bottoms (which we all were) are accustomed to trusting their Tops to make the final decision about when it's time for a rope scene to finish. In this large group situation, no one wanted to disappoint anyone else, no one had enough information to make an informed decision, and we were all used to trusting our mutual Top. These are four of the five main factors that often conspire to keep people from safewording: (1) not wanting to disappoint others (usually the other people directly involved in the scene, but sometimes the audience as well); (2) insufficient information to actually assess danger, particularly since kinky people often do things that are risky and so are not always able to correctly evaluate the difference between mild and serious risk in the heat of the moment; (3) habitually trusting the other person (usually bottoms trusting Tops); (4) mostly having fun and not wanting the fun to stop for anything that isn't perceived as very serious; and (5) not wanting to attract undue and alarmed attention from others.

There's another class of scenes that are negotiated "to red," meaning that people are going to do a psychologically and/or physically brutal scene with someone and keep going until the person safewords. People about to do them usually warn the dungeon monitors about those scenes beforehand so the DMs won't get worried. I witnessed an extremely vicious "takedown" scene in which four men kicked and hit another struggling man on wrestling mats in a dungeon. It resembled a gang attack in a movie, and virtually everyone in the dungeon gathered around to watch the unusual display of violence (most of the people I talked to agreed squeamishly that it "wasn't hot"). The scene had been planned in advance and the dungeon monitors knew that it was going to continue until the bottom called, "Red," at which point the Tops did, in fact, stop kicking and hitting their consenting victim. The story related in chapter 1 of Jezebel, who had a rattle to drop at the point where she wanted her gang rape scene to end, is another example of this type of scene. Although they make for compelling stories, these types of push-to-red scenes are pretty rare.

Despite the pressure in the Scene not to say "red," especially in public places, most bottoms will say "yellow" (i.e., caution) or something like it with relative ease. In practice, bottoms often use "yellow" more like the official BDSM literature presents "red." Rather than calling everything to a grinding halt because of discomfort, people say "yellow" to make adjustments to what is happening or to seriously warn their tops that they will need to stop soon. In recent years, the Scene has become increasingly aware that bottoms often don't safeword. Rather than trying to minimize the stigma of safewording, the Scene has mostly encouraged Tops to negotiate with bottoms more carefully before scenes and carefully "read" bottoms' body language.

Rule #2: Respect the Scene

The second most common formal dungeon rule is: "Don't interrupt someone else's scene." In keeping with the principle of nonjudgment ("Your kink is not my kink, but your kink is okay") and the principle that things that look terrible might be cathartic and therapeutic for the folks involved, the Scene strictly teaches kinksters not to interfere with each other's play. The formal rules mandate that uninvolved people must maintain respectful distance from other people's sex and kink activities and not interrupt, verbally or physically. Active spectators must maintain a respectful distance (although not everyone agrees how far that's supposed to be), and unsought participation is absolutely forbidden. Uninvited participants are not supposed to flirt, ask questions, or correct someone's technique in the middle of a scene.

Most dungeons also have related rules about noise. For instance, one dungeon says, "Please keep conversation, laughter, and comments to a minimum around play." My favorite dungeon sign ever said, "Please Scream Quietly." This principle is in place both to keep people from disturbing each other's scenes and, in some buildings, to keep people from disturbing the neighbors. In many dungeons, the music is so loud that people have no need to moderate their voices to respect other people's scenes. In others, there's no music, or the music is sufficiently quiet that people are required to talk quietly in confined space. It's common for multiroom dungeons to have a "quiet dungeon" where there is no or low music and where people talk quietly and engage in relatively low-key scenes. Quiet dungeons often feel a little like libraries where people are tying, whipping, or beating each other. For some, the quiet provides a sense of intimacy and privacy, while for others keeping quiet while being hurt is just another kind of consensual torture.

In practice, there is a lot of variation in how well these rules are followed. Kinksters often adhere to the principles very seriously, and I've literally seen people wait around for an hour at a party so they could say good-bye to a lover who was involved in a lengthy scene they didn't want to interrupt. In general, however, there are unacknowledged systems for breaking the rules of interruption gracefully (or just barely not breaking them) in permissible ways in special circumstances. For example, sometimes friends or lovers will hover close by a scene in progress and make eye contact with the Top in the scene, who will acknowledge the interrupter before the interrupter actually speaks. Generally speaking, this type of interruption is unacceptable from strangers other than DMs.

On the other hand, while not technically interrupting scenes, strangers often huddle in groups around scenes, making fairly audible comments to one another (but not to the participants). Veteran kinksters can usually discern the palpable (but completely intangible and invisible to the inexperienced) difference between what are functionally public exhibitionistic spectacles versus intimate private scenes that happen to be taking place in a public space. The "audience" interacts more freely and casually in relation to these exhibitionistic scenes compared to private-public ones. For example, my partners Arielle and James—who were well-known exhibitionists—were playing in a dungeon one time with a cape draped over them for warmth. At one point when they took a brief break from what they were doing, a good friend of Arielle's came over to complain that the cape was spoiling her view, and Arielle laughingly rearranged it and resumed. Such an interruption would usually have been perceived as "weird" or "creepy" from someone they didn't know, but because the interrupter was a friend who knew they were exhibitionists and had waited for a break in play, they were both amused by it.

The interruption of scenes highlights the way that public dungeons often end up with both genuinely public and semiprivate scenes. "Public" scenes in dungeons mostly happen in the center of the dungeon, and people's movements are often larger and showier. The participants also tend to be relatively loud in terms of both their verbalizations and their screams. In these types of highly exhibitionistic scenes, Tops will sometimes start engaging with their audience—with eye contact, by asking for assistance holding objects, or by getting someone to fetch gloves or other implements to facilitate the scene. For example, I witnessed a Top controlling his bottom who was riding a sybian (a large vibrating sex machine). He was constantly asking their audience if the bottom was allowed to "come" (orgasm) yet and what she would have to do to be allowed to do so. The audience was providing enthusiastic suggestions. Exceptionally performative and unusual scenes will sometimes get spontaneous applause from kinksters watching, and it's pretty common at camp for people to literally bring popcorn or other snacks and just chill out at a "respectful" distance from friends to watch them put on kinky shows.

"Private" public scenes, on the other hand, often occur more around the edges of the dungeon—in darker corners or sometimes in separate adjacent rooms that aren't considered the "main dungeon." These scenes frequently involve smaller and more intimate physical movements. They're also usually quieter, and Tops and bottoms are much more likely to whisper to one another than yell. Instead of putting on a show, participants seem to be carving out a private space for themselves, even in the midst of a crowd.

People (almost always men) who kinksters refer to as "creepers" sometimes hover too close to these personal scenes and interrupt them in spite of the rules. However, most kinksters know better than to interrupt these scenes without good reason or even to conspicuously watch them. I've lost count of the number of times people have told me after a scene, "Sorry, I couldn't help but notice how hot the scene you did with So-and-so was last night," thus preserving the illusion of privacy in the midst of public space. That type of apology is especially likely to precede a comment about a scene that happened in a secluded alcove or back room with the door open—places where real privacy obviously doesn't happen, but people can sometimes trick themselves into believing in it if they want.

Rule #3: Share and Take Care of the Equipment

Another common rule in dungeons is to keep scenes to about an hour during high-traffic times so as to share the equipment with others. The rules also say that people should keep the equipment clean and undamaged, but the community hotly debates the precise implications of this rule. Some dungeons specifically forbid naked genitals from touching their equipment and expect people to use "chux" (large disposable absorbent underpads usually used for people who are incontinent or training puppies) on the equipment if they're naked. The rules forbid engaging in acts likely to make equipment "dirty" (namely, sex) without chux. Shoes (and especially high heels) on soft equipment are always forbidden. Traditional etiquette says that people should wipe down equipment before using it and after. Despite what many people fear, almost every piece of gym equipment I've ever come in contact with at a public gym smelled worse than any piece of public BDSM furniture, so I think someone is usually doing an okay job of taking care of it.

In practice, conformity to these rules is iffy. It's easy to get swept up into a moment and forget to clean the equipment. More experienced people are usually more trustworthy around equipment, partly because they've developed the habit of cleaning up before and after themselves. It's also common for female submissives to clean up equipment before and after scenes for their male Dominants, even if the sub wasn't involved in the scene herself (I have never personally seen a male sub do this for a female Dom). After one large event I attended with a mix of experienced and inexperienced kinksters, there was a scandal because people had treated the equipment so poorly; someone had even intentionally vandalized equipment. People had left heel tears in a cushion, mutilated a wooden suspension frame by using chain on it instead of the intended rope, and written "Fuck you" in permanent marker on valuable equipment. Appalled by what happened, the rest of the community quickly banded together through FetLife and raised more than $2,500 to replace the damaged items, which someone had lent to the event. That's the only story I know of like that. At many large dayslong events, the dungeons never close and they're monitored for only a few hours a day, but people are generally responsible.

People are much worse about sharing equipment. People who are deeply immersed in their scenes often have no sense of time, so it's hard for them to be strategic about allotting time. Moreover, many dungeons forbid having cell phones out (because of the possibility of taking pictures), so people often don't have a normal timepiece. Kinksters sometimes actually get into arguments over the use of rare or unique equipment. There are even some funny passive-aggressive norms about setting one's own things down near a piece of furniture that someone has been using for too long to signal to them that you'd like for them to move along, as well as standing "rudely" close to the furniture and pointedly looking at the people involved. DMs are sometimes empowered to tell people to move on when they take too long, but they rarely do because they don't like interrupting scenes unless absolutely necessary.

Rule #4: (Un)Dress Appropriately

Most dungeons have a rule that goes something like, "Nudity is permitted inside the dungeon, but not in any other rooms of the club or outside it." I've seen specific rules like, "Nudity is only permitted behind the black curtain" because the reception area of the club has very large windows. Officials at the desk in the reception area will tell people to put on more clothes if they try to step beyond the curtain boundary when underdressed. Most clubs and events maintain that when visible to vanillas, people must maintain "better than street-legal" attire (so, for instance, I was once sent back behind the curtain even though I was in street-legal pasties and underwear). Local ordinances occasionally create strange variations of this rule. In Philadelphia, the law forbids alcohol and visible nipples or genitalia in the same place, so a party that I attended there strategically divided its space so that alcohol was consumed downstairs and nudity was only allowed upstairs.

Individual parties often have a theme that participants are encouraged to dress up for (and costume contests may provide further incentive). Many holiday seasonal themes inevitably appear (Halloween, Christmas, Valentine's Day, etc.), but I've been to parties throughout the year themed around superheroes, the cult classic television program *Serenity/Firefly*, Steampunk, and the Renaissance, among many others.

In practice, kinksters rarely hang out in dungeons completely naked. People often strip completely for scenes, within certain unspoken guidelines, while they're playing. The most important of these guidelines is that bottoms usually strip, but Tops don't—nudity implies vulnerability. (This really only applies for people who are cisgender, because trans folks almost never get naked in the Scene.) Stripping is logically necessary for most bottoming activities (whips and floggers can easily get caught in clothes, and ropes are supposedly more stable on skin than on clothes). On the other hand, Topping is often very strenuous physical activity, and I've seen many Tops literally dripping with sweat remain stubbornly dressed in their sweat-soaked, seasonally inappropriate attire. Stripping is also logical for having sex, but most sexual activities in dungeons occur with the participants at least partially clothed. At the conclusion of their scenes, most people (usually bottoms) put their clothes back on. Indeed, seeing all the participants fully or mostly dressed is often a cue to others that the scene is really finished, but almost no kinksters I've met are consciously aware of this norm.

Rule #5: Sex?

Across the United States (although less so within particular regions), dungeons vary wildly in what types of sexual activity are permitted. Kinksters refer to events and parties that allow sex as "sex-positive," although there's no generally agreed-upon term for the parties and events that forbid it. There's no real logic in the sex positivity variation, and many venues allow sex under one set of circumstances, then forbid it for another. The strictest antisex rules I've ever seen were in a New England dungeon that says, "There is no sex allowed on the premises. This includes vaginal, oral, or anal," and then adds, "If more than one people [sic] are in the bathroom, the door must remain open." I've also been to events that allow sex but require it to be protected with barriers (gloves, dental dams, and/or condoms). As you might imagine, those rules are difficult and tedious to enforce (and DMs at these events often roll their eyes and refer to themselves as the "condom police"). At the opposite end of the spectrum, one large event posted an official rule: "If you are having unprotected sex, we will assume that you are fluid bonded with your partner(s) and not an idiot with a death wish. Please don't prove us wrong." In a weird gray area in between, I attended an event where sex was technically forbidden (even though the club was a swinger club on alternating nights), and when I asked a party organizer if sex was "really" against the rules, she winked at me and said, "Welllll . . . just don't do it where anyone can see you."

The community used to hotly debate whether sex should be allowed at large kink events. Two of the largest hotel kink events in the mid-Atlantic for several years maintained polar opposite rules about sex: one initially declared that "nothing organic may penetrate anything else that is organic." (My friend Alex snarkily pointed out that this rule meant that French kissing was forbidden but strap-on sex was permitted.) By contrast, the other event organized a large room adjacent to the dungeon proper filled with beds and sex furniture like wedges (a giant pillow that looks exactly like it sounds), as well as jars of condoms, lube, and vinyl gloves for safer sex, accompanied by a helpful sign that said, "Fuck Here!" When I began studying the Scene in 2012, many more large BDSM events forbade sex than they did by 2017, by which time most of the big events that forbade sex either shut down or changed their policies (including the one with the funny "organic" rule). Many older kinksters claimed that as the specter of AIDS faded, the community opened up more toward sex, and events outside of New England mostly came down in favor of it.

Despite the broad spectrum of dungeon rules regarding sex, there isn't a lot of variation among dungeons in people's actual sexual behavior, because sexual activity in dungeons is pretty uncommon. When people do have sex in clubs or at events, it mostly happens in the designated sex spaces rather than in the dungeon proper. The sex that happens in most dungeons, regardless of whether the dungeons technically allow sex, tends to involve women receiving hand jobs or vibrators. Although cock-and-ball torture is also common for male bottoms, it rarely involves any real sexual stimulation the way that torturing vaginas does. By contrast, the use of Hitachi's massage wands as vibrators on vaginas is so common that kinksters have verbed the word, as in, "I Hitachi'd her until she couldn't remember how many times she came." Vibrators are an efficient way to "torture" clitorises with excessive orgasms (many people find excessive orgasms to actually be quite painful) but conveniently skirt the legal definition of sex. Hand jobs and "fisting" (trying to get most or all of one's hand into a person) are also popular dungeon sexual activities—again, mostly with women receiving. At one event I attended where sex was supposedly forbidden, the event nonetheless sponsored a poorly attended "Fist-a-Thon"—a fisting orgy—in the dungeon. Likewise, people who regularly go to the dungeon mentioned earlier with the extremely strict antisex policy have told me hand jobs and fisting are not merely tolerated, but encouraged there.

Less frequently, in the places that permit it, dungeon sex involves oral sex (cunnilingus or fellatio), although often under clothes (for example, women giving blow jobs to men who are still wearing kilts). More rarely, dungeon sex involves vaginal or anal intercourse. People are much more likely to have more sex in dungeons where there is furniture explicitly intended for that purpose (particularly sex swings). Even when the sex involves some form of intercourse, people often leave most of their clothes on. I've almost never seen two entirely naked people of any gender fucking in a dungeon. Because the official rules usually discourage people from using dungeon furniture for too long, people don't tend to have much sex on the dungeon furniture itself. Consequently, sex tends to happen on couches, wrestling mats, and actual sex furniture.

Although I've never seen a written rule that forbids masturbation, the informal rules of all dungeons basically forbid solo masturbation (with exceptions for someone who was obviously being ordered to masturbate by someone else). Kinksters tend to label people—especially men—who masturbate in dungeons while watching other people play "creepy." There are also no formal rules forbidding gay sex, but I've almost never seen two cis men engaging in sexual activity without a woman's involvement in a pansexual kink dungeon. Although many men in the pansexual Scene self-identify as heteroflexible or even bisexual, they almost never have public sex with (or even engage in BDSM play with) other men in public spaces. Cis women, on the other hand, have sex with all genders in public freely. But regardless of the gender configuration of the participants, public sex in dungeons proper is not really common.

Rule #6: Acceptable Violence?

It's normal for dungeons to forbid play involving guns, anything gunlike, and sometimes swords. Other than that, it's rare to see any real limitations on the permissible (consensual) violence. All events reserve the right to stop anything they deem too disturbing or dangerous, but they usually do so at potential social cost. That said, much of the play in dungeons feels and looks violent without actually being particularly dangerous. People rarely punch others in the face or head and are usually very careful to avoid impact to the stomach or kidneys. People often yank others around by the hair, but usually while trying to protect the person's neck. Many kinksters have formal training in violence (usually from the military or martial arts), and they mostly employ that training to carefully hurt people in a manner designed not to harm them.

Rule #7: Don't Drink and Kink; No Illegal Drugs

As I mentioned in chapter 5, adherence to the "Don't drink and kink" rule is pretty high. When they drink more than two or so drinks, most people don't play. But there's an important exception to this anti-intoxication policy: smoking pot. Pot use is almost normalized at large events, even when it's illegal and technically forbidden (which it functionally always was during my fieldwork in 2012). Twice, when I sat down to interview someone during my fieldwork, they politely offered me a joint. (I refused.) That said, pot smoking tends to still be a *little* bit furtive, mostly happening on the literal edges of things rather than at the center. Nonetheless, entire areas of BDSM camping events often smell like pot, and no one seems to care. I've only heard people say, "I can't play, I'm stoned," when they were very, very high. If anything, many kinksters seem to think smoking small amounts of pot enhances their kinky and sexual experiences. Cigarette smoking, vaping (by 2015 or so), and cigar smoking are also fairly normalized. As bisexuals are much more likely than straight people to smoke (Ward et al., 2014), it's no surprise that the rate of cigarette smoking appears much higher around the Scene than we would otherwise expect from a white, middle-class subculture. Occasional cigar smoking is *extremely* popular and much more normalized than pot or cigarettes, with an entire cluster of kink practices surrounding it. Tops put cigars (and much more rarely, cigarettes) out on bottoms, put hot ash on their tongues, blow smoke on them, and expect bottoms to prepare and serve them cigars.

Rule #8: Aftercare Matters

The Scene has semiformal norms expecting Tops to take care of bottoms after scenes, especially ones that are physically and/or psychologically brutal. This post-scene caretaking is referred to as "aftercare," and it's so expected that most dungeons include an official rule asking people to "remove themselves from dungeon equipment for aftercare so as to make the furniture available to others," and often have a separate adjacent space labeled with a sign for aftercare. Conventional aftercare consists of food, drink, and/or cuddles; I know a number of kinksters who half-joke that sex is their aftercare, but the term is never traditionally used that way. For many people, aftercare consists of dealing with the care of the equipment and a quick hug, but for others, it's much more elaborate and may involve everything from stuffed animals to specific words. Traditionally, aftercare was mostly directed at bottoms, but

kinksters increasingly talk about "Top aftercare" as well, generally emphasizing Tops' need to know that the bottom actually enjoyed what happened
to them, that they still like the Top, and that they're okay. Natalie explained
that when she was Topping, it was essential for her to provide good aftercare for her bottom in order for *her* to feel good. She said that after doing a
particularly brutal scene with a bottom, "I told him he had to give me a half
hour afterwards [for aftercare]. And had him clean up, got him hydrated, all
that kind of stuff, and made sure he was okay. He must be doing really okay.
He's already checked in with me today, so I didn't scare him off too bad."
The idea of post-scene "check-ins" between a Top and bottom often serves as
a kind of Top aftercare.

Performing aftercare well is often one of the ways Tops show that they're
good Tops. Many Tops emphasize that taking care of their bottom after a
scene is their highest priority, superseding other concerns. Luke said that
when someone complained that he had left his rope gear on a piece of equipment long after he had finished his scene and thus kept the equipment from
being used, he defended his actions, saying his bottom

> needed much more aftercare than I expected. She was, like, the first point of
> my attention. I needed to take care of her. So I couldn't really pay too much
> attention to cleaning up, which I should have. I'm like, that's [taking care of
> your bottom], actually what you're supposed to do.

At the other end of the spectrum, I've heard some bottoms in conversation
make it a point of pride not to "need too much aftercare." However, almost
all of the mentions of aftercare in my interviews were from Tops, not bottoms, suggesting to me that in general Tops may feel the need to provide
aftercare even more than bottoms feel the need to receive it.

Rule #9: Don't Be a Dick

Many events actually have an official rule: "Don't be a dick." The rule is
intended to encompass an intentionally vague array of behaviors, particularly things like racism, sexism, and intentionally or repeatedly misgendering
someone (e.g., referring to them as "her" when they tell you they're "him").
Frequently, events list those behaviors explicitly as well, and most people
appear to at least attempt to follow them. People seem to have the most
difficulty with and least motivation for correctly gendering people, but most
kinksters seem to take a dim view of making no effort at all.

The other big issue that falls under the "Don't be a dick" umbrella is avoiding doing scenes that are intended to piss other people off or gross them out. There are several "taboo" kinks that are tacitly (and occasionally explicitly) understood to be inappropriate for standard public play. These include things like race play (Weiss, 2011), which is any type of play that highlights race in the interaction, especially in derogatory or humiliating ways; Nazi play, which is functionally a specific type of race play that usually involves someone roleplaying as a Nazi and someone else as Jewish; any form of cannibalism, meaning that part of another person gets eaten; and, to a much lesser degree, nonviolent "rape" play, meaning roleplay coercion or date rape. Kinks involving vomit ("rainbow showers") and feces ("scat play") tend to be explicitly forbidden for sanitation reasons, although urine ("piss play" and "golden showers") is generally accepted or even encouraged at outdoor events. Most of these kinks are well known to be objectionable, and I actually saw a party advertised on the West Coast that was specifically geared toward taboo kinks, with race play and Nazi play specifically listed as permissible.

Kinksters draw some of these lines of acceptability in places that must seem very strange to outsiders. (Actually, they seem pretty strange to me, and I've had years to get used to them.) Feces and vomit play are perceived as revolting, but urine play is just kind of normal. Violent abduction and rape scenes are common, and many kinksters seem to consider watching or participating in them as the height of cool, yet nonviolent "rape" scenes are so rare that I can't remember ever having personally witnessed one (although I've done them). Cooking and eating human flesh is totally gross by Scene standards, but I've watched kinksters enthusiastically have human blood–drinking parties. Although kinksters mostly seem to follow their own principle that "Your kink is not my kink, but your kink is okay," there are still common lines in the sand where most kinksters seem to generally agree that *that* kink maybe isn't really okay—at least not "here," in public.

ENFORCING THE RULES: OFFICIALLY

Galilee-Belfer (2020) analyzed the way official BDSM organizations present their enforcement strategies for rules, but as with most social organizations, there is frequently a chasm between the way BDSM organizations idealistically present and imagine their enforcement strategies and the way things are actually enforced (Holt, 2016). At events hosted in large public venues like hotels, kinksters often have to contend with official professional security personnel (and sometimes actual police) who know little about BDSM. Not having to contend with these people is part of why kinksters often love the freedom of BDSM camping events. However, in most circumstances, the people technically responsible for enforcing safety norms, as well as all the rest of the dungeon rules, aren't professional security personnel but rather (mostly volunteer) designated dungeon (or playspace) monitors or other event staff/management. (Note that many private parties, even the ones held in public dungeons, often don't have any real enforcement authorities other than the host.) In most venues, DMs wear reflective orange or yellow vests to clearly mark them out in dark dungeons. Ostensibly, their job is to make sure that kinksters follow basic safety rules (e.g., cleaning the equipment or not suspending people from unsustainable points) and that people aren't doing things that will damage equipment, and to be a last line of defense if consent violations occur. In reality, the reliability and consistency of this enforcement tends to be mediocre at best. DMs are often poorly trained volunteers who face constant ambiguity about when to actually interfere in scenes. My friend Alex, who worked as head DM for several events, explained some of these problems. Alex said that for many parties, DMs are like party hosts—the formal representative of an event—but at the same time they're supposed to serve as sort of security personnel for people who are often their friends (and sometimes partners and lovers). Like everyone else in the Scene, DMs are drilled in the refrain to not interfere in a scene. But DMs are asked to overcome that socialization in favor of selective interference when they judge it necessary. Alex said that another head DM once told him that "DMs are like condoms: everyone wishes we could get along without them because they feel annoying and constraining, but we need them for safety."

Experienced players know to tell DMs ahead of time when they're going to play in ways that would typically cause alarm. Sofia, who worked as a head DM on several occasions, recounted the first time she saw Dan and Antonia playing in a dungeon at which she was working:

> "Having a good time" is a very broad definition in kink, and that's one of the things you have to teach DMs. Just because a person looks like they're not having a good time, you don't know that. You don't know to interrupt, unless, you know, there's a physical or equipment safety issue. But I think responsible Tops playing in public spaces—it behooves them to check in with

the staff to say, "We're going to do something that looks nonconsensual." When I first met Dan and Antonia and they came and played in the dungeon, Dan came up to me as the head DM that night and said, "You should know she cries and screams a lot." And they played, and everyone in the dungeon kind of went "whoa." And she cried a lot, and there was something very beautiful about that, but there were people who were very upset by it.

Sofia's story emphasizes some of the challenges DMs often face, since theoretically, if enough people complain to them about a scene, they might feel obliged to interrupt even if they don't personally want to. There was no rule against loud play in the dungeon Sofia was working in, but Alex and their partner were stopped by a DM at a dungeon at a different event because Alex's partner was screaming loudly enough that other people were annoyed. Raucous scenes also sometimes garner complaints from people nearby who are trying to do quiet, serious ones. Faced with these complaints, DMs have to make a call about whether to tell the complainers to get over it or tell the people being complained about to tone it down.

As mentioned earlier, people call "red" in public dungeons so infrequently that DMs rarely have to dramatically intervene on behalf of consent. Indeed, most dungeons are so loud that it would take a healthy pair of lungs and a DM with keen hearing to actually hear someone say "red." Experienced head DMs like Alex will sometimes station a DM near a scene they're worried about so they'll be able to intervene quickly if something goes amiss. But DMs can't be everywhere, and they often can't predict the situations that are likely to cause the most trouble.

ENFORCING THE RULES: UNOFFICIALLY

Because DMs can't be everywhere at once, Scene norms depend heavily on the idea that anyone can step in and enforce fundamental rules they see being broken. Many kinksters gain a sense of security from a feeling of Foucauldian-style surveillance (Foucault, 1979)—the sense that people (mostly Tops) won't break the rules as long as other people are watching or might walk in at any time. Luke captured the spirit of this sentiment when he explained why he felt such a profound experience bottoming in private:

> Because there was the atmosphere of being secluded and in a space [where you couldn't escape]. Of course, there were safewords, but I didn't use a

safeword once because I don't like doing that anyway. And if you would be in a public scene, although nobody will interrupt a scene, you still have this idea, like, "Hey, there's other people. I'm going to be okay." Which might be a false interpretation, because there have been situations where people did not intervene even though they probably should have.

As Luke says, being in public lets bottoms *feel* like they'll be safe, even though kinksters are programmed not to interfere in others' scenes, so they generally don't.

Ironically, the existence of DMs actually helps to discourage bystander intervention (Fischer et al., 2011) at kink events because their existence creates an awkward sense of "I'm not actually authorized to intervene here" combined with "This is really not my job." In general, psychology experiments indicate that bystander intervention is pretty difficult to manifest in large public areas, in part because of what psychologists call "diffusion of responsibility" (Darley and Latané, 1968): that is, in situations where multiple people *could* intervene, everyone assumes someone else will. Kinksters rarely find themselves in public situations where they're the *only* person around who ought to intervene in a scene, so they don't know who's actually supposed to take responsibility, especially because bottoms so rarely safeword. Most kinksters have little to no experience intervening and no training in it. All these factors combined mean that most of the stories I've heard of scene interventions from bystanders were ones of delay or failure to intervene more than successful intervention.

MATERIAL CULTURE

Costuming

The material culture of dungeons and the Scene manifests in three main ways: the dungeon furniture, norms of costume and dress, and "toys," described below. The Scene, as a place of performance, is a place where appearance matters, although not so much in conventional norms of appearance—kinksters don't at all look like the sorts of people you see in fashion magazines. Rather, there's a preference for a geek/goth aesthetic, which for feminine presentation I like to refer to as Suicide Girls Chic (a reference to a popular soft-core porn website that closely mirrors the Scene's aesthetics for feminine people). That aesthetic includes bright Manic Panic–style hair colors (especially for more feminine and genderqueer people) and large and colorful tattoos, although only within certain traditional constraints (namely, no tattoos on the hands, neck, or face). Many body piercings, especially nipple and genital piercings, are also valued (though not precisely common), although as with tattoos, excessive facial piercings are less popular. The Scene's body modification aesthetics are definitely much more mainstream than in the actual body mod subculture (Irwin, 2003; Klesse, 1999).

As a subculture (though often not individually), kinksters love to dress up, and costume contests and awards for the "best dressed" are common at events and parties. This propensity for dressing up means that someone hoping to see a lot of people wearing very little would do much better to go to an average beach than an average dungeon. Indeed, when kinksters do go around naked, they often get ironic (although generally sincere) compliments from others about how they "like their outfit." When parties have themes, which they often do, most people usually at least make a token attempt to dress to the theme of a party; those who don't often apologize or look a little uncomfortable. Much like people on a cruise, at dayslong events, where people literally spend much of the day and much of the night in each others' company, most people wear casual clothes during the day and then "get dressed" for the evening in the types of standard kink attire described below every night.

Without a specific theme, geek, goth, and steampunk subcultures (which are all heavily overlapped with the kink subculture) strongly influence kinksters' attire. Like most mainstream dress-up attire, kink attire tends to follow fairly exaggerated gender displays—but those gender displays don't necessarily match people's sex or usual gender identities. It's normal (although not precisely common) to see people who identify as women dress in masculine attire and people who identify as men dress in feminine attire. Feminine attire includes heavy makeup, slinky dresses, gartered stockings, high heels (especially boots), very short skirts, visible thongs and g-strings, lace, and corsets. Masculine attire includes nice jeans and T-shirts (often with pithy sayings, like the one I made for my husband that says, "Geek in the streets/Freak in the sheets"), leather clothing, goth kilts (utilikilts), vests, goth pants, and dark slacks and button-down shirts. For both genders, black is the most popular color, with red the second most popular color for feminine clothes and brown the second most popular color for masculine clothes. Genderqueer attire tends to eschew conventional dressing up entirely (just showing up in deliberately casual beat-up jeans and a T-shirt) or follows more Queer

Two men in utilikilts doing "impact play" with a woman positioned against a St. Andrew's cross. *Photo: Nightowls1206*

Feminine attire tends to be scanty and gothic-inspired, with metal adornments on black clothes. *Models: Kaylee and GoodFoxy, Photo: Kaylee*

Some kinksters take great pride in getting very dressed up. This photo shows a man and a woman in unusually fancy steampunk attire.
Photo: Nightowls1206

cultural norms of dress (glitter, rainbow tutus, bodysuits—the same kinds of styles that are popular at Queer dance parties outside the Scene).

Gothic clothes are almost always black, include platform boots with gratuitous buckles and heavy heels, are often made of rubber or vinyl, and have lots of lace and ruffles. In the masculine version, more gothic clothes tend to mean skinny (form-fitting) pants, and in the feminine version, large black skirts and/or bustles. Gothic attire usually includes silver accessories, although kinksters almost always eschew the traditional crosses. While similar in many respects, steampunk clothes are more likely to be brown than black and accented with brass rather than silver. Feminine steampunk clothes involve less lace and more buckles, with keys and gears as accents. Masculine steampunk clothes are much more distinct from gothic clothes. Masculine steampunk attire avoids jeans or form-fitting attire and instead favors vests, dramatic jackets with many pockets, dress shirts with cravats, dress shoes, and dress pants.

In practice, without a theme, feminine people usually dress up for dungeon parties and masculine people mostly show up in relatively casual attire. I have frequently heard men complain that they don't "know how to dress for kink parties." I've never heard this complaint from experienced women, suggesting that the sartorial norms for masculine attire are much less defined than they are for feminine attire. A few men I know solved the problem for themselves by always wearing suits to dungeons, a choice that often gets a good reaction from women. The fact that several of my interviewees spontaneously discussed clothes—but mostly talked only about women's clothes (whether they were women or men)—suggests that kinksters tend to care more about what women wear than men.

The guidelines for how much flesh to show are very different for masculine versus feminine attire. For feminine attire, less is usually more, with many clothing items making only a token effort to cover flesh, functioning much more like lingerie or actually being lingerie. Masculine attire, on the other hand, is usually street legal and mostly covers flesh. Breasts are often completely bared in dungeons, but men rarely wander around without shirts (let alone without pants). However, as usual, in the Scene, it's hard to separate norms of Dom/sub roles from norms of gender. Nudity and bared flesh are strongly associated with bottoming (especially submission), while clothing is strongly associated with Topping (especially Domination). Ben vividly recalled his first night in a public dungeon:

> A man was having his slave walk around in high heels blindfolded, going up and down stairs even. So, very tentatively, very shyly, very slowly, a beautiful woman wearing a garter and mostly just a lot of silvery chains draping the beautiful curves over her body parts—just looking majestic in really sexy garb.

Masculine bottoms are also often expected to wear very little, whether in public or at home. Lily, a female Dom, explained that when her male sub was visiting her house, "he had to do everything naked, and I like to keep subs in the house naked when everybody else is clothed. I feel like that's the way things should be."

Toys

There's no question that kinksters are an acquisitive folk. Weiss (2011) specifically focused on materialism in the Scene, and she critiqued it heavily for what she perceived as an excessive focus on material belongings that made it difficult for poorer folks to access. She missed a few important details about the nature of that materialism I'll elucidate briefly here.

First of all, kinksters don't just randomly value more stuff; they value very particular kinds of stuff. They value stuff pertaining to BDSM specifically (namely, clothes and BDSM toys), but they value things assembled and made in the spirit of do-it-yourself (DIY) most of all. Subculturally, kinksters don't care about fashion labels or brand names; I've never even heard a conventional brand name mentioned at an event. What they value are things that are handmade or creatively assembled. Many kinksters wear fancy clothes, but they're often purchased from thrift stores, and the most fashion-conscious kinksters I know make and sew their own clothes. Kinksters scorn BDSM toys purchased from Spencer's or other readily accessible stores almost exclusively in favor of handmade items purchased directly from vendors at events or from known kink vendors. I bought a new whip during my fieldwork, and the first question everyone asked me was, "Who made it?" For many years, the norm for bondage photos posted on FetLife and Twitter included credit for the rigger (the person who tied), the model (the person tied up), the photographer, and the person who made the rope. There's nothing that Scene culture thinks is as cool as making your own toys. Kinksters were often fascinated when I used rope that my husband and I made, and they were far more interested in the knives he forged for me than they were in any of the machine-made wares vendors usually sold.

Toys have different meanings for Tops and bottoms, and for people with different levels of experience. Bottoms usually have only a few toys, typically things they personally love or that are "fluid-bonded" to them. (For

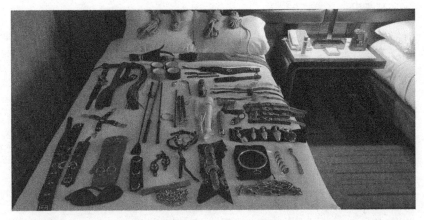

It's not unusual for kinksters (usually Tops) to display their massive toy collections in person and in photos. *Photo: Dirty Archangel*

example, it's difficult to satisfactorily wash the common kinds of bondage rope that has been in or on someone's naked crotch, so bottoms who really enjoy "crotch rope" typically carry their own piece with them for their Top to use.) Tops, on the other hand, often have an entire arsenal of toys that they bring with them to use on potential bottoms. Most experienced Tops I know note that when they first got into the Scene, they used to travel with a car full of toys to parties and events, but after a couple of years, they reduced everything to two or three treasured items. Newer kinksters often haul massive trunks of toys around with them to parties and events, and I half-jokingly refer to them as "mating displays" for Tops. The toys are a way to demonstrate potential fun for bottoms, and the display makes Tops look a little more powerful and interesting in the eyes of potential bottoms, who often magically appear in response to these displays. Many experienced Tops say they prefer doing things that require fewer accoutrements (especially just hitting people with their hands), and they also don't need to put on such displays to attract bottoms once they have established partners and reputations.

It's easy to erroneously believe that only rich people can get into the Scene and be successful there because of the cost of entrance to parties and events and the expectations surrounding costumes or toys. In reality, the people who are the most successful in the Scene are often living in near poverty, and many of their most valuable belongings are gifts from others. Swap meets where people exchange various toys and clothes they no longer want are common at events, and kinksters often trade various services (such as helping someone build BDSM equipment in their home) in exchange for toys; richer kinksters frequently give away their older, lightly used toys to poorer friends and acquaintances when they upgrade or decide they don't need them anymore. No matter how rich the Scene might *look*, its material customs, like these, demonstrate otherwise.

NONMATERIAL CULTURE

Performing Safety

In addition to performing things like aftercare or displaying toys to attract bottoms, Tops also often make a point of performing safety. As I've said before, "safety" tends to be a pretty nebulous and somewhat arbitrary concept in the Scene, but there are some normative ways that kinksters perform the *appearance* of safety in the course of their scenes. These safety performances are often most elaborate for Tops doing suspension bondage or needle play. Suspension bondage Tops frequently make a point of swinging from their "hard points" (the point they'll be suspending their bottom from) to check that they're sturdy, push on suspension frames to test their integrity, and ostentatiously lay out "bondage shears" (which are usually bandage shears). The purpose of these performances, ostensibly, is to ensure that their bottoms are unlikely to fall because of equipment failure and to enable them to cut their bottoms out of their rope in an emergency. In reality, bondage equipment failures are extremely rare and the vast majority of rope injuries happen due to other causes; almost no one cuts someone out of rope in a suspension because it's usually a terrible option. When things go seriously wrong, most rope suspension bottoms are saved by some combination of strong helping hands nearby to lift them, strategically applied climbing carabiners, and/or chairs or stools for them to stand on. But the safety performance norms are so deeply ingrained that many dungeons require rope Tops to have visible shears to be allowed to tie.

The elaborate safety rituals of needle Tops could take up an entire chapter. Most needle and other piercing Tops ostentatiously emphasize the supposed sterility of their play environments, setting up complicated layouts of "uncontaminated" gloves, needles, special cleaning supplies, and sharps disposal containers. While the general format of their safety protocol follows those of many professional body modification artists such as tattoo artists, their protocols are *far* more elaborate than any acupuncturist I've ever visited (most of whom don't even wear gloves). Indeed, most needle and piercing scenes seem to try to make it look like they're occurring in a high-quality body modification studio rather than the often decidedly unsterile dungeons where they're actually happening. Unlike the bondage safety rituals, to the best of my knowledge, the safety rituals of needle Tops at least sort of make sense. But they're still done in a highly performative way, as if to assure bottoms, DMs, and anyone else watching that this needle Top really does care about safety.

I could go on and on about the way that kinksters perform safety for their scenes, from whip Tops changing the crackers on the ends of their whips between bottoms if they get blood or other bodily fluids on them to knife Tops putting cavicide (a medical cleaning agent) on their knives to clean them. While many of these safety protocols make sense, kinksters have had to invent almost all of them without much basis in real scientific research, since most scientists don't spend time researching the disease-spreading properties of whip crackers. All the actual scientists and medical professionals I've spoken with in the Scene tend to agree that most of these deeply ingrained safety practices are probably not harmful but also are mostly unnecessary. Yet kinksters faithfully perform them anyway to meet the expectations of others.

What Makes an "Awesome Scene"?

Dungeons, rules, equipment, clothes, toys: these are all ingredients (or, in the terms of the classical dramaturgical theory of Goffman [1959], setting, stage, costume, and props) for the performances kinksters come to dungeons for—their "scenes." Although I think it's important to reemphasize here that most kinksters stay involved in the Scene in general for the social experiences they have there, kinksters tend to go to *dungeons* because they want to play and/or watch others play. Thus, during my interviews, I asked my interviewees to tell me about an "awesome scene" they had witnessed. The things they found memorable were not always the things they themselves liked to do, but there were certain commonalities among their responses, which I will recount in no particular order.

Kinksters said they enjoyed watching things that were aesthetically interesting and/or sensually appealing to them. Several people specifically mentioned watching any scene involving fire play (which involves actually physically touching a person with fire while trying not to burn them). Vicky explained that fire play is "gorgeous and I love how the whole experience is sensual. There's the auditory, there's a scent involved, there's the physical feeling of the warmth, the visuals—all just gorgeous"—yet she said she doesn't actually personally like to Top or bottom for fire play. Kinksters also enjoy watching the connection between the people playing, which they often talk about in terms of "energy." Luke described an "extreme" scene involving bondage and a man shocking a woman's clitoris with 750,000 volts, saying that throughout the vicious scene,

> there was a lot of energy going on between the two of them. And somebody later made a picture of them when she had come down and was untied. And he was sitting next to her and they were both smiling and it was just, like one of these really, really beautiful pictures. Because we saw this connection and energy between them.

Conventional mainstream observers might refer to this type of "connection" and "energy" as "chemistry," but whatever you call it, kinksters learn to highly value it in what they observe and do.

Post-rope-suspension "connection" photos that show the Top and bottom embracing while the bottom still has conspicuous rope marks are classic shots for kink photographers. Pictured here are two people in a "rope studio" setting after finishing their tie. *Models: Javi and Airune; Photo: Alexander*

They also enjoyed watching Tops who they felt had great skills. Tom said the scene that made a great impression on him was one where "a woman was double-Florentining some guy" so skillfully that he couldn't tell "if she's left- or right-handed." Florentine flogging (or "Florentining") involves wielding a flogger in each hand in an artful alternating pattern and is quite difficult to master. Will likewise said he enjoyed watching any scene that involved "those who really have the skill, who really do fantastic things with knots and rope work and you can tell that their brain is just working overtime, or people who really know how to work a flogger."

The parallel pleasure for watching bottoms was for ones who were highly reactive. Emma explained that a scene she had really enjoyed watching involved

single tails [whips] and flogging and some caning and paddling. She [the Top] was pretty rough. People get rougher when they get cheered on. And he [the bottom] squealed and howled and carried on. He's very, very noisy, which is why we love him. He's a lot of fun to observe in a scene because he was so noisy in the way he reacted and everything.

David remembered his first experience witnessing a bottom in agony a lot less cheerfully than Emma did, explaining that he watched a woman rip a "clothespin zipper" (a line of clothespins applied to the body strategically so they can be ripped off more or less all at once) off another woman, and then heard "a scream like I had never heard before. And I almost ran out of the club that day and never returned. I was like, 'Holy shit, this is fucked up!'" As Newmahr (2011) observed, Tops are generally noted for their skills, while bottoms are generally noted for their (especially loud) reactions.

Finally, they enjoyed watching things that seemed creative or unusual, especially if they were also a little bit flashy. Tony and another interviewee both separately described the same scene they had witnessed that took place on an unusual piece of dungeon equipment that is basically a half-hemispheric jungle gym made of metal bars. Tony said,

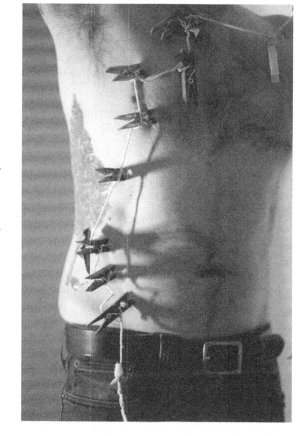

Clothespin zippers vary wildly in the number of clothespins and their complexity but always involve a fair bit of time to set up, and usually a very short but painful moment when all the clothespins are pulled off at once. *Model and photo: ThatPorcupine*

They kind of played a game of Twister with it where they colored the vertices of the bars. And they had a pair of rope bottoms and a pair of riggers and each of them had a rope around each wrist and each ankle. And so "left hand red" became untie the left-hand rope and retie it to the red. Probably my favorite thing about that is it's the one thing that's happened to me in the kink community that I have seen that I am almost positive does not exist on the internet, because I'm pretty sure it's something that one of the people who did it thought it up.

Connor, who had been around the Scene for a very long time, said it took a lot to impress him. But when he attended a Queer kink event, he was astounded to see

a group of dykes pin down this really curvy, like, 300-pound dyke, and fill her with needles. And they had a helium tank in the dungeon, and they filled it with helium balloons and like, lifted her tits up, like, her big, massive tits up with helium balloons. And then they ran another line out here with a bigger helium balloon, and from it they hung the Canadian flag. And they turned her into a pony and made her pull a woman who was in a wheelchair around the dungeon while she had to sing the Canadian national anthem.

In case you're wondering, that also remains the weirdest thing I've ever heard of happening at a kink event as well.

CONCLUSION: THE PERFORMANCE

It's easy to equate performance with superficial action. For the entire first year that I was in the Scene, I felt like it was full of shallow displays between people with shallow connections to one another. I still think there's some truth to that observation, but I don't think it's reasonable to accuse people of superficial connections when deep ones aren't really the point; for instance, at a tango convention, people practice passionately dancing with one another without really seeking deep emotional ties because that isn't really the goal (Törnqvist, 2018). For many kinksters, things like flogging, bondage, and fire play all work very much like a form of skillful dance that they practice on many partners. The better costumed and accessorized they are, and the more appreciative and enthusiastic their audience, the better their scenes. Many experienced kinksters learn how to create the kinds of scenes that will gather a crowd, like the ones described above. But almost all experienced kinksters learn to tell the difference between the spectacles and the intimate moments many people actually describe as their own most powerful scenes.

Despite its power and passion, the Scene's emphasis on display and performance creates many problems for establishing a valid system of personal accountability. For better and mostly for worse, public performances often become the foundation for cherished status and reputation in the Scene. This construction of social status ignores the inconvenient fact that even for those heavily involved in the Scene, most of their relationshipping and BDSM activities don't occur in public spaces. Moreover, watching public displays often doesn't really give kinksters an opportunity to conduct penetrating character studies of their fellows. Worse, these performances sometimes create the *illusion* that kinksters know someone well when in fact they really only know their public personas, making it easy to think someone is a good Top because of their skillful and careful public persona even though their private behavior is reckless and/or abusive. The Scene has never systematically reconciled its love of a good show with the reality that BDSM relationships are, in the end, mostly private affairs.

CHAPTER SEVEN

THE DEVIANT ELITE

Reputation and Social Status in the Scene

"CELEBRITIES" AMONG US

When you first arrive in the Scene, everyone you meet appears more or less equal. There are clusters of people that seem to be a bit larger than others, but that's about it. Some people have little "Presenter" ribbons attached to their name badges at large events, but that doesn't seem like a big deal. Everyone is at the same party, plays in the same dungeons, and socializes in the same places. It took me about two years of being in the Scene to slowly realize that those "Presenter" ribbons were highly coveted and often came with an inordinate amount of respect. In the Scene, presenters are usually formal teachers and sometimes also performers, activity leaders, and demonstrators. There were presenters and players (meaning kinksters who didn't teach or officially perform, but who were known for putting on good scenes) who other kinksters talked about in reverential tones—people they desperately desired but who they would never be brave enough to proposition for play or sex because they considered them so far out of their reach. They often just assumed that everyone felt the same; the other night, a kinky friend asked rhetorically, "Really, who here would kick [famous kinkster] out of bed?" The idea that everyone mostly desired the same few people was just assumed, and the idea that those people could have practically anyone they wanted was equally taken for granted (although it was totally untrue).

As a sociologist, reputation and status is the subject that has fascinated me the most about the Scene since I arrived. Kinksters have always depended on reputation to fulfill a wide array of social functions, particularly substituting for meaningful policing/enforcement in the Scene (Holt, 2016). Understanding the way that reputation was constructed in the Scene from 2010 to 2017 is one of the keys to analyzing the crisis the Scene found itself in by late 2017. Any functionalist sociologist can tell you that it's often only

211

a short step from a highly functional social system to a highly dysfunctional one when, say, social circumstances change and people continue to try to employ the same strategies that used to work well to manage the new situation or when people begin to rely too heavily on a single social mechanism to solve problems it is ill-equipped to manage. Both approaches apply here, because the social world of the Scene changed greatly after the appearance of FetLife in 2009.

Because I think reputation in the Scene is both extremely important and complex, I'm going to tackle the issue from different angles with multiple approaches. Kinksters don't understand their own system of reputation at all, so I can't directly rely on their explanations and descriptions to analyze it. The chapter begins with a very brief historical overview of reputation in the Scene. Then I'll analyze the qualities that people *said* in their interviews give people good reputations, followed by the characteristics of people interviewees nominated as having good reputations. Next I'll try to unpack some of the things kinksters *actually* care about and describe the experience of "fetlebrity" and elite status in the Scene. Finally, I'll move to a discussion of how interviewees believed people get bad reputations and how bad reputations spread, and explain why reputation is so messy and complicated in the Scene.

REPUTATION MATTERS A LOT

One of the semiformal norms of the Scene involves not judging other people's kinks—associated with the phrase "Your kink is not my kink, but your kink is okay." Kinksters do a mediocre job of following their own rule here, but it doesn't stop them from constantly judging each other's *execution* of their kinks. They may not be judging you for being into rope bondage, but there's a good chance they're judging you for being into "sloppy bondage." Kinksters are also judging you for how cool you are by the standards of the Scene. Many dayslong events give out awards at the end that all the attendees vote on, and the awards show the kinds of things kinksters care about: "Best Dressed," "Best Bruises," "Dungeon Slut" (for the person who played in the dungeon the most), and—always the pièce de résistance—"Camp Slut" (usually for the person who apparently slept with the most people). People sometimes actively compete for these awards, offer all sorts of bribes for votes (which are anonymous anyway), and even hold gangbangs to win camp slut. All over the Scene, a group of people who will almost universally tell you they were the geeks, weirdos, and outsiders in middle and high school formed a social group that was so obsessed with popularity and reputation that it would make a teenager blush. It's hard to exaggerate how obsessed the Scene is with reputation, status, and popularity. Forty-one percent of kinksters with high levels of Scene involvement strongly agreed with the statement, "I work hard to maintain my good reputation in the Scene," versus only 22 percent of those with medium involvement (with 78 percent of those with high involvement agreeing or strongly agreeing versus 61 percent of those with medium involvement). Hypothetically, reputation, status, and popularity are sociologically distinct, but they're so closely intertwined here that I'm going to end up treating them as one thing.

Reputation is theoretically very sociologically functional for the Scene: the Scene lacks much in the way of objective methods to distinguish "abusers" from "kinksters" and is even shorter on solid methods of enforcing judgment against people deemed unsuitable—so it settles for reputation. At the local level, good or bad reputations often spread jaw-droppingly quickly, thanks to communication on FetLife and to the tight-knit and gossipy social networks of kinksters. At the national level, good or bad reputations spread much more slowly and are usually relevant only for people who travel extensively. The Scene clusters in geographic microcultures, and people have to really make an effort to travel beyond their own microculture in order to achieve a larger reputation. As we'll see, actual reputation is often rather nebulous, so kinksters frequently substitute visible popularity for genuine reputation.

HOW FETLIFE CHANGED REPUTATION IN THE SCENE

The appearance of the social networking website FetLife in 2009 changed a lot of things about the Scene. To be clear, I arrived in the Scene myself in early 2010, so everything I know about the pre-FetLife Scene mostly comes from talking to people who were around for a long time before that. The following are some of the important changes that FetLife created:

- It made the Scene a lot bigger (at least temporarily), because people had an easy way to communicate about events. Gone were the days of complex event notification and management; in 2012, a party was canceled at the last minute (on FetLife) and my partner Curtis and I were able to organize (a much smaller) one at my house within a couple of hours—all through FetLife. Moreover, FetLife made it possible, for basically the first time ever, to easily have international kink events.

- It provided a way to share art and ideas that previously weren't available much in the community. FetLife allows people to readily post personal (typically kinky) photos and writings, and sharing these things almost instantly became an important part of Scene culture.

- It helped establish vast webs of social networking, especially among people who became kink influencers. Through just a few well-connected people, it became possible to reach almost everyone who was heavily involved in the community in less than 24–48 hours. Most heavily involved kinksters I know pretty much always have at least one tab on their phone browser with FetLife up that they check multiple times throughout the day.

- Within the first two years or so, FetLife created a feature it called "Kinky & Popular," which would highlight photos and videos that people were "loving" and commenting on regularly. For a couple of years, at least, kinksters cared about this, too, and would congratulate their friends on "going K&P"—that is, having something featured on K&P. Kinksters stopped caring much about this feature at the point where too many not-very-kinky men had joined the website and most of the K&P photos were just selfies of young, naked white girls.

I could go on about the way FetLife changed life in the Scene, but I'm going to leave the list here so that I can focus specifically on the way it changed reputation in the Scene.

Prior to FetLife, most kink parties and even the larger events were still relatively small; the organizers often knew most of the people attending them, and they were often functionally just gatherings of friends. People had good reputations because lots of people *actually knew them*. If they personally annoyed the organizers, the organizers kicked them out. I don't want to idealize this system. Being so crony-based, it had the serious flaw that if someone reported Problem Person to the event organizer, the chances were pretty high that the organizer would ignore the complaint because Problem Person was their friend.

After FetLife, many parties and events were springing up overnight that were large and full of people the organizers had never heard of. Kinksters often arrived at these new events with supposedly glowing reputations they'd earned in completely different states or parts of the country, spread for them via FetLife by a bunch of people who had never met them in real life. Often, they didn't even have reputations based on anything traditionally meaningful to the Scene—they had reputations based on sexy K&P photos or clever writings. Kinksters quickly coined a term for this new generation of kinky superstars: *fetlebrities*. Although their credibility was sometimes dubious at best, the fetlebrities' status in the Scene was buoyed by the need for all these frantically competing new events to find some way to stand out from the crowd. Most kink events are always on the cliff edge of financial viability, so their strategy to draw crowds was to advertise the presence of these fetlebrities at their events and to beg them to advertise the events to their many followers on FetLife (and later on Twitter as well). Thus the fetlebrity's status became apparently legitimated through the attention and approval of event organizers. Eventually, even the few people who had been well known in parts of the Scene prior to FetLife started using FetLife to cement their status as well, which lent further credibility to the nouveau fetlebrities. The combined effect meant that whereas in the old days, events had been reluctant to kick Problem Person out because there was a decent chance they were friends with the organizer, now events were reluctant to kick Problem Person out because they were relying on Problem Person to help sell their event. And besides, Problem Person's 2,000 FetLife "friends" couldn't all be wrong, could they?

Unfortunately, only a very, very small circle of kinksters who were deeply embedded in the inner workings of events have ever really been aware of the fragile realities of this status system. Connor, an international kink teacher and organizer, was the only person cynical enough to answer my interview question, "How does someone get a good reputation in the Scene?" with "Give John Baku [the creator and admin of FetLife] a blow job." When I asked Connor if he was being literal or figurative, he said, "Both." Unlike Connor, most of the people with high status in the Scene—who were usually the only ones in a position to fully understand the arbitrary nature of their status—never wanted to openly acknowledge the arbitrariness of that status (possibly for fear of undermining it). The people who were in the best position to understand it were people who had been in high-status positions since long before FetLife appeared, so they looked like they were whining about the upstart newcomers if they complained about things (and most of them started utilizing FetLife to solidify their own position anyway). The Scene teaches new kinksters to have a lot of faith in its reputation system, and when they first enter the Scene, most of them do. To some degree, experience teaches them to be cynical and start to doubt it, but many members of the kink elite also have faith in the system (which has the benefit of justifying their status).

WHAT KINKSTERS SAY GETS YOU A GOOD REPUTATION

In order to understand reputation in the Scene, I asked interviewees who were sufficiently involved to tell me about a couple of people in the Scene they felt had good reputations and what those reputations were, or to describe kinksters they admired and why. For people who had been involved in the Scene a long time, I also asked them more generally how they thought someone got a good reputation. (I asked the same questions about bad reputations, which I'll discuss later.) I'll start by looking at the qualities people said were important, and answers were fairly consistent. The Ideal Kinkster possesses "integrity without ego" (a quote from Sofia); takes their responsibilities to themselves, their partners, and their community seriously but doesn't take *themselves* too seriously; is knowledgeable and/or skillful about certain aspects of BDSM; demonstrates authenticity and vulnerability in their interactions with others; and "shows their humanity" (a quote from Connor). In terms of play, the Ideal Kinkster is one who respectfully and consensually pushes their own and others' boundaries; likes to play publicly a lot, preferably with many different people; makes a serious effort to follow the rules but admits when they make mistakes; and engages in their play because they love it and not because they're trying to impress other people. Vera managed to list most of these things all by herself, saying that kinksters get good reputations through

> creativity, responsibility, treating your people well, clear communication. There's a leadership thing—you can be thought of well without having it, but it helps. Ethicalness, and being able to own when you've fucked up. Skill. Being a decent human. Being kind as well as being "evil" [i.e., a sadist]. Also, having [your kinky self] not be all of who you are. You have to have a whole personness to you and be willing to show your feet of clay.

Some of these qualities are a little bit vague (e.g., "integrity") and some of them are pretty specific (e.g., not just playing to impress other people). But one thing they all have in common is they're mostly subjective and very, very hard to measure. I made a point of interviewing several of the people others described as having good reputations. I had hoped to be able to try to gauge whether the people kinksters nominated as having good reputations actually possessed the qualities that were supposed to accompany having a good reputation. But there wasn't really a way to do that because the qualities associated with having a good reputation were so subjective.

The qualities people ascribed to the individuals they admired tended to be a little more objective. The most popular quality by far was play style or specific BDSM skills, which 22 people mentioned. Emma summarized the main point of this characteristic: "Liking to play is a big thing in the Scene. If you're known as someone who's always ready and willing to play and try all kinds of crazy shit, and you're a good, honest, reliable person, then you're going to have a good name." Notice that it's not just about how somebody plays, but whether they play often with many people. Also, although my interviewees tended to take it for granted, what they really wanted was people who frequently played *in public*. Public play both contributed to the general atmosphere of fun and pleasure in the Scene and was presumed to show that you had nothing to hide. If you played in public, others (believed they) had an opportunity to see for themselves that you can do "crazy shit" and still be safe about it.

The next most often mentioned quality was contributions to the community, which interviewees usually framed as happening through organizing social events or parties and/or mentoring newer people. Fifteen people mentioned this characteristic in describing someone with a good reputation. Getting people talking about issues and looking for ways to improve life in the community was also a way to earn a good reputation. The last characteristic most often mentioned for bringing good status was being a "presenter." Sometimes people specifically admired a presenter's skill at teaching, and sometimes they admired their wisdom and personality. Connor described a presenter he admired, saying that

> even in the things that have been really messed up along her journey, she still presents them in a way that has them be—not necessarily positive, but—understood that she has learned a lesson that has helped her grow through that experience. And when I become a silver-haired beautiful creature, I hope that I have half the grace that she does.

In these kinds of descriptions, kinksters tended to be consistent about respecting others they thought of as knowledgeable, humble, and relatable.

During my time studying the Scene, the prestige of presenters grew considerably, in large part due to the fetlebrity factors I discussed earlier. The Scene has no formal system for declaring someone knowledgeable about any particular kink or BDSM activity, so the closest way people have to prove their authority is to say that they've taught it somewhere officially. There's a common misconception among many kinksters that presenters are invited and paid for what they do and that teaching is thus an honor and a profession in the Scene. In reality, nearly all presenters are volunteers, and they sometimes have to aggressively pursue the "opportunity" to present. Rather than paying presenters, events often give them VIP status instead, allowing them to attend the event for free and sometimes giving them special lodging and free food, advertising them in programs, and just generally treating them like rock stars. ("Come to this happy hour, featuring Fetlebrity X!") By 2015 or so, virtually all the highly promoted presenters were fetlebrities, at least to some degree. For kinksters who are involved in the larger "national" Scene, meaning that they attend many of the big dayslong events, "presenter" is basically interchangeable with "good reputation." Indeed, when I asked most of the well-known presenters (who were all heavily involved in this large event circuit) that I interviewed how a person gets a good reputation in the Scene, most of them took for granted that I was asking how *presenters* get a good reputation. Meanwhile, kinksters who were involved only in their local Scenes (who are the vast majority of kinksters) were much less likely to mention presenters when asked to name someone they admired in the Scene. Those kinksters usually mentioned skilled local players or the people who hosted their local parties and gatherings. For kinksters going to their local clubs on Saturday nights, fetlebrities were generally a lot less important than the person who first taught them how to use a whip and showed them around. But more experienced kinksters learned to revere a list of well-known presenters who they were often much more personally removed from.

If you're wondering if kinksters' ideas about reputation changed much over time, the answer is "no," as far as I can tell. I gave a talk in 2019 at a kink event and asked people how someone gets a good reputation in the Scene. The answers from that audience, at least, were mostly the same, word for word, as the ones my interviewees gave in 2012.

WHAT ACTUALLY GETS YOU A GOOD REPUTATION

I had long suspected that gender played an unacknowledged role in whether or not people got a good reputation and that men were more likely than women to have good reputations. But when I analyzed the names people mentioned as having a good reputation, the numbers were split almost perfectly evenly between men and women, which suggests that gender doesn't really matter. Though gender doesn't matter here, BDSM role *absolutely* does. Even though not one single person I have ever spoken with in the Scene has listed BDSM role as a way to good reputation, Tops turn out to have far more status and good reputation than bottoms or switches. The difference was pretty extreme: 26 of my interviewees described admirable Tops, but only four described admirable bottoms. Indeed, that difference is almost certainly a massive underestimate, since people's descriptions often seemed to take someone's Topping more or less for granted. For instance, Harry, a Dom, described a man in the Scene as his "mentor," saying, "I just sort of learned by watching him." I could reasonably deduce from this description that the mentor was probably a Top, but since the description didn't specifically mention skills, in the spirit of conservative coding, I didn't count the mentor as a Top. Also, there were many people I personally knew were Tops but didn't count as Tops because they weren't described that way by the interviewee. It's important to understand that bottoms often *do* have status in the Scene, but it's almost always from organizing and other forms of community service, writing, and/or teaching, rather than from their BDSM skills. Indeed, of the four bottoms who were praised for their skills, two of them were presenters.

In the previous section, I followed my interviewees' descriptions and talked about "BDSM skills" as if these were neutral and applied equally to everyone. In reality, when kinksters described "skills" related to BDSM, they were almost always referring only to the skills of Tops. Sometimes, their admiration was very specific and focused on a physical skill. Andrew described the skills of a Top he admired, saying, "That man can knock a single wing off a fly with a single tail [whip] at 15 feet!" For others, admiration focused more on the way Tops did something rather than their physical ability. Jackson emphasized the way a Top he admired put him at his ease when he was bottoming to her for needle play (which he was very anxious about) for the first time. He said, "She did my needles, and she talked. She walked me through it in a very friendly, compassionate way, and I had no problem. She just has a way of connecting with people." And then there were Tops who were admired for their attitude and presentation/performance of kink. Derek described my partner Damien thus:

> First of all, the guy is the Energizer Fucking Bunny. He just goes and goes. He's tying people all damn day, all damn night. He doesn't stop and, you know, he's kind of a goofy guy. He kind of dresses a little funny, but he does his thing. There's no shame in his game—he's fucking good, and he doesn't give a shit [what other people think], and I love that.

Despite the variation in their kinks, for all of these admired skilled players, the skill (and even the energy in Damien's case) was described as belonging to Tops.

Much more rarely, people described admiration for a bottom's skills. On the relatively rare occasions when people express admiration for bottoms in the Scene, the compliments tend to take three forms: (1) admiring them aesthetically—frequently describing them as "beautiful," (2) admiring their masochism (i.e., their ability to endure and/or enjoy physical hardship), and (3) admiring their skills of service, meaning the bottom (usually identifying as some variation of "slave" or "service submissive") is good at performing acts of service for their Top and sometimes others. Typically, the main way bottoms get status as "beautiful" is by posting pictures of themselves on FetLife, but no one mentioned any praise for that in my interviews. Martin was the only person who expressed traditional BDSM/Leather admiration for hard-core masochism, describing a scene he had done long ago with a partner of his: "She's a brutal young lady. [She takes] amazing punishment. I don't understand how anyone likes it that hard, but she does." However, most of the compliments my interviewees offered for bottoms were for service submission. Vanessa was effusive in her praise of a well-known slave's "anticipatory service," which she felt he accomplished perfectly:

> Seeing Craig in the morning, he's up before his Master. And he already knows without hearing Vince [Master] call for him when Vince is starting to stir. So Craig already has tea ready, and already knows what kind of meal that Vince is going to want that morning. Just being able to hold deep theological conversation one minute and being able to be happy rubbing feet the next minute.

Kinksters were happy to praise service submissives like Craig, but service submissives are pretty rare in the Scene (which is probably part of why they get good reputations). In general, bottoming rarely brings good reputation and status in the Scene, and kinksters are largely oblivious to this disparity.

Although it didn't show up in my interviews, another way this status difference manifests is in the expectations kinksters have for accomplished Tops versus bottoms. It's normal to hear kinksters make disparaging remarks about "21-year-old guys who say they're a 'Master,'" but there are no complementary disparagements for the (much more common) "21-year-old women who say they're a 'slave.'" Implicit in these disparagements (and lack of them) is the assumption that ownership/Topping is more difficult than being owned/bottoming—that Topping is a skill that must be learned over time and through experience, but bottoming is something people can just do. Indeed, traditional Leather cultural practices (which is primarily where the Master/slave dynamic comes from) expect aspiring Masters to work their way up through the ranks by bottoming and serving other Masters before earning their status as a Master themselves. Only people who had completed this service phase could legitimately claim to be a "true" Master (even though, as we saw in chapter 4, according to many of the same people, true Masters are born, not made). While I rarely heard of folks in the pansexual Scene following this tradition to become Masters, I did meet and interview kinksters who had been submissives as an intentional path to becoming Dominants.

No interviewees ever expressed admiration for switching as a skill or even referred to someone they admired as a switch (e.g., "it's amazing to me that he's such a good Dom and then can turn right around and get beaten up").

Because the Scene heavily implies that high status is equally available to Tops and bottoms, and this implied equal opportunity is largely unquestioned in the subculture, it usually takes a certain type of cynicism or cheerful obliviousness to this cultural narrative to observe what seemed to me the *real* ways people often gained status. I was fortunate enough to interview Duncan, whose observations about how people (Tops) often gain status pretty much perfectly coincided with my own observations. In response to my question about how someone gets a good reputation in the Scene, he said,

> Putting on a public scene that's extravagant, flashy objects, screaming women, well-orchestrated. It's showmanship. Some people are very talented. Some people practice with their single tails, rope. If you're out there playing, and you play with a lot of people, then you will get a reputation. I was here

last year, and I met a couple of guys who were like "Hey, we want to fuck some women," and it was their first time to one of these things. "How do we do this? Do we just walk up to a woman and say, 'You want to fuck?'" I said, "No, you go to a class, pick a subject, any subject you want that appeals to you. Whips, chains, rope—learn it, get really good at it. Ask a girl if she wants to get tied up, if she wants to do a scene. She wants to show off, she wants to be noticed, she wants attention. Develop your skill set, play with a couple of people, do an awesome scene. And then you will have girls come up to you and want you to tie them up. Aka, tie them up and then fuck them afterwards."

There are many things to unpack here. First of all, Duncan didn't really present this information with a tone of cynicism, which was remarkable to me. Usually when I had casual conversations with kinksters who said essentially the same thing, they made the observations grumpily or as a sneering, snide remark. Duncan, however, seemed sincere in his explanation and advice. Second, in implicit keeping with many other kinksters I talked to, Duncan's description basically assumes that reputation is something Tops need and is irrelevant for bottoms. Third, the intense heteronormativity of his account—assuming that straight men would want to be Tops and that the women who would want to fuck them were probably bottoms—was mostly backed up by the statistics we saw in chapter 4. However, I'll say as a side note that experience and observation showed that the same technique worked just as well (if not better) for women as Tops: female Tops who put on a good display usually had women swarming them afterward. Fourth, the assumption that BDSM was basically just a very effective seduction strategy was really in violation of the Scene's common "nonsexual BDSM for BDSM's sake" cultural narrative that we've seen throughout this book—even though most kinksters say that BDSM is mostly sexual for them. Finally, notice the implication in Duncan's statement that one of the ways Tops get status is by having "screaming women"—not just one stoic bottom, but *multiple screaming bottoms* who are all loudly showing their pleasure in what's happening. Years of observation and experience have taught me how true this is: there's no faster way to a good reputation in the Scene than having two bottoms at once obviously enjoying a single Top's sadism. Again, gender is more or less irrelevant for that.

Related to showmanship, there was general admiration for being a badass and being kind of reckless. I described my tornado suspension debacle in chapter 5 and how its stupidity garnered me and the others involved in it perverse respect from fellow kinksters. The Scene thinks it's kind of hot when people bend (but do not break) the rules, and people who can get away with bending them habitually often acquire reputations mixed with admiration and fear (both the sexy kind of fear that many kinksters enjoy as well as the kind of fear that makes people genuinely nervous). None of the Tops I saw with shady reputations for safety or even a rather blasé attitude toward consent were ever short on bottoms to play with—on the contrary, they were often in very high demand. Mike, who had been in the Scene for a very long time and was a Top who had a good reputation and enthusiastic play partners, said,

> There are people who don't play with me because they think I'm unsafe, and I'm not going to argue with them, because I'm not entirely sure I would clas- sify me as "safe." I mean, I go out of my way to make sure the person is safe. [But] let's face it. I do hanging scenes, scenes that involve choking and stran- gling, the other person passing out or choking out. That is not, according to BDSM 101, what you're supposed to do. In the end, it depends on what the person [bottom] wants to do. They're all happy, so that should help.

Mike's comments highlight how much experienced kinksters expect to be allowed to bend the formal rules, and I think the status of people like him shows how much the Scene admires the sorts of Tops who do—and how many bottoms desire that kind of play. Since one of the main ways the Scene measures a Top's reputation is by the number of happily "screaming" bottoms the Top has, if lots of bottoms line up to play with someone, other bottoms and Tops often assume that Top must be doing something important right— even if they're not strictly following the rules of the BDSM 101 playbook. Back to the point in chapter 5 about bottoms being the ones with real power in BDSM interactions, I think this type of status could really be summarized as "We're fine with whatever makes the bottoms happy."

Overall, my observations led me to think that Duncan's path to reputa- tion and status in the Scene was at least as, if not more, effective than the paths described earlier focusing on integrity, humility, and so on. I don't mean to suggest that having integrity, humility, and the like *aren't* paths to good reputation in the Scene—they definitely are. But when push comes to shove, I think the Scene prefers a good show over all those honorable qualities. Indeed, many of the Tops I knew with the best reputations were really cocky—because cocky people tend to put on much flashier shows than humble people—and were at best sometimes successful at maintaining false humility. I might concede that honor is the long path to good reputation in the Scene and flashy Topping is the short path. There are certainly people who are known for both, but they're few and far between. Perversely, being able to put on a good show tends to make people a lot less likely to believe bad things about a Top, and several male Tops who put on a good show were able to maintain loyal followings for a long time in spite of a conspicuous lack of integrity, honesty, humility, and so on. Whether as a Top or a bottom, it's nearly impossible to get a good reputation in the Scene without engaging in public play, preferably with lots of people. But once your reputation is established, putting on a good show often becomes irrelevant to kinksters' reputations, which may rest more on a foundation of teaching and organizing.

CONFESSIONS OF THE KINK ELITE

I went out of my way to learn how the fetlebrities and high-status presenters of the Scene—who I'm calling the "kink elite"—live. I interviewed many of them, I dated them, I played with them, they stayed at my house, I chatted with and befriended them, and eventually, I more or less became one. Let me give you a little taste of what life in the kink elite is like, because you can really achieve some pretty weird levels of micro-fame. In the Scene, you really know you've hit elite status when you start to occasionally get a genuine article before your name in introductions. Thus, at some point, when I introduced myself to someone in the Scene with, "Hi, I'm IPCookieMonster [my scene name]," and they responded—without a trace of sarcasm—"*The* IPCookieMonster?" I knew I had arrived. After a while, I got so tired of kinksters fanboying/fangirling at me that I often didn't introduce myself with my Scene name at all. I felt like it became increasingly difficult to have authentic interactions with kinksters, who often seemed to perceive me as some sort of intimidating fount of knowledge and sexy rather than as a real person.

In the kink elite, you can sometimes get into parties for free just because the owner likes you or with the expectation that you and your comped partners will play. (This works on the same principle that dance clubs will comp or pay good dancers to come and get the party started). When you travel as an elite kinkster, people often treat you like visiting royalty. I went to Iceland and casually RSVP'd to a party there on FetLife. (I knew absolutely no one in Iceland.) Within 24 hours, the party organizer sent me an excited message asking if I would teach a class (for pay) and come to the party for free with my partner. Faraway dungeons that are "members and their guests only" are no obstacle to the kink elite. You post to FetLife that you're visiting, and the owner or a member either already knows you or pretends they do to get you in.

Despite these many advantages, being part of the kink elite often makes it perversely difficult to play (or have sex) with as many people, especially in public. Most of the kink elites I interviewed were reluctant to talk much about how their status affected their lives in the Scene, but both Amelia and Dylan were extremely Scene-famous presenters who said they almost never played in public anymore. Both of them framed it more as a personal choice and an inevitable part of their life course development as kinksters (as if they'd simply grown out of it over time). Pat, like several other high-status presenters I spoke to, said he was very careful when playing at events where he also taught that he always followed his own rules, "to make sure that people don't think that it's okay to do something one way just because they saw me do it that way." A feeling of all-eyes-on-you pervaded many of the discussions I had with kink elites about playing in public that only the hard-core exhibitionists could really get over.

While enjoying certain privileges, elites run into other related problems. Among my elite interviewees, only Connor and Doyle were extremely analytical and open about the way their status had affected their lives in the Scene. Doyle said that he loves the perks of his job as a professional presenter (who, in order to be professional presenters, have to be Scene famous), such as being able to take for granted that he'll be accepted to present at major events, getting kink toys for free, and feeling "rich in social capital." But he was perpetually borderline broke and complained that he found it increasingly difficult to play with his partners in public or private because it felt too much like doing a job. He said that his life looks a lot more glamorous on the surface than it really is, but most kinksters refuse to believe that:

[An event] put me and my partner up in a condo on Maui for a week, and I got to go snorkeling—I mean, wonderful, wonderful stuff. But at the same time, [kinksters] don't realize the things you give up for that kind of thing, like medical insurance, dental insurance, a retirement plan—the number of relationships I've had that really probably disintegrated because I travel too much. Even things like petty cash. Yes, I could be flying to an exotic location, but I may be flying to that exotic location with $5.00 in my pocket, and it's because everything else is taken care of. But there's this impression people have of it being this life of a superstar kind of a situation, and most of the time it's nothing like that. It's lugging your luggage around Manhattan in the middle of the night because you're going to be sleeping on your friend's couch, and she lives on the fourth floor of a walk-up. When you're carrying a lot of gear that's really heavy, it's not very glamorous, and you can't afford a cab so you take a bus. I say all this in the interview with the full knowledge that nobody will believe it. They ought to, but at the same time they have this impression that "Oh, if I do this, if I can become a hotshot presenter! I will have an endless supply of sex, I will make a lot of money off of doing what I absolutely love, and, you know, everybody will think I'm the shit." They're probably right about the third thing. Everybody will think that you're the shit, but the other parts are not necessarily there. It's a job, and the odds of me actually having a sexual scene with [some free new] rope with someone who is emotionally and directly involved with me is very slim. I could count on one hand the number of times I've had that situation. It's like the price you pay for going on this ride is not what you think it is.

When I asked him if people propositioned him frequently, he said they did, but he "learned to be discerning" because so many of them were "crazy."

Connor picked up on Doyle's theme of people who were interested in him for the wrong reasons. Connor said he felt insecure about people being drawn to a superstar image of him rather than his actual self—"I want people to play with, but especially to be in a relationship with [real name], not [Scene name]. And that's challenging." He also said it was very difficult to play in public dungeons without raising lots of expectations and getting attention that he didn't really want. He said he intentionally went to a kink event he'd never been to before so that he could bond and play with his partner, but as soon as they put on a flashy scene in the dungeon, they were instantly recognized and people started asking him if he was a "surprise presenter" at the event. He admitted,

It's one of those mixed blessings, because I hate double standards, but there's a part of me that's an egoic asshole that loves double standards, and I own that fact. Where [people say to other people], "Oh, I'm sorry, nobody can do that kind of play in the dungeon, blah blah blah," or, "This is a [special] event, you can't show up," and I'm like, "Hi, my name's [Scene name]," and they go, "Oh!"—I mean, not all the time, but it's like, I've played the card a few times. But I'd say the difference with the Scene with the presenting side versus whatever [i.e., being lower status], there's that piece, which is the star fuck, but also the "How do I get to just experience life as a normal kinkster again?"

The answer generally was: you don't.

The vast majority of kinksters have no idea what the lives of kink elites are really like. There's a deep sense of *cool* that comes with being part of the kink elite, but there's also an awkwardly discordant sense of fake fame, which I've discussed with many elites. Inside the 400-person event you're teaching at, you might be one of the most desirable people there, but when you leave the event and go to lunch, no one at the restaurant knows or cares who you are. They also struggle with the sense that others are interacting with a character the elite person has created far more than with the real person. Added to those challenges is borderline poverty. Like Doyle and Connor, the vast majority of kink elites are seriously struggling financially. In general, kink just doesn't pay well, and the only people who are willing or able to spend large amounts of time crisscrossing the country to teach BDSM and organize kink events tend to be the sorts of people who don't have conventional careers. Most kink elites try to pretend they're financially fine in front of their main audiences (i.e., other kinksters) because pretending success becomes part of their job—which, to some degree, is fulfilling the fantasy that other kinksters have of them as Successful Kinksters.

THE BAD BOYS' CLUB

People like Doyle and Connor worked for years to develop their good reputations in the Scene. But I've seen people get bad reputations in the Scene in a matter of days, almost always because of some sort of public complaint on FetLife. Getting a bad reputation in the Scene is no joke, as kinksters will functionally shun people who get irredeemably bad reputations. Formally, that means not allowing people to attend most public events and typically refusing to invite them to private parties; informally, it includes things like shaming anyone who continues to be involved with the banned person, cutting off ties of friendship with that person, not freely admitting that the person taught or mentored you, and often not even mentioning them in casual conversation. I went out of my way to interview three men whom I knew had dubious reputations within the Scene (all of whom were eventually banned), in part to see if their perspectives on reputation and status were noticeably different than that of their peers when talking to an interviewer; they weren't.

While good reputation doesn't seem to be especially gendered, bad reputation is mostly a problem for men and people with penises in the Scene. When I asked my interviewees to tell me about someone in the Scene who'd gotten a bad reputation, 23 people mentioned men, but only three mentioned women. That 23 count is a serious underestimate, as many other people intentionally concealed the gender of the person they were talking about. Despite the concealment, I was 99 percent sure that most of those vague stories were about men (especially since they were sometimes repeating the same story that someone else had told me), but I didn't count them. My survey results also showed that all people with penises were statistically significantly more concerned about their reputations than people with vaginas, and nearly all gender groups agreed that it was harder for men to keep a good reputation in the Scene than it was for women.

Although I can't really show it with concrete data, I can say anecdotally that this reputation difference doesn't entirely seem to be the product of people with penises *causing* all the problems. In all the time I've been in the Scene, my consent has been flagrantly violated by only three people: two women and one man. But the Scene subjects people with penises to much greater social scrutiny, so behavior is perceived as "threatening," "creepy," or "gross" when people with penises do it but is tolerated or even encouraged when women/people with vaginas do it. For example, I've walked around with one of my male submissive partners at events and watched multiple cis women simply casually grope him over the course of an evening—behavior that would almost certainly earn a cis man doing it to me a serious rebuke and possibly a one-way ticket out of the event. I can't easily separate out the effects of gender and BDSM role there, but I definitely don't see anything like that happening when I walk around with female submissives. The Scene doesn't see people with vaginas as threatening (even when they're Dominants), so it interprets their behaviors differently than that of people with penises—and teaches them to interpret their own behaviors differently.

Bad reputation is not only mostly the problem of men—it's also mostly the problem of Tops. It may seem somewhat perverse, but in exactly the same way—and for the same reasons—that Tops get so much more social status than their bottoms, Tops are much more vulnerable to bad reputations. My interviewees rarely directly mentioned the role of a person with a bad reputation when describing them, but when they described unsafe or problematic play, it was almost always Tops they were calling out (often with the implicit assumption that a bottom was being taken advantage of or naively abused). For most people, "unsafe play" and the bad reputation that accompanied it functionally meant Tops who were playing unsafely with their bottoms (who were usually framed as victims). One person mentioned a knife scene gone wrong that damaged the Top's reputation (knife scenes aren't expected to result in serious cuts for the bottoms, so if Tops cut them more than a few accidental nicks, their reputations for skill tend to suffer). Several interviewees also mentioned their own or others' reputations suffering as the result of "botched rope suspensions"—again, only as Tops. To be clear, rope suspensions are extremely difficult to safely manage, and many things can go wrong in them that often aren't remotely the fault of the Top or the bottom, but the community tends to blame the Top anyway (and many Tops blame themselves). Only two people specifically described bottoms getting a bad reputation, and in both cases it was for "being drama" (explained below).

Ostensibly, the rules for getting a bad reputation are the same across the board, for all genders and all BDSM roles. Interviewees said that kinksters get a bad reputation by playing unsafely, "not respecting boundaries," being "predators," being "creepy," being dishonest, not respecting the consent of their partners, being arrogant/showing hubris/taking themselves too seriously/getting hung up on their own egos, not respecting privacy of others, and creating "drama." I'll explain each of these qualities, starting with "not respecting boundaries." Tony, who had helped manage a small kink group, said there was one guy who had

> boundary problems. He was just really, really cuddly and affectionate with people and didn't—I've never been able to get a good read on him, really. And I think it's possible that it's just something that comes so naturally to him that he doesn't realize that it doesn't for other people and that you need to establish boundaries and consent for that. And it's possible that it's more complicated than that. But he's also sort of someone that I've always been a little bit, like, he's always made me slightly uncomfortable, and I haven't really been able to get a read on him. But he doesn't feel sort of predatory to me, it's just more of a, like, I'm just not sure what I'm dealing with here kind of a thing.

I've left Tony's comments completely unedited here because the hesitations in them so perfectly capture the way kinksters in general tend to describe problem guys like the one he's describing: with hesitation, uncertainty, and a reluctance to pass negative judgment, even as intuition wars with available information. Even through the hesitations, you can start to get a more concrete sense of what it means to have "boundary problems": usually it means consistently failing to get explicit consent for some behavior or interaction that Scene norms expect explicit consent for (particularly physical touching).

Notice that Tony contrasts his "boundary problem" guy with a "predator," which is an often used but ill-defined term in the Scene. Several interviewees used the term to negatively talk about people, but few provided a clear sense of what it meant. Kinksters generally described predators as people who intentionally took advantage of others, especially newbies, in order to find play partners who were too naive to be able to really protect and stand up for themselves. They almost always described predators as older male Doms who were preying on young, naive female subs. Andrew described a common predatory scenario, imagining an arrogant predatory man, "Super Dom, He Who Must Be Obeyed," who takes himself much too seriously and lures naive 24-year-old bisexual women into becoming his submissive. Elijah also described a man he said was "predatory" and "underhanded" who he encountered when he and his girlfriend were new to the Scene. He said the man would pretend to be sympathetic with Elijah over challenges he experienced as a new kinkster and use that as an excuse to play with Elijah's girlfriend. This behavior wasn't really violating any rules; it was just sleazy. This type of behavior is a common problem with predators in the Scene: they often don't break any formal rules, but they're perpetually hunting for loopholes and technicalities.

On my survey, I sought the closest efficient approximation I could find to encapsulate predatory behavior and asked for people's response to the statement, "I worry about getting a reputation as someone who pressures people to play or have sex." Although most people disagreed with the statement, there were still very significant and large gender differences in their responses. Twenty-four percent of gender-nonconforming people with penises agreed or strongly agreed, as did 25 percent of men, but only 8 percent of women and 12 percent of gender-nonconforming people with vaginas did. In short, the Scene's narrative that men are predators affects people's consciousness of their own reputational maintenance so that people with penises are much more concerned about being perceived as predators compared with people with vaginas. I tried controlling for BDSM role but found no differences once I did.

Even as the Scene struggles to clearly define and understand who the predators are, it has an even harder time defining who the "creeps" are. While the term "creepy" has a rather ambiguous meaning in mainstream culture (Kotsko, 2015), in the Scene, "creepy" is one of the most stigmatized labels. It's also dangerously arbitrary, since no one really has a clear set of criteria for what constitutes a creep. In interviews or in casual conversations, kinksters consistently struggled to explain what "creepy" meant in practice. Melissa said, a little hesitatingly,

> But it's somebody that has—I would say it would have to be the men who are just—they're standoffish. They're just watching. You can't really read them too well, and they kind of have this creep vibe to them. That's the only way I can explain it. Their energy just comes off as that's nothing that you really want to mess with.

As in Melissa's explanation, Scene cultural narratives almost always frame creeps as men, but in practice I saw many people labeled "creepy" who were GNC-Ps. On my survey, both men and GNC-Ps were about equally likely to agree or strongly agree with the statement, "I worry about other people perceiving me as creepy in the BDSM Scene" (55 percent for the GNC-Ps and 50 percent for men), but the GNC-Ps (24 percent) were much more likely than men (14 percent) to *strongly* agree with the statement. Both groups were vastly more likely to worry about this perception than women (1 percent strongly agree/12 percent agree) or GNC-Vs (2.5 percent strongly agree/17 percent agree). Because of the vagueness of the criteria for "creep," many people with penises I know have expressed concern that other kinksters might interpret even the most innocent-seeming behaviors as creepy.

However, of all the labels the Scene stigmatizes most harshly, "violator" is clearly the worst. "Consent violations" rarely fit the imaginary paradigm BDSM 101 tends to frame of a Top ignoring a bottom's safeword; usually, they involve pressure, assumed consent, or stepping beyond reasonable boundaries rather than something as blatant as ignoring a safeword. Drake explained how arrogance and consent violation often went hand in hand, saying that a man he had known "thought he was God's gift to everyone, the Top Master Dominant you know. He'd come in in black leather and expect everybody to kneel to him. And he got a bad reputation because once he got you in a private party, he would just literally destroy you." To clarify, this Top was "destroying" female bottoms, and Drake said he was eventually kicked out of the Scene. In order to actually get a bad reputation as a violator, someone (almost always a man and pretty much always a Top) typically had to violate the consent of *multiple* bottoms, *and* those bottoms had to happen to communicate enough to be able to realize that the problem was habitual. Until that point, violators usually just had a hazy reputation if one or two bottoms talked badly about them to their friends.

Not respecting boundaries, being predatory, being creepy, and violating consent all had rather unpredictable consequences for most of the period from 2012 to 2017 because there was no real system for clearly defining and identifying the behaviors. But there was one behavior that was almost certain to get someone permanently uninvited from a venue or event: being reckless with privacy. Several interviewees mentioned men who had gotten in trouble over illicit photographs taken at events, which was a blatant violation of the formal rules. Another interviewee told a story about a woman who was intentionally causing "drama" at a party and yelling at another woman by her real name (as opposed to her Scene name)—earning the yeller a permanent disinvitation.

The most ambiguous of all the routes to a bad reputation was "being/having drama"—something that would rarely get someone banned from the Scene by itself. It was also a quality more often associated with women and submissives than any of the other negative characteristics I've just described. None of my interviewees provided a clear definition for "drama," but the idea is that someone continually exaggerates small problems or seems to constantly be dragged down by problems others perceive as insignificant. There's a pretty strong social stigma against causing/being/having drama in the tiny social world of the Scene, even though there aren't really any formal rules against it or formal consequences for doing so. But one of the main ways many kinksters worry they might cause drama is by actually telling other people that someone violated their consent or hurt them.

SKEPTICISM AND DOUBT

We saw earlier that most highly involved kinksters said they worked hard to maintain their good reputations in the Scene. But given that so many people, including at least three of those I interviewed, enjoyed good reputations in parts of the Scene but had bad reputations in other parts, kinksters who had been around long enough to witness these kinds of discrepancies inevitably started to doubt the legitimacy of reputation. Several event organizers and promoters themselves argued that *all* event organizers and promoters inevitably became unpopular in certain circles (a point I tend to agree with) because being in charge meant that someone (or whole groups of people) inevitably thought you did a bad job or didn't respond to them satisfactorily. Fifteen of my interviewees expressed a great deal of skepticism about the reliability of reputations in the Scene in general. Most of these skeptics were highly involved in the Scene but were not presenters or organizers. People with less involvement and/or experience usually said they felt like they knew little about the reputational system in the Scene and/or seemed to believe it was reasonably reliable; kinksters who had been around longer had many more doubts.

My interviewee Oliver, who was still fairly new to the Scene but already heavily involved, was suspicious that reputation didn't mean much. He said he thought the Scene wasn't really special in its hierarchies and that the main way people got good reputations was through "networking, ass kissing, and probably just the same way they do [in any other context]." Mary, who had been involved in the Scene for many years, strongly hinted that she thought the main way people got good reputations was just by sticking around for a long time and playing in public. I think her concern was fair, and the problem with these assumptions of good reputation was that they were circular: kinksters assumed someone had a good reputation because they'd been around for a long time, and so the person continued to have a good reputation because they'd been around for a long time. Moreover, as the Scene slowly learned, public play wasn't always a great reflection of how somebody played in private. Indeed, it eventually became clear from the reports of anguished bottoms that a major strategy of abusers was playing carefully in public to seduce both the bottom and the audience into believing in the Top's respectability, then getting the bottom alone and treating them very differently—causing dissonance for the bottom and skepticism from the audience the bottom reported to. These kinds of common problems led people like Mark to say that he thought reputations didn't mean much because the Scene was constantly hushing up its problems. When I asked him about reputation in the Scene, he said, "I'm fairly sure that there's quite a lot of abuse that's going on [in the Scene], but it's usually not reported, or it's underreported or swept under the carpet. The community prides itself on being far safer than any normal [vanilla] gathering or party, but I'm not entirely sure it is."

At least five interviewees specifically mentioned people they felt had undeserved good reputations. Lucy, who in chapter 5 strongly recommended bottoms get references about Tops before playing with them, frustratedly described an abusive Top who nevertheless enjoyed a good reputation:

> Everybody talked about how skeevy he was. But he's also one of the biggest names in the area, was on some national boards [of BDSM organizations], and had all these other people saying what a fabulous, wonderful person he is. He's had a couple scandals that he's gone through, and people still think that he's like this fabulous, wonderful person because he raises a lot of money for charity and he donates a lot of money.

I don't know who Lucy was describing specifically, but I can personally think of multiple people at the time who would probably fit the basic outline of her description. The fact that this type of story was sufficiently common that multiple people would fit the profile speaks to why experienced kinksters often become jaded about the nature of reputation in the Scene.

Conversely, one of my interviewees, Mila, indignantly described a casual partner and friend who she felt had gotten an undeserved bad reputation, saying he had always carefully checked on her when the two played together to make sure that she was okay with everything that was happening. She said, "I can't fathom why anybody who actually knows this person would think that he is a threat. There are people with bad reputations. I try to take it upon myself to, if I meet them, if I encounter them, to have a conversation and make my own judgment call."

Kinksters often cared more about their own personal interactions with others than the abstract interactions of those people with someone else. They also generally had more faith in their own opinions than in those of strangers, and when the two opinions conflicted, they trusted their own judgments. A reputation system starts to break down when it too frequently asks people to feel like they're denying the legitimacy of their own experiences and observations in favor of a very different judgment. When I asked Harriet, an experienced kinkster, about her ideas about reputation, she said, "I tend to stay out of that trouble; everyone has their own opinions, and you can't judge someone because of one person's opinion."

With so many of my interviewees expressing doubts about it, the Scene's reputation system was bound to have serious flaws, since reputations are meaningful only when people believe in them. But it wasn't just skepticism that drove problems in the Scene's reputation system: the biggest problem was that the Scene taught kinksters not to actually say anything bad about each other. We saw that kinksters said again and again that causing drama would lead to a tarnished reputation, and one of the ways people (bottoms) got accused of causing drama was by voicing complaints about violation and abuse. There was also a general Scene norm about not talking badly about others, so deeply ingrained that interviewees would often tell me about people with bad reputations in only the vaguest of terms—even when the people were long gone and there was no way that I could have done any social damage to them. For example, Alice, who was still fairly new to the Scene, told me a story about a Top who had initiated sexual activities with her without previous negotiation (going so far as to put on a condom), which is a pretty serious problem by Scene standards. He stopped when she told him "no," but when I asked her if she would tell other people about him, she said,

> No, not exactly, because I don't think he's dangerous or predatory; his style just didn't work well with me. So if I thought someone was a poten-tial abuser, I might—or would—try to steer people away. But if it was just someone who enjoys playing in a way that I don't, I don't see a reason to tell people to clear off.

Since this Top adhered to the letter of Scene norms, stopping when Alice asked him to, she concluded that his play style didn't match hers. I don't think that's the conclusion that many other experienced kinksters would have drawn from her description, since the spirit of Scene norms generally emphasizes more sound negotiation ahead of time and less in the middle of play—but since she wasn't really telling anyone about it, no one could tell her it was a problem.

Both Elijah and Lucy expressed vehement frustration at people's general unwillingness to tell unwelcome truths about other people. Elijah, who we saw earlier had a bad experience with a predator when he first entered the Scene, later learned that this man was infamous for his behavior, but no one told Elijah until it was too late. Elijah exclaimed that he wanted fellow kinksters to "say that shit!" adding, "I'm protecting people coming in. I don't want anybody to have the experience I had." Lucy summarized the situation baldly, saying,

> I have known several people in the Scene that I've met that I feel are dangerous, unsafe, and predators. But then this is where it comes down to who's policing who? Who is going to say something about them? Sometimes people will say, "Don't play with them, they're not good," but they won't tell you why. They don't want to damage someone's reputation, say things that could completely ruin someone. I understand that. But if somebody has done something unsafe or hurt someone in a nonconsensual way, then I think that those things need to be talked about.

My interviewees certainly illustrated Lucy's and Elijah's frustrations, as most of them hadn't told other people when bad things happened to them at the hands of fellow kinksters. On the rare occasions when people did tell others about their bad experiences, they usually only told people they were fairly close to—typically their Leather families or the partners of the people who hurt them. But of course, talking to the people close to them did nothing to help new people coming in—like Elijah—who lacked these kinds of connections. Kinksters' well-socialized hesitancy to pass global judgments, absolutely ruin reputations, and "cause drama" meant that the reputational system they prided themselves on and depended on became less and less meaningful.

Throughout my official research period, from 2012 until 2017, I almost never heard anyone more than casually question the idea that bottoms could deserve bad reputations as much as Tops—it was just accepted that Tops were the ones usually responsible for problems in scenes, relationships, and the community in general. By 2019, I was starting to see more murmurings countering that trend, but consent and status in the Scene remained mostly focused on protecting women bottoms, with almost total disregard for other groups.

APPEARANCES AND SHOW

The Scene's reputational system was built on a foundation (really a facade) of cronyism, truthiness, and showmanship, so it's little wonder that it began to collapse spectacularly in mid-2017. Indeed, the only surprise was that it lasted as long as it did. As more and more (usually men) Tops with great reputations were revealed to have taken advantage of many (usually women) bottoms, kinksters began to wonder what—if anything—their reputation system had been based on. The semiformal values that were supposed to get someone a good reputation (honor, integrity, humility, experience, and skill) awkwardly coexisted alongside a set of tenuously connected, more informal values that seemed to bring good reputation much more quickly (being well connected to established people, putting on a good show, and playing with a lot of people). The Scene remained fairly oblivious to this awkward co-existence, mostly refusing to acknowledge the importance of this informal system next to its semiformal system. Even as the system started to collapse, kinksters never seemed to notice that their status/reputation system had been almost entirely directed at Tops to the exclusion of bottoms and much more focused on people with penises than people with vaginas. The idea that the system was so fragile in part because this deep inequality was built into it from the start never seemed to occur to anyone. With so little status available to bottoms, they were easy prey, and with such weirdly differentiated sex/gender norms, everyone was confused about what responsible behavior really looked like. After all, by all appearances, the system had been built to *protect* bottoms and people with vaginas. But by any analysis I can come up with, the people who seemed to benefit the most from the system were male Tops who could put on a good kinky show.

CONCLUSION

What Is It That We Do?

Kinksters have a very old euphemism to describe BDSM in vanilla company: "What it is that we do." Researching the Scene as an insider made this euphemism feel more like a question: What is it that we do? As I frolicked my own switchy way through the Scene, the answers I arrived at, both personally and professionally, were that what we do—BDSM—is a constantly evolving, wildly subjective, experiential thing. Even after all these years, I still don't understand what BDSM really is. The best answer I have is physical and psychological experiences focusing on control and pain for purposes of mutual gratification. A clear and easy definition for *BDSM* still remains as elusive to me as one for *sex*.

The Scene, for all its murky edges and amorphous complexity, is much easier for me to understand than the thing it claims to celebrate: BDSM. By the time I became thoroughly immersed in the Scene in 2012, it was hard for me to imagine my life without it. I felt cool, and I felt like I belonged somewhere for the first time in my life. I hope you've seen that these feelings are common in the Scene and gotten some sense for why the people who love it often love it *so* much. For many kinksters, BDSM is full of intense psychological and physical pleasures they simply don't get anywhere else, and the social world of the Scene is full of friends and acceptance they don't feel anywhere else. No matter how strange our lives might look to outsiders, "what it is that we do" fulfills cravings many of us have felt our entire lives—cravings that society told us made us deviants, weirdos, freaks, or even criminals. We share that sense of rejection among ourselves and collectively reassure one another that we're still good people and that in the protective bubble of our own world, we're normal.

But that rosy picture of the Scene is much *too* rosy; the Scene is full of imperfect people and constructed on some very flimsy social foundations that often collapse with the slightest push. As far as I can tell, the majority of people who ever love the Scene don't love it for long: the Scene experiences rapid turnover, and many of the people I interviewed in 2012 who were the most heavily involved left within one or two years. Some people just get busy, while others get bitter and disillusioned, saying the Scene's promises of acceptance were ultimately shallow and unfulfilling. I've known others who said as they grew older, the idea of a wild party just didn't seem that necessary anymore, and they'd rather stay home and chill with people they loved. Even large, annual dayslong events usually only persist for about 3 to 10 years after their initial appearance. Social groups, parties, events, and fetlebrities all come and go stunningly quickly within the Scene. I talked to many people who took two or three years away from the Scene for various reasons and said that when they got back, they barely recognized it. The norms stayed basically the same, but the people and events changed rapidly.

The multidimensional portrait of the Scene I've tried to paint in this book has to capture this paradox: the Scene as a place of belonging and intense passion *as well as* a gossipy "dramatastic" mess that isn't nearly as well ordered as it tries to be. As a collection of human beings interacting passionately in a very small space in a minute social universe, the Scene is full of problems and flaws. Moreover, though they have much in common with each other, the disordered conglomeration of microcultures that make up "the Scene" are sometimes completely at odds with one another. There are many parties and events I went to for research purposes that I would never want to attend again; there are others that became part of the basic fabric of my social and personal life. Some of those parties and events I disliked are quite large and bring many kinksters great joy, and those same people are unimpressed with parties and events I love. My interviewee Gabe, describing some of his own frustrations with divisions in the Scene, said, "But really, we're all kind of after the same thing, you know? Maximum fun and pleasure and massive kinkiness and getting it on—and why can't that common goal be something that unites rather than bifurcates the Scene?" I've tried to stick to the details in this book of patterns that seem to hold true across large swaths of the Scene, but I think there are great opportunities for future researchers to explore more about differences between various parts of the Scene and the individuals within it.

BORN THIS WAY

There are many things kinksters as a group often say they want from the rest of the world: acknowledgment, respect, and the understanding that what we do isn't abuse tend to be high on that list. Luther said in frustration, "The world doesn't understand us. Well, they do—they like it, they just don't want to deal with it. They want it in one hand and don't want it in the other hand. That's the way of the [vanilla world]—'Let's use sex and advertise with it, but let's not talk about it'—that type of stuff." This sense that "vanilla" people wanted what "we" had was especially poignant when I was doing my interviews in 2012 with Rihanna's "S&M" playing on the radio and *Fifty Shades of Grey* at the top of the bestseller list. The more it felt like the rest of the world fetishized our lifestyle, the more offensive it became when (as happened during my fieldwork) kinksters lost their jobs or were demoted for being involved in it. During my time in the Scene, sexual orientation protections in mainstream society increased considerably for gays, lesbians, bisexuals, and queers, but kinky and poly remained conspicuously unprotected statuses. Mainstream society bought the argument that gays, lesbians, maybe bisexuals, and possibly even trans folks were "born this way," but seemed pretty uninterested in the idea of kinky and poly as possible sexual orientations. As far as mainstream society seemed concerned, we had made a choice to live the way it seemed like everyone else fantasized about, and they expected us to pay for our good times by keeping our mouths shut about our lives.

But there's always a tension among kinksters about how normal and accepted they really want to be. Only two of my 70 interviewees adamantly described themselves as "normal"; most of the rest of them, like folks in the Scene in general, delighted in being weird. Lily, as one of those two, really stood out in her comments about her life as a Dominant, poly woman:

> I'm not somebody's walk on the wild side. I'm not a freak show. I know a lot of people in this Scene identify as freaks, but I'm shockingly normal. I have a normal job. I'm very well educated, I'm well traveled, I'm cultured, I like wine. I'm pretty boring—except I do like knee-high boots and to beat people. I don't like it when people treat me like I'm a freak instead of like I made a lifestyle choice. But the way I identify is the same way—I don't want to offend a whole bunch of gay people here—but the same way gay people deal with their sexual orientation. We live in a time in society where it isn't kosher anymore to look at someone who's gay and be like, "Freak." But not too long ago, that was what was happening. And I feel like that's where we need to move with alternative lifestyles—with polyamory, BDSM, female-led relationships. We need to take it out of, "Oh, the only way I can be involved is because I'm a big freak," and be like, "No. I have been a dominant personality, if not dominant sexually, my entire life. So I'm pretty sure I was born this way." And it does not make my partner weak.

Even though most people in the Scene enjoy being weird—and often truly eroticize it by getting sexual thrills from socially taboo acts and desires, I think Lily's comments still speak to what many kinksters want in terms of social acceptance and recognition. While it might be fun to shock and titillate sometimes, I've heard many kinksters complain about how exhausting it is never to have an answer to the question, "Are you seeing anyone right now?" that the questioner will understand. Yet I'm not sure that kinksters can ever reach acceptance in mainstream society without making a lot of compromises with "normalcy" that most of them don't really seem prepared to make. We've made difference a point of pride for so long that I don't know what we'd do if society suddenly did start accepting us.

ARE WE ACTUALLY BETTER AT THIS?

Because the Scene had always defined itself in terms of difference from the rest of the world, it was a little bewildered circa 2012 to encounter such incontrovertible evidence that much of the world at least fantasized about what we did. Rather than opening its arms to all the people who had discovered how much they fantasized about BDSM and were buying up BDSM-related gear at Spencer's and Target in unprecedented numbers, the Scene doubled down on its difference from these "wannabes" and chose to highlight how much more authentic and "right" its BDSM practices were. The Scene, through institutions like the National Coalition for Sexual Freedom (NCSF), created a kind of party line to defend our lives to vanillas. Here's a quote from the NCSF's website of a "sound bite" to give to reporters about consent: "The educational and social kink groups constantly discuss issues of consent, which is the basis of safe, sane, and consensual sexual education"; it then goes on to define "consensual" as "respecting the limits imposed by each participant. One of the ways to maintain limits is through a 'safeword'—in which the person being stimulated can withdraw consent at any time with a single word or gesture." This simplistic rhetoric is designed to draw a not-so-subtle line between "us" and "those idiots you read about in the news who strangled someone during a bondage scene." I think most kinksters genuinely believe that these differences are the ones that distinguish "us" from "them," but I don't know if they are. I think it's true that kinky folk outside the Scene probably don't care about safety and consent the way that kinksters in the Scene do, but I'm not sure how much that matters. And we certainly don't use safewords the way we claim we do.

Rather than focusing on the differences of BDSM practices per se, the differences I see as the most glaringly obvious between the vaguely defined "us" and the even more vaguely defined "them" are much more a matter of culture and normative expectations. You can go to the table of contents of this book to get a pretty good sense of what most of those differences are: doing BDSM with an increasing sense of kinky identity, not just doing it for good times; de-emphasizing the sexual motivations for BDSM in favor of other motivations; doing BDSM with the assumption that you're doing it with multiple people; doing BDSM with the assumption that roles of Dominance and submission are deeply meaningful, as is the fantasy of 24/7 relationships; establishing an elaborate system of educational programming and rules for how to practice BDSM "right," including monitoring and enforcement; and doing BDSM as an exhibitionistic performance for an audience of fellow kinksters. In the Scene, BDSM often becomes a "life-style," and there's no way that a lifestyle is going to feel or look the same as something a person dabbles in after reading a sexy story. (Unlike so many kinksters I know, I don't say that with any sense of judgment; it's just as a statement of fact.)

Rather than emphasizing how the Scene turns BDSM into a lifestyle, most kinksters I encountered in the Scene tended to emphasize how much "better" they were than folks outside the Scene at doing BDSM. For example, when I watched the first *Fifty Shades* movie in the theater with a large group of kinksters, several of them expressed disgust at the "incompetent" rope bondage in the film and what they perceived as the poor consent and negotiation that occurred between the characters. As I explained in chapter 6, there are many safety ideas that float around the Scene as truth with little scientific support. But kinksters learn to pride themselves on the idea that they know things about BDSM safety that kink-curious folks outside the Scene don't, assuring ourselves and each other that our carefully tying knots, not punching each other in the kidneys, and not dragging our single-tail whips across the floor takes what we do from being "potentially dangerous" to "reasonably safe." Meanwhile, a lot of experienced kinksters like me have argued in frustration that almost everything we do, even at the extremes, is safer than riding in a car and safer than most sports, yet we still tell these stories of safety to comfort ourselves and outsiders.

CONCLUSION

I believe (although my belief is obviously biased) that the Scene *is* much safer for both sex and BDSM than the vanilla world outside. I have no concrete data to support this claim, since gathering data on rape, abuse, and consent violations is always incredibly messy and even more difficult in a context where the line between "assault" and "BDSM" is sometimes literally a quick nod of the head. For what it's worth, I do have statistically significant evidence from my survey that kinksters are much more likely to use condoms the first time they have penis-in-vagina sex with a new person than are kinky people outside the Scene, which at least suggests that kinksters have successfully addressed one objective aspect of sexual safety. And while it's possible that kinksters are able to promote this kind of safety because of their cultivated relationship, sexual, and kink communication skills, I think those things are probably less important than the rigorous normative environment of the Scene. For example, kinksters don't tend to "negotiate" or even talk much about condoms, in my observation and experience; they've just created a normative context where people understand and agree that condoms are expected unless someone suggests otherwise.

I'm pretty sure that there are some important differences in how kinksters and vanillas manage safety and communication, but they're not really the ones the Scene tends to emphasize. The first, and I think most important, difference is the strongly antisubstance culture of the Scene. For instance, even though group sex is popular in the Scene, the whole concept of "drunken hookups" and "drunken threesomes" isn't really part of its culture, unlike outside of it (Morris, Chang, and Knox, 2016). All other things being equal, I'm reasonably certain that two (and especially three) drunk people are probably not as good at negotiating a satisfactory sexual/BDSM experience as two sober people are, but drunken hookups are very common for new sexual partners outside the Scene. I think the kinkiest thing about life in the Scene is that we do most of what we do sober—whereas vanilla-identified folks often only seem to engage in group sex or experiment with BDSM while drunk or high.

Second, the Scene uses intense social monitoring to help try to minimize assault and consent violations. Even though kinksters may roll their eyes at dungeon monitors, I have abundant observational evidence that their presence makes kinksters more self-conscious and aware about what they're doing than when they play by themselves. That said, I think DMs are relatively insignificant in terms of social monitoring compared to the way gossip makes or breaks reputations in the Scene. Even though lots of people got away with repeated consent violations for years, the sense that reputations are fragile was pervasive. In my interviews with Tops who became notorious in the Scene for consent violations, they were at a bare minimum parroting most of the party lines about the importance of reputation, and I doubt anyone could have distinguished theirs from the remarks of other kinksters as the words of violators.

And finally, the Scene has defined expectations about when people are supposed to have a conversation about their desires and expectations—and who's supposed to initiate that conversation. Whereas sexual scripts in vanilla contexts have become extremely muddy (Jozkowski and Peterson, 2013), kinksters have a straightforward normative context to "negotiate" about what they're comfortable with. Somebody asks somebody else to play, and then at the point where they're about to do something together, the Top is supposed to ask the bottom about their "limits" and preferences. But in the vanilla world, it's not clear who's supposed to ask who what, how they're supposed to respond, what it's acceptable for someone to admit desiring, or when you're supposed to have a conversation. The Scene created a normative expectation of a pre-play/sex discussion that traditional dating and hookup norms have no provision for. That said, the Scene's discussion norms don't seem to work as well for sex as they do for BDSM play, and whenever I've taught classes on "negotiating sex for scenes" in the Scene, many kinksters have said in astonishment, "I've never heard anyone talk about this before!" The discussion norms the Scene created are aimed at negotiating BDSM play, and they don't seem to work as well for negotiating sex.

In sum, the Scene *believes* that it's the safest and best context for doing BDSM and that it knows the best practices for it. There's absolutely no objective way to assess the truth of that conviction, but I'm reasonably sure that both beliefs are more or less true, at least for the more complex aspects of BDSM for which kinksters emphasize the importance of education, like elaborate suspension bondage or 24/7 D/s relationships. If you're in the company of other people who've already experimented and know a lot of the pitfalls of what you're about to do, you can at least share information about your mistakes. That system starts to break down a bit when people become ashamed of admitting their mistakes (which happened a lot in the bondage community particularly, thanks to all the reputational issues I talked about in the last chapter). Yet the Scene has several social mechanisms in place that have the unintended consequence of making people less safe. Safewords, presenter worship, and a strong subcultural norm of not "interrupting" other

245

people's scenes or "judging" their kinks all create a much less safe culture than the Scene aspires to. However, it would be a grave error to suggest that the imperfections of the Scene make it worse than its easiest alternative—people muddling through this all on their own.

DIRECTIONS FOR FUTURE RESEARCH

While I've provided an extensive overview of life in the Scene from 2010 to 2017 in this book, there are many important research questions I hope others will explore and answer. In particular, I hope future researchers will look at changes over time in the way the Scene teaches and manages norms about consent, negotiation, and responsible Topping and bottoming. It's hard to imagine these norms remaining unchanged after all the consent-related chaos the Scene experienced in 2017–2018. Adding to all of the normative issues I've discussed in this book, I hope that more American and Canadian researchers will build on Haviv's (2016) work on the Israeli BDSM Scene and Holt's (2016) work on the Florida Scene studying the social institutions kinksters have in place to try to manage rulebreakers. My own observations and experiences suggested that those institutions were extremely weak everywhere I knew of prior to 2017, but in the wake of increasing worries about consent violators in the Scene, many kinksters hoped these institutions would become stronger.

During my time in the Scene, there were many changes in the way bottoming and bottoming education were constructed. I have barely touched on these issues in this book, and I hope that future research can explore more about how the Scene came to take bottoming education more seriously. Whether the role of bottoms will change as a result of that and other social changes in the Scene is another research question ripe for study.

Although I've discussed the overlapping subcultures around the Scene a fair bit in this book, I think there's still much left to explore—especially looking at the overlaps between the Scene and geek cons like DragonCon. With a few exceptions for poly, previous research on kinksters has mostly explored them in social isolation, but the BDSM subculture overlaps so heavily with poly, Pagan, Ren Faire, geek, and to a lesser degree burner subcultures that it's problematic to try to understand the Scene without reference to the others. Presumably, changes in one subculture might create ripples in the other subcultures that wouldn't be obvious to most members of either, and there is very little sociological research on the idea of overlapping subcultures at all.

Relatedly, we need more research on the role of race in the Scene. Though Cruz (2016) studied Black women's representation in pornography and professional domination, only one study has looked at American kinksters' experiences with race in depth (Erickson et al., 2021). As discussed in chapter 5, I think any analysis of race in the Scene needs to incorporate analysis of race in the (likewise almost entirely white) overlapping subcultures mentioned above. The Scene's excessive whiteness isn't really special, but it would certainly be interesting to explore whether different minority groups have created their own mini BDSM Scenes that are mostly off the radar of the "mainstream" pansexual Scene (van Dorn, 2019).

And finally, we need more research on BDSM and the Scene from kinky insiders. There's plenty of value in having outsider perspectives, but we've let their perspectives monopolize the academic conversation for far too long. We need more kinksters to tell *our* story.

EPILOGUE: THE BREAKDOWN

I've written this book in much the same way I rewatch the movie *Moulin Rouge*: starting it when things are good, then abruptly turning it off right before things get sad, with the full knowledge that that's how the story goes. Although the Scene was never explicitly political, because it is a fundamentally deeply liberal subculture, Donald Trump's election in 2016 was very bad for it—especially in the DC area. Instead of going to parties on the weekend, kinksters were going to protests, and the overall grim sociopolitical context of the nation took the party spirit out of a lot of people. In one of the most profound explications of this sense of general hopelessness I've encountered, Amal Graafstra, the owner of a high-tech body implant company (think science fiction, but real), explained that sales of his product had been steadily increasing until Trump's election, at which point no one bought one for a solid week. Once he'd processed this fiasco, he determined that

> really it just comes down to people that are excited about the future in a very
> basic sense. I think one way or another, people lost faith in humanity, and

in a sense lost faith in the future. And they had much more pressing current concerns than, "What am I going to do with this cool implant?" (Robertson, 2017)

While I personally know only a few kinksters who've bought Graafstra's products, the zeitgeist problem he described was every bit as troublesome for the Scene as it was for his company. Although fundamentally escapist, the Scene isn't nihilistic; people needed hope to want to participate, but the kinds of people who usually participated had lost hope. Then, to make matters worse, unemployment rates plummeted for the next couple of years, which was good for the American economy but bad for the Scene, which heavily depends on the labor of un/deremployed people to function.

Though kinksters remained mostly unaware of their influence, these larger social factors formed the backdrop for the disastrous state of the Scene by the summer of 2017, when so many male Top presenters and organizers started to get called out by others, mostly female bottoms, for histories of violation and abuse. These repeated revelations sparked outrage and a mostly unproductive process of reflection as kinksters tried to figure out what deep underlying problems had led them to this dark place. Many large events closed or struggled to continue, happy hours and munches devolved into arguments and fell apart without being replaced, and I heard from organizers who literally shut down educational events because they felt like they couldn't protect the reputations of presenters from an increasingly furious mob of kinksters. Throughout 2018 and much of 2019, as I traveled around the country writing this book, I heard the same demoralized story from kinksters everywhere about once-thriving Scenes that had been reduced to an occasional happy hour or party.

The vast majority of these stories of abuse were depressingly similar: scene-famous male rope Tops who had been taking sexual advantage of female bottoms they played with or who had persuaded uneducated newbie bottoms into much more intense D/s dynamics than they were comfortable with—usually for years. I think it would be inaccurate to say that the #MeToo movement caused this change, especially since the Scene's own version of #MeToo started several months before it did in the larger culture; rather, the social climate of gendered mistrust and frustration that led to the #MeToo movement led to the same general experience in the Scene. Kinksters quickly adopted the language of #MeToo to describe what was happening in the Scene but still mostly treated the Scene's problems as basically separate from those of the broader culture.

I hope that any sociologist brave enough to tackle this transition in the Scene in the future will find a roadmap in my book to see some of the specific problems the subculture had that led to these troubles. Chief among them were:

- A complete failure to reconcile competing norms about BDSM being extremely intimate with other norms that make it appear not very intimate at all (Chapters 2 and 5)
- Deep ambivalence about the role of sexual desire and expression in BDSM (Chapter 2)
- Failure to acknowledge that bottoms have lower self-esteem than Tops (Chapter 4)
- Failure to appreciate that the process of learning one's "limits" usually requires breaking them at some point (Chapter 5)
- A massive and almost completely unacknowledged contradiction between semi/formal norms about safe, sane, and consensual behavior and informal norms about these things for more experienced kinksters (Chapter 5)
- Ambivalent construction of what bottoms' role in consent should be (Chapter 6)
- Heavy dependence on a deeply flawed reputation system that experienced people often lost faith in and that wasn't really based on the criteria most people wanted to believe it was (Chapter 7)
- Failure to acknowledge that the Scene's status and reputation system almost entirely focused on Tops to the exclusion of bottoms (Chapter 7)
- An idealization of presenters and kink elites that was deeply disconnected from the reality of their experiences and expertise (Chapter 7)

By constructing a culture with so much ambiguity around intimacy, sexuality, BDSM roles, and responsibility for consent, it was easy for some Tops to intentionally and unintentionally exploit the gray areas of these interactions in ways that took serious advantage of bottoms—occasionally drifting into the territory of plain old rape or abuse. The community had a pretty low tolerance for behaviors that unambiguously violated its rules (e.g., ignoring safewords), but most of the problem people weren't doing anything so obvious, so even on the rare occasions when bottoms actually spoke up, no one was really sure how to respond.

But Hey, It's Home

I intentionally stopped studying the Scene after it became so chaotic in June 2017. I had too much emotional investment in that story to be able to tell it with even a hint of objectivity—it would have felt like trying to narrate the story of my own breakup. For the next year, instead of doing interviews naked in the sweltering heat, my study of the Scene increasingly came down to crunching survey statistics on my computer at home. That was just as well, because even though I still found plenty of joy at them, my experience of BDSM events for the next couple of years would be full of disappointments and personal tragedies—which weren't really just personal at all because they were shared throughout the community.

I felt like the community was tentatively trying to put the pieces of itself back together by mid-2019 or so, but of course, only a few months later, in early 2020, there was no more live BDSM Scene or any other kind of scene or clubs or even much in-person socialization because of the COVID-19 pandemic. DC was one of the few places in the country where the Scene re-opened in July 2021—the clubs and events most everywhere else had folded due to economic pressures. With one of the oldest scenes in the country, it was probably no surprise that when the clubs reopened to vaccinated-only people in the summer of 2021, the lines to get in stretched around the block. The arguments and infighting and uncertainty hadn't stopped, and now they had an extra burden of COVID anxiety and accompanying gener- alized anxiety to manage as well. But here in DC at least, the ongoing party resumed. There were a *lot* fewer in-person parties, socials, house gatherings, and large-scale events than in the past, but the public events that persisted locally flourished.

Back yet again at Camp O-Town in September 2021 after a heart- wrenching absence of two years, everyone was bewildered and awkward after so long without mass contact. The drug use norms had clearly changed some- what, as people were using so much pot you could practically get high just from walking around the tents. The dungeon was almost empty the first few nights as people slowly tried to remember "how to people" (a phrase I heard a lot) again: how to socialize, how to approach people to play, how to negotiate play, and how to learn the body and being of a new person—or even just how to play with familiar people in front of an audience. But people were trying hard to recapture the spirit of what had moved them before they were locked out of normal social contact for well over a year. I played so much that every night I staggered into bed in delirious exhaustion, barely able to stand up. Surrounded for the first time in literally years by the sounds of screams and orgasms, I was powerfully reminded of all the things we come together to do in pleasure and joy that other people find confusing, terrifying, violent, cruel, weird, silly, arousing, or just plain dull. Collectively, we try to gratify complex psychological and physical desires that society doesn't even want to acknowledge exist. At our best, we constantly strive to find new and better ways to manifest desires many of us didn't even know to dream before we arrived. What it is that we *really* do is continually try to build and rebuild a space to explore innumerable carnal and connective possibilities.

It's not perfect, but hey, it's home.

METHODOLOGICAL APPENDIX

ETHNOGRAPHY

Observing and writing about the BDSM Scene is an ethically challenging undertaking. Although the chair of my ethics board was initially skeptical about the ethics of BDSM itself, let alone my studying it, I did finally manage to persuade them to approve my study. By the traditional code of researchers, many BDSM events are basically public affairs in that anyone who pays the admission price can go to them. On the other hand, there's an explicit expectation of privacy at most of them, since they often make you sign paperwork before going in assuring the staff that you're just there for your own enjoyment and you aren't a journalist. When I was formally conducting my fieldwork in 2012, all the officials at the events and parties I attended were aware that I was doing research in addition to being there for my own amusement. No one ever questioned my legitimacy or presence, and I only ever heard of one instance where someone who personally disliked me tried to discourage the board of an event from allowing me to attend. (They let me in anyway.) Even in 2012, when I was still relatively new to the Scene, many people knew who I was and were delighted to talk to me about my research and writing. I was actively participating everywhere I studied (I think there was only one party and one event I attended during my fieldwork where I didn't play), and my enthusiastic participation seemed to inspire a lot of trust from the people around me. I looked like I belonged, I acted like I belonged, and most of the kinksters I talked to said they trusted me to tell the truth about them (which they felt hadn't happened with previous researchers). Most of the events I attended forbade the use of recording devices, but no one ever complained when I used one for my interviews, and I often interviewed the event organizers themselves without anyone even commenting that I was technically breaking the rules.

During the period of my formal fieldwork, from May through September 2012, I functionally immersed myself in the Scene. I attended a variety of multiday hotel and camping events, each of which was attended by hundreds of people, including two BDSM events in hotels, three BDSM camping events, two adults-only "sacred sexuality" Pagan camping events that were heavily infused with BDSM, and two multiday "family-friendly" Pagan camping events that were heavily attended by BDSM participants (but did not actually include BDSM). I attended private or public parties in DC, Baltimore, Philadelphia, and New York City nearly every weekend that I was not at an event, attended numerous BDSM happy hours, and was perpetually connected to other Scene participants through FetLife. In the years since the conclusion of my official fieldwork, I've remained extremely involved in the Scene, attending parties and events and teaching classes throughout the United States, Canada, and even Iceland and Jamaica. These diverse experiences allow me to compare and contrast the very geographically diverse BDSM Scenes and develop a better sense for what "the Scene" really consists of beyond the Scene around the mid-Atlantic region.

I've mostly treated any information that you can obtain with a quick Google search (such as the names of prominent BDSM organizations and the rules of various dungeons and events) as public. (In contrast, all interviewee names are pseudonyms. Friends were named at their request.) These days, even the names and addresses of specific dungeons and major BDSM events are generally public, too, but many weren't when I started my research, so I've kept up the pretense of privacy for them. In order not to compromise the privacy of what goes on at events, I've gone out of my way in this book not to provide details of my observations of scenes (BDSM encounters) and people who didn't give me explicit permission to include their stories. I've provided a lot of information about general norms and rules of behavior, but I've mostly intentionally removed details unless I could ask people's permission to include them. One major exception was the stories that interviewees provided for me about "awesome scenes they had seen," of which I have included several. I struggled with whether or not it was appropriate to include those stories, but none of them includes any notable identifying information about the people involved, so I have judged them okay. My standard was that if the people involved were unlikely to recognize themselves in the stories, they were okay to include in this book. There are a few stories in this book of scenes that were kind of "local legends" (both good and bad), which were undoubtedly recognizable by the people involved and that I heard told again and again, and I treated those stories (none of which I saw firsthand) as community property.

INTERVIEWS

During the summer of 2012, I conducted interviews with 70 people who identified as kinky in some way. Interviews covered a wide array of topics, from how people became involved in the Scene to their favorite things about the Scene and BDSM to their relationship dynamics to their spirituality. Although I highlighted my insider status through dress and conversation, I tried to maintain the kind of social distance I think implied by Simmel's (1950) concept of "the stranger"—someone who is like the interviewee but doesn't know them personally. In keeping with that principle, I intentionally interviewed people who were outside of my own social network as much as possible. I talked about all the issues in my interviews with my friends and acquaintances regularly, so I already had their perspectives anyway. When I was at BDSM events or social gatherings, I casually talked to random people about my research and was able to quickly find enthusiastic participants. With the permission of moderators, I posted to different FetLife discussion forums about my research and recruited many interviewees through the internet. I recruited everyone who wasn't really involved in the public Scene through FetLife. Occasionally, friends introduced me to people they thought I should talk to, and if the people were unfamiliar to me, I interviewed them. All my interviews took place in person and were recorded and then transcribed.

I had to make a few exceptions to my stranger principle for several people. One was a friendly acquaintance, Grace (who I came to know much better later), whom I interviewed because I was interested in talking to more people who felt that BDSM defined their sexuality, and they were hard to find randomly. All the rest were people I judged "key informants" (Payne and Payne, 2004), who for my purposes were people who had taught at or organized at least two BDSM events in the last six months and who had been involved in the Scene for at least five years. About half of my 10 key informants were part of my social network. Although I don't regret any of those interviews, there were usually certain quality costs from them. While close friends will often freely tell of the problems with their boyfriend, and total strangers will often tell of those problems, the key informants I was interviewing were in between friends and strangers and thus sometimes seemed more nervous about revealing that type of information. The possibility that I might break their confidentiality and go tell my friends—who were also their friends—about their personal problems loomed much larger in those interviews.

I refused to formally interview anyone I had ever played with, and I also refused to interview any of my current partners' current partners. However, I informally interviewed (meaning I did not record them or take notes) several people who fit that description, partly because they were so eager to participate in my research. It was clear to me that some of my interviewees (all the obvious ones were men) agreed to be interviewed with the hope that the interview would function like a date or foreplay. I worried that my sex appeal (such as it was) constituted something almost potentially coercive in getting people to agree to be interviewed, even though I tried never to engage in behavior with interviewees that I thought would be interpreted as flirtatious. Even though I knew that I wasn't going to sleep with them, I couldn't establish good rapport with my interviewees if I started off my interviews saying, "Just so you know, I'm not planning to sleep with you—ever." However, failing to do so probably brought about certain expectations on the part of some of them. At least two of the interviews that resulted from these awkward expectations were of very low quality, as the interviewees were cagey with information and seemed to be trying to impress me; ironically, another two were some of the most open and engaging interviews that I did. Interviewees would occasionally hit on me after our interview; only one was blatant enough to do so during our interview, but he was a key informant who was so far inside my own social network that the flirtation was more cute than weird or threatening.

I don't think I ever approached an ideal "saturation point" in my interviews, meaning that I had enough people to answer all the questions I really cared about. Kinksters' experiences vary so much by a complex overlap of gender, age, BDSM role (Dominant, submissive, etc.), and level of Scene involvement that I would have had to carefully recruit about 300 people in order to hope to reach a saturation point. That wasn't practical, so I did something that I think was even better: I administered a large-scale survey.

SURVEY

In April 2017, I created a survey designed to test several hypotheses about the demographic and statistical trends in the Scene. I formulated a draft survey and piloted it through several acquaintances in the community before making it publicly available online. The Scene networks very heavily through the internet, mostly through FetLife and to a lesser degree through Twitter and blogs. Virtually everyone in the public Scene really was on FetLife or a kinky Twitter hub at the time, so I had access to literally almost the entire community through these websites. Many BDSM events wouldn't let people attend without RSVPing to the event on FetLife. I posted a link to my survey on FetLife, Twitter, and Facebook and asked friends to share it; within 24 hours, I had nearly 800 initial responses, with a final sample of more than 1,600. The link was spread widely, and 92 percent of the final sample had FetLife accounts (which is actually remarkably low for the Scene at the time and shows how widely the link was spread).

It's impossible to gauge how representative my sample is of the population of interest. Being "in the Scene" is a pretty ambiguous concept to begin with, and there's no census to measure its population. The best proxy is FetLife, but while basically all publicly involved kinksters are on FetLife, most FetLife users aren't involved in the public Scene. There are unpublished analyses of active FetLife users (which, though banned by the website, are still publicly available) that contain information about their age, gender, BDSM role, and geographical location and can provide a reasonable population estimate for age, gender, and BDSM role against which to measure a survey sample, and mine appears to be in line with these estimates. The most reliable of these was age, and my sample matches the median ages of FetLife users by gender—35 for women and 39 for men. Overall, 1,743 people answered the second question on the survey and 1,447 answered the last, leaving a survey completion rate by this measure of 83 percent. (As many questions did not apply to all respondents, it's difficult to provide a more comprehensive completion rate.) For most of my results, my sample is about 1,600.

There's no way to know the gender composition of the Scene, so there's no way to gauge how representative my data are by gender. Observations and unpublished estimates suggest that as much as two-thirds of the Scene might be men, but, like many entirely voluntary survey samples (Smith, 2008), my survey respondents are heavily biased toward women: based solely on a question about self-described gender, only 31 percent of the sample identified as masculine, but 51 percent identified as feminine (and the remaining 18.5 percent identified as other). Fortunately, analysis of variables that I hypothesized were gender-neutral, such as level of Scene participation, showed no significant or marked differences between genders, suggesting that there were no unexpected differences in the types of men and women who responded to the survey. All my survey results that don't control for gender are probably biased as population estimates. However, since level of Scene participation is one of my main variables and is not skewed by gender, estimates comparing different levels of participation are still *relatively* (just not always absolutely) accurate.

Gender was the most difficult characteristic to measure on my survey. I gave respondents six categories to describe their gender: feminine, butch/demi-woman, genderqueer/genderfluid, soft masculine/demi-man, masculine, and other (nearly all of which I recoded as genderqueer). Kinksters don't often self-identify, when asked, as anything other than feminine, masculine, or genderqueer/genderfluid, but 6 percent of people with vaginas on my survey identified as butch/demi-woman, and 11 percent of people with penises identified as soft masculine/demi-man. I also asked questions about sex assigned at birth as well as current genitalia (which sociologists generally refer to as "sex"). To create my "gender" variable, I divided the sample into feminine people with vaginas (who I treat as cis women, even though there are a handful of them who have undergone medical transition), masculine men with penises (who I treat as cis men, even though there are also a handful of trans men here), and other. In more nuanced analyses, I combined measures of gender with measures of sex to create a kind of gender-sex variable that separates out feminine people with vaginas (who I generally just refer to as "women" in the text), nonfeminine people with vaginas ("gender-nonconforming person with vagina/GNC-V"), nonmasculine people with penises ("gender-nonconforming person with penis/GNC-P"), and masculine people with penises ("men"). Many Queer folks in the Scene were extremely critical of my focus on genitalia, but in the culturally pansexual Scene, I decided to treat the importance of genitalia as an empirical question. Sometimes it proved highly significant; other times, the only thing that mattered was gender identity. For more statistically complex analyses (particularly multivariate regressions), I could only use gender instead of gender-sex due to sample size constraints. I don't use terms like assigned male at birth because a handful of people had undergone total gender confirmation surgery, and I was more interested in sexual and gender display in the sexually open world of the Scene than I was with identity.

SAMPLE STATISTICS

In this section, I provide brief summary statistics about my sample, with numbers in parentheses indicating how many cases.

- *Gender-sex:* Women 48 percent (793), median age 35; Gender-nonconforming with vagina (GNC-V) 11 percent (179), age 32; Gender-nonconforming with penis (GNC-P) 9 percent (150), age 33; Men 32 percent (520), age 39
- *Region:* United States and Canada 86 percent (1574); Europe 11 percent (193); Australia and other 3 percent (60)
- *Level of Scene Involvement:* Low 16 percent (304); Medium 52 percent (984); High 32 percent (615)
- *Race:* White 90 percent (1422); Black 1.5 percent (23); Asian 1.6 percent (26); Multiracial and other 7 percent (107)
- *Education:* Less than high school .5 percent (8); High school 6 percent (98); Some college 27 percent (427); Associate's degree 11 percent (173); Bachelor's 32 percent (502); Master's 17 percent (266); PhD/Professional degree 7 percent (111)
- *Spirituality:* Pagan 22 percent (352); Buddhist/Taoist 7 percent (107); Jewish 3 percent (37); Christian 16 percent (254); Nothing/atheist/agnostic 45 percent (720); Other (mostly "spiritual") 6 percent (97)

REFERENCES

Abramson, Corey M., and Darren Modzelewski. (2011). "Caged Morality: Moral Worlds, Subculture, and Stratification among Middle-Class Cage-Fighters." *Qualitative Sociology* 34, 143–75.

Adler, Patricia A. (1993). *Wheeling and Dealing: An Ethnography of an Upper-Level Drug Dealing and Smuggling Community.* New York: Columbia University Press.

Akers, Ronald L. (1977). *Deviant Behavior: A Social Learning Approach.* New York: Transaction.

Allison, Rachel, and Barbara J. Risman. (2013). "A Double Standard for 'Hooking Up': How Far Have We Come toward Gender Equality?" *Social Science Research* 42, 1191–206.

Bauer, Robin. (2010). "Non-Monogamy in Queer BDSM Communities: Putting the Sex Back into Alternative Relationship Practices and Discourse." In Meg Barker and Darren Langdridge (Eds.), *Understanding Non-Monogamies* (pp. 142–59). New York: Routledge.

———. (2014). *Queer BDSM Intimacies: Critical Consent and Pushing Boundaries.* London: Palgrave Macmillan.

Becker, Howard S. (2008). *Outsiders.* New York: Simon and Schuster.

Bennion, Janet. (2022). "Polyamory in Paris: A Social Network Theory Application." *Sexualities* 25, 173–97.

Besbris, Max, and Shamus Khan. (2017). "Less Theory. More Description." *Sociological Theory* 35, 147–53.

Bezreh, Tanya, Thomas S. Weinberg, and Timothy Edgar. (2012). "BDSM Disclosure and Stigma Management: Identifying Opportunities for Sex Education." *American Journal of Sexuality Education* 7, 37–61.

Blumberg, Antonia. (2014). "Morning Glory Zell-Ravenheart Dead." *Huffington Post.* https://www.huffpost.com/entry/morning-glory-zell-dead_n_5324410

Bogle, Kathleen A. (2008). *Hooking Up: Sex, Dating, and Relationships on Campus.* New York: NYU Press.

BRC. (2014). *Black Rock City 2014 Census.* https://burningman.org/about/history/brc-history/afterburn/2014-afterburn-report/brc-2014-census/

Brents, Barbara G., and Teela Sanders. (2010). "Mainstreaming the Sex Industry: Economic Inclusion and Social Ambivalence." *Journal of Law and Society* 37, 40–60.

Broad, Kendal L., Sara L. Crawley, and Lara Foley. (2004). "Doing 'Real Family Values': The Interpretive Practice of Families in the GLBT Movement." *Sociological Quarterly* 45, 509–27.

Butler, Judith. (1990). *Gender Trouble: Feminism and the Subversion of Identity.* New York: Routledge.

Callis, April S. (2013). "The Black Sheep of the Pink Flock: Labels, Stigma, and Bisexual Identity." *Journal of Bisexuality* 13, 82–105.

Carlström, Charlotta. (2017). "Gender Equal BDSM Practice—A Swedish Paradox?" *Psychology & Sexuality* 8, 268–79.

———. (2021). "Spiritual Experiences and Altered States of Consciousness— Parallels between BDSM and Christianity." *Sexualities* 24, 749–66.

Carpenter, Laura M. (2005). *Virginity Lost: An Intimate Portrait of First Sexual Experiences.* New York: New York UP.

Chambers, Wendy C. (2007). "Oral Sex: Varied Behaviors and Perceptions in a College Population." *Journal of Sex Research* 44, 28–42.

Clarke, Victoria, and Kevin Turner. (2007). "V. Clothes Maketh the Queer? Dress, Appearance and the Construction of Lesbian, Gay and Bisexual Identities." *Feminism & Psychology* 17, 267–76.

Colosi, Rachela. (2017). *Dirty Dancing: An Ethnography of Lap Dancing.* London: Willan.

Comella, L. (2017). *Vibrator Nation: How Feminist Sex-Toy Stores Changed the Business of Pleasure.* Durham, NC: Duke University Press.

Cote, Rachel V. (2015, December 3). "Even More Sex Industry Performers Accuse James Deen of Abuse, Violence." *Jezebel.* https://jezebel.com/even-more-sex -industry-performers-accuse-james-deen-of-1746108988

Cox, Daniel, Juhem Navarro-Rivera, and Robert P Jones. (2016). "Race, Religion, and Political Affiliation of Americans' Core Social Networks." *Public Religion Research Institute.*

Critelli, Joseph W., and Jenny M. Bivona. (2008). "Women's Erotic Rape Fantasies: An Evaluation of Theory and Research." *Journal of Sex Research* 45, 57–70.

Cruz, Ariane. (2016). *The Color of Kink: Black Women, BDSM, and Pornography.* New York: NYU Press.

Darley, John M., and Bibb Latané. (1968). "Bystander Intervention in Emergencies: Diffusion of Responsibility." *Journal of Personality and Social Psychology* 8, 377.

Daum, M. (2001). *My Misspent Youth.* New York: Better World.

DeGroot, Jocelyn M., Heather J. Carmack, and Margaret M. Quinlan. (2015). "'Topping from the Bottom': Relational Convergence of Meaning in Domestic Discipline Relationships." *Sexuality & Culture* 19, 85–102.

REFERENCES

DiPrete, Thomas A., Andrew Gelman, Tyler McCormick, Julien Teitler, and Tian Zheng. (2011). "Segregation in Social Networks Based on Acquaintanceship and Trust." *American Journal of Sociology* 116, 1234–83.

Dougherty, Kevin D. (2003). "How Monochromatic is Church Membership? Racial-Ethnic Diversity in Religious Community." *Sociology of Religion* 64, 65–85.

Durkheim, Emile. (1897). *Suicide*. Glencoe, IL: Free Press.

Durkheim, Emile, and Joseph W. Swain. (2008). *The Elementary Forms of the Religious Life*. New York: Courier Corporation.

Erickson, Jennifer M., Anna M. Slayton, Joseph G. Petersen, Hannah M. Hyams, Lori J. Howard, Shane Sharp, and Brad J. Sagarin. (2021). "Challenge at the Intersection of Race and Kink: Racial Discrimination, Fetishization, and Inclusivity Within the BDSM (Bondage-Discipline, Dominance-Submission, and Sadism-Masochism) Community." *Archives of Sexual Behavior* 2, 1–12.

Ezzy, Douglas. (2014). *Sex, Death and Witchcraft: A Contemporary Pagan Festival*. London: Bloomsbury.

Fahs, Breanne. (2011). *Performing Sex: The Making and Unmaking of Women's Erotic Lives*. Albany: State University of New York Press.

Farmer, Melissa A., Paul D. Trapnell, and Cindy M. Meston. (2009). "The Relation between Sexual Behavior and Religiosity Subtypes: A Test of the Secularization Hypothesis." *Archives of Sexual Behavior* 38, 852–65.

Ferrer, Jorge N. (2018). "Mononormativity, Polypride, and the 'Mono–Poly Wars.'" *Sexuality & Culture* 22, 817–36.

Fine, Gary A., and Michaela De Soucey. (2005). "Joking Cultures: Humor Themes as Social Regulation in Group Life." *Humor: International Journal of Humor Research* 18, 1–22.

Fischer, Peter, Joachim I. Krueger, Tobias Greitemeyer, Claudia Vogrincic, Andreas Kastenmüller, Dieter Frey, Moritz Heene, Magdalena Wicher, and Martina Kainbacher. (2011). "The Bystander-Effect: A Meta-Analytic Review on Bystander Intervention in Dangerous and Non-Dangerous Emergencies." *Psychological Bulletin* 137, 517.

Fennell, Julie. (2018). "'It's All about the Journey': Skepticism and Spirituality in the BDSM Subculture." *Sociological Forum* 33(4), 1045–67.

Flood, Michael. (2008). "Men, Sex, and Homosociality: How Bonds between Men Shape their Sexual Relations with Women." *Men and Masculinities* 10, 339–59.

Foucault, Michel. (1979). *Discipline and Punish: The Birth of a Prison*. New York: Vintage.

———. (1990). *History of Sexuality: An Introduction*. New York: Vintage.

Galilee-Belfer, Mika. (2020). "BDSM, Kink, and Consent: What the Law Can Learn from Consent-Driven Communities." *Arizona Law Review* 62, 507.

Gathorne-Hardy, Jonathan. (2004). *Kinsey: Sex the Measure of All Things*. Bloomington: Indiana University Press.

REFERENCES

Giddens, Anthony. (1992). *The Transformation of Intimacy: Sexuality, Love, and Eroticism in Modern Societies*. Stanford, CA: Stanford University Press.

Gilsdorf, Ethan. (2010). *Fantasy Freaks and Gaming Geeks: An Epic Quest for Reality among Role Players, Online Gamers, and Other Dwellers of Imaginary Realms*. Guilford, CT: Lyons Press.

Giordano, Peggy C., Monica A. Longmore, and Wendy D. Manning. (2006). "Gender and the Meanings of Adolescent Romantic Relationships: A Focus on Boys." *American Sociological Review* 71, 260–87.

Goffman, Erving. (1959). *The Presentation of Self in Everyday Life*. New York: Doubleday.

———. (2009). *Stigma: Notes on the Management of Spoiled Identity*. New York: Simon and Schuster.

Gopnik, Adam. (2015, January 12). "The Outside Game." *New Yorker*.

Guttmacher Institute. (2017). "American Adolescents' Sources of Sexual Health Information." https://www.guttmacher.org/fact-sheet/facts-american-teens-sources-information-about-sex

Hagle, Timothy M. (1991). "But Do They Have to See It to Know It? The Supreme Court's Obscenity and Pornography Decisions." *Western Political Quarterly* 44, 1039–54.

Hammers, Corie. (2014). "Corporeality, Sadomasochism and Sexual Trauma." *Body & Society* 20, 68–90.

Harrington, Lee. (2016). *Sacred Kink: The Eightfold Paths of BDSM and Beyond*. Anchorage: Mystic Productions Press.

Harviainen, J. T. (2011). "Sadomasochist Role-Playing as Live-Action Role-Playing: A Trait-Descriptive Analysis." *International Journal of Role-Playing* 2, 59–70.

Haviv, Noam. (2016). "Reporting Sexual Assaults to the Police: The Israeli BDSM Community." *Sexuality Research and Social Policy* 13, 276–87.

Hebdige, Dick. (1979). *Subculture: The Meaning of Style*. London: Routledge.

Holt, Karen. (2016). "Blacklisted: Boundaries, Violations, and Retaliatory Behavior in the BDSM Community." *Deviant Behavior* 37(8), 917–30.

Holvoet, Lien, Wim Huys, Violette Coppens, Jantien Seeuws, Kris Goethals, and Manuel Morrens. (2017). "Fifty Shades of Belgian Gray: The Prevalence of BDSM-Related Fantasies and Activities in the General Population." *Journal of Sexual Medicine* 14, 1152–59.

Inbar, Yoel, David Pizarro, Ravi Iyer, and Jonathan Haidt. (2012). "Disgust Sensitivity, Political Conservatism, and Voting." *Social Psychological and Personality Science* 3, 537–44.

Irwin, Katherine. (2003). "Saints and Sinners: Elite Tattoo Collectors and Tattooists as Positive and Negative Deviants." *Sociological Spectrum* 23, 27–57.

James, E. L. (2011). *Fifty Shades of Grey*. New York: Vintage.

REFERENCES

Johnston, Erin F. (2013). "'I Was Always This Way . . .': Rhetorics of Continuity in Narratives of Conversion." *Sociological Forum* 28, 549–73.

Jost, John T., Jack Glaser, Arie W. Kruglanski, and Frank J. Sulloway. (2003). "Political Conservatism as Motivated Social Cognition." *Psychological Bulletin* 129, 339.

Jozkowski, Kristen N., and Zoë D. Peterson. (2013). "College Students and Sexual Consent: Unique Insights." *Journal of Sex Research* 50, 517–23.

Kaestle, Christine E., and Carolyn T. Halpern. (2007). "What's Love Got to Do with It? Sexual Behaviors of Opposite-sex Couples through Emerging Adulthood." *Perspectives on Sexual and Reproductive Health* 39, 134–40.

Kaldera, Raven. (2009). *Dark Moon Rising: Pagan BDSM & the Ordeal Path.* Morrisville, NC: Lulu.

Kanazawa, Satoshi. (2010). "Why Liberals and Atheists Are More Intelligent." *Social Psychology Quarterly* 73, 33–57.

Kao, Grace, Kara Joyner, and Kelly Stamper Balistreri. (2019). *The Company We Keep: Interracial Friendships and Romantic Relationships from Adolescence to Adulthood.* Washington DC: Russell Sage.

Kapsalis, Terri. (1997). *Public Privates: Performing Gynecology from Both Ends of the Speculum.* Durham, NC: Duke University Press.

Keenan, Jillian. (2014, August 18). "Is Kink a Sexual Orientation?" *Slate.* http://www.slate.com/blogs/outward/2014/08/18/is_kink_a_sexual_orientation.html

Kington, Candie S. (2015). "Con Culture: A Survey of Fans and Fandom." *Journal of Fandom Studies* 3, 211–28.

Kinsey, Alfred C. (1948). *Sexual Behavior in the Human Male.* Bloomington, IN: Indiana University Press.

Klesse, Christian. (1999). "'Modern Primitivism': Non-Mainstream Body Modification and Racialized Representation." *Body & Society* 5, 15–38.

———. (2005). "Bisexual Women, Non-Monogamy and Differentialist Anti-Promiscuity Discourses." *Sexualities* 8, 445–64.

———. (2009). "Paradoxes in Gender Relations: [Post] Feminism and Bisexual Polyamory." In Meg Barker and Darren Langdridge (Eds.), *Understanding Non-Monogamies* (pp. 109–20). London: Routledge.

———. (2011). "Shady Characters, Untrustworthy Partners, and Promiscuous Sluts: Creating Bisexual Intimacies in the Face of Heteronormativity and Biphobia." *Journal of Bisexuality* 11, 227–44.

———. (2014). "Polyamory: Intimate Practice, Identity or Sexual Orientation?" *Sexualities* 17, 81–99.

Kotsko, Adam. (2015). *Creepiness.* Lanham, MD: John Hunt.

Kraemer, Christine H. (2012). "Gender and Sexuality in Contemporary Paganism." *Religion Compass* 6, 390–401.

Krueger, R. B. (2010). "The DSM Diagnostic Criteria for Sexual Sadism." *Archives of Sexual Behavior* 39, 325.

REFERENCES

Kuipers, Giselinde. (2008). "The Sociology of Humor." *Primer of Humor Research* 8, 361–98.

Lamont, Ellen. (2017). "'We Can Write the Scripts Ourselves': Queer Challenges to Heteronormative Courtship Practices." *Gender & Society* 31, 624–46.

Lehmiller, Justin. (2018). *Tell Me What You Want.* Boston: Da Capo.

Lin, Kai. (2017). "The Medicalization and Demedicalization of Kink: Shifting Contexts of Sexual Politics." *Sexualities* 20, 302–23.

Lindemann, Danielle. (2010). "Will the Real Dominatrix Please Stand Up: Artistic Purity and Professionalism in the S M Dungeon1." *Sociological Forum* 25, 588.

———. (2011). "BDSM as Therapy?" *Sexualities* 14, 151–72.

———. (2012). *Dominatrix: Gender, Eroticism, and Control in the Dungeon.* Chicago: University of Chicago Press.

Livingston, Gretchen, and Anna Brown. (2017). "1. Trends and Patterns in Intermarriage." *Pew Research Center's Social & Demographic Trends Project.* https://www.pewresearch.org/social-trends/2017/05/18/1-trends-and-patterns -in-intermarriage/

Maines, Rachel P. (2001). *The Technology of Orgasm: "Hysteria," the Vibrator, and Women's Sexual Satisfaction.* Baltimore: Johns Hopkins University Press.

Martinez, Katherine. (2018). "BDSM Role Fluidity: A Mixed-Methods Approach to Investigating Switches within Dominant/Submissive Binaries." *Journal of Homosexuality* 65, 1299–324.

———. (2021). "Overwhelming Whiteness of BDSM: A Critical Discourse Analysis of Racialization in BDSM." *Sexualities* 24, 733–48.

Matza, David, and Thomas G. Blomberg. (2017). *Becoming Deviant.* London: Routledge.

McClure, Amy I. (2017). "'Becoming a Parent Changes Everything': How Nonbeliever and Pagan Parents Manage Stigma in the US Bible Belt." *Qualitative Sociology* 40, 331–52.

Meepos, Devin. (2013). "50 Shades of Consent: Re-Defining the Law's Treatment of Sadomasochism." *Southwestern Law Review* 43, 97.

Mendes, Kaitlynn, Jessica Ringrose, and Jessalynn Keller. (2018). "#MeToo and the Promise and Pitfalls of Challenging Rape Culture through Digital Feminist Activism." *European Journal of Women's Studies* 25, 236–46.

Merton, Robert K. (1938). "Social Structure and Anomie." *American Sociological Review* 3, 672–82.

———. (1949). *Social Theory and Social Structure.* New York: Free Press.

———. (1967). *On Theoretical Sociology.* New York: Free Press.

Mills, C. W. (1959). *The Sociological Imagination.* New York: Oxford University Press.

Mitchell, Valory. (2008). "Choosing Family: Meaning and Membership in the Lesbian Family of Choice." *Journal of Lesbian Studies* 12, 301–13.

REFERENCES

Morris, Hannah, I. J. Chang, and David Knox. (2016). "Three's a Crowd or Bonus?: College Students' Threesome Experiences." *Journal of Positive Sexuality* 2, 62–76.

Moser, Charles. (2016). "Defining Sexual Orientation." *Archives of Sexual Behavior* 45, 505–8.

Newmahr, Staci. (2010). "Rethinking Kink: Sadomasochism as Serious Leisure." *Qualitative Sociology* 33, 313–31.

———. (2011). *Playing on the Edge: Sadomasochism, Risk, and Intimacy.* Bloomington: Indiana University Press.

Nordling, Niklas, N. Sandnabba, Pekka Santtila, and Laurence Alison. (2005). "Differences and Similarities between Gay and Straight Individuals Involved in the Sadomasochistic Subculture." *Journal of Homosexuality* 50, 41–57.

Oerton, Sarah. (2004). "Bodywork Boundaries: Power, Politics and Professionalism in Therapeutic Massage." *Gender, Work & Organization* 11, 544–65.

Oosterhoff, Benjamin, Natalie J. Shook, and Cameron Ford. (2018). "Is That Disgust I See? Political Ideology and Biased Visual Attention." *Behavioural Brain Research* 336, 227–35.

Orne, Jason. (2011). "'You Will Always Have to "Out" Yourself': Reconsidering Coming Out through Strategic Outness." *Sexualities* 14, 681–703.

———. (2013). "Queers in the Line of Fire: Goffman's Stigma Revisited." *Sociological Quarterly* 54, 229–53.

———. (2017). *Boystown: Sex and Community in Chicago.* Chicago: University of Chicago Press.

Payne, Geoff, and Judy Payne. (2004). "Key informants." In *Key Concepts in Social Research*, 135–38. New York: Sage.

Peters, Jeremy W. (2014). "The Decline and Fall of the 'H' Word." *New York Times*, March 23, 2014.

Plante, Rebecca. (2005). "Sexual Spanking, the Self, and the Construction of Deviance." *Journal of Homosexuality* 50, 59–79.

Plummer, Deborah L., Jeroan Allison, Rosalie Torres Stone, and Lauren Powell. (2016). "Patterns of Adult Cross-Racial Friendships: A Context for Understanding Contemporary Race Relations." *Cultural Diversity & Ethnic Minority Psychology* 22(4), 479–94.

Rambukkana, Nathan. (2007). "Taking the Leather out of Leathersex: The Internet, Identity, and the Sadomasochistic Public Sphere." *Queer Online: Media Technology & Sexuality* 40, 67.

Randall, Holly. (2018, April 11). "Casey Calvert" (Episode 39) [Audio podcast episode]. In *Holly Randall Unfiltered*. Holly Randall Productions. https://www.pleasurepodcasts.com/hollyrandallunfiltered

Richters, Juliet, Richard O. De Visser, Chris E. Rissel, Andrew E. Grulich, and Anthony M. Smith. (2008). "Demographic and Psychosocial Features of Participants in Bondage and Discipline, 'sadomasochism' or Dominance and Submission (BDSM): Data from a National Survey." *Journal of Sexual Medicine* 5, 1660–68.

Robertson, Adi. (2017, July 21). "I Hacked My Body for a Future That Never Came." *The Verge.* https://www.theverge.com/2017/7/21/15999544/biohacking-finger -magnet-human-augmentation-loss

Rosenberg, Eli S., Patrick S. Sullivan, Elizabeth A. DiNenno, Laura F. Salazar, and Travis H. Sanchez. (2011). "Number of Casual Male Sexual Partners and Associated Factors among Men Who Have Sex with Men: Results from the National HIV Behavioral Surveillance System." *BMC Public Health* 11, 189.

Roxiefoley. (2018, April 5). "Ethical Non-Monogamy and the UCMJ." *Polyamory and the Military.* https://polyamoryandthemilitary.com/2018/04/05/ethical-non -monogamy-and-the-ucmj/ (accessed August 2019)

Rubin, Gayle. (2000). "Sites, Settlements, and Urban Sex: Archaeology and the Study of Gay Leathermen in San Francisco." In Robert A. Schmidt and Barbara L. Voss, *Archaeologies of Sexuality*, 62–88. London: Routledge.

Rubin, Rachel. (2012). *Well Met: Renaissance Faires and the American Counterculture.* New York: New York University Press.

Rudder, Christian. (2014). *Dataclysm: Love, Sex, Race, and Identity—What Our Online Lives Tell Us about Our Offline Selves.* New York: Crown.

Ryan, Christopher, and Cecilda Jetha. (2010). *Sex at Dawn.* New York: Harper.

Schilt, Kristen, and Laurel Westbrook. (2015). "Bathroom Battlegrounds and Penis Panics." *Contexts* 14, 26–31.

Scoats, Ryan, Lauren J. Joseph, and Eric Anderson. (2018). "'I Don't Mind Watching Him Cum': Heterosexual Men, Threesomes, and the Erosion of the One-Time Rule of Homosexuality." *Sexualities* 21, 30–48.

Sheff, Elisabeth. (2006). "Poly-Hegemonic Masculinities." *Sexualities* 9, 621–42.

———. (2011). "Polyamorous Families, Same-Sex Marriage, and the Slippery Slope." *Journal of Contemporary Ethnography* 40, 487–520.

———. (2013). *The Polyamorists Next Door: Inside Multiple-Partner Relationships and Families.* Lanham, MD: Rowman and Littlefield.

Sheff, Elisabeth, and Corie Hammers. (2011). "The Privilege of Perversities: Race, Class and Education among Polyamorists and Kinksters." *Psychology & Sexuality* 2, 198–223.

Sherry, John F., and Robert V. Kozinets. (2007). "Comedy of the Commons: Nomadic Spirituality and the Burning Man Festival." *Research in Consumer Behavior* 11, 119–47.

Simmel, Georg. (1950). *The Sociology of Georg Simmel.* Translated by Kurt H. Wolff. New York: Free Press.

Simula, Brandy L. (2012). "Does Bisexuality 'Undo' Gender? Gender, Sexuality, and Bisexual Behavior among BDSM Participants." *Journal of Bisexuality* 12, 484–506.

———. (2019a). "A 'Different Economy of Bodies and Pleasures'?: Differentiating and Evaluating Sex and Sexual BDSM Experiences." *Journal of Homosexuality* 66, 209–37.

REFERENCES

———. (2019b). "Pleasure, Power, and Pain: A Review of the Literature on the Experiences of BDSM Participants." *Sociology Compass* 13, e12668.

Simula, Brandy L., and J. Sumerau. (2019). "The Use of Gender in the Interpretation of BDSM." *Sexualities* 22, 452–77.

Sloan, Lorca J. (2015). "Ace of (BDSM) Clubs: Building Asexual Relationships through BDSM Practice." *Sexualities* 18, 548–63.

Smith, G. (2008). "Does Gender Influence Online Survey Participation?: A Record-Linkage Analysis of University Faculty Online Survey Response Behavior." ERIC Document Reproduction Service no.ED 501717.

Sprott, Richard A., Jules Vivid, Ellora Vilkin, Lyle Swallow, Eliot M. Lev, Julius Orejudos, and Danny Schnittman. (2020). "A Queer Boundary: How Sex and BDSM Interact for People Who Identify as Kinky." *Sexualities* (online).

Stephens, Paul, Andy Leach, and Laura Taggart. (1998). *Think Sociology*. Cambridge, MA: Wakefield Press.

Suschinsky, Kelly D., and Martin L. Lalumière. (2011). "Prepared for Anything? An Investigation of Female Genital Arousal in Response to Rape Cues." *Psychological Science* 22, 159–65.

Taliaferro, Lindsay A., Kari M. Gloppen, Jennifer J. Muehlenkamp, and Marla E. Eisenberg. (2018). "Depression and Suicidality among Bisexual Youth: A Nationally Representative Sample." *Journal of LGBT Youth* 15, 16–31.

Taormino, Tristan. (2008). *Opening Up: A Guide to Creating and Sustaining Open Relationships*. San Francisco: Cleis Press.

Taylor, Gary W., and Jane M. Ussher. (2001). "Making Sense of S&M: A Discourse Analytic Account." *Sexualities* 4, 293–314.

Taylor, Julia. (2018). "Bisexual Mental Health: A Call to Action." *Issues in Mental Health Nursing* 39, 83–92.

Thompson, Mark (ed). (1991). *Leatherfolk: Radical Sex, People, Politics, and Practice*. Boston: Alyson.

Thrasher, Steven W. (2015, September 27). "Burning Man's Black Campers Explain Why They Are the 1%." *The Guardian*.

Törnqvist, Maria. (2018). "Rethinking Intimacy: Semi-Anonymous Spaces and Transitory Attachments in Argentine Tango Dancing." *Current Sociology* 66, 356–72.

Twenge, Jean. (2017). *iGen*. New York: Simon and Schuster.

Twenge, Jean M., Ryne A. Sherman, and Brooke E. Wells. (2015). "Changes in American Adults' Sexual Behavior and Attitudes, 1972–2012." *Archives of Sexual Behavior* 44, 2273–85.

van Dorn, Niels. (2019). *Civic Intimacies: Black Queer Improvisations on Citizenship*. Philadelphia: Temple University Press.

Vilkin, Ellora, and Richard Sprott. (2021). "Consensual Non-Monogamy among Kink-Identified Adults: Characteristics, Relationship Experiences, and Unique

Motivations for Polyamory and Open Relationships." *Archives of Sexual Behavior* 50, 1521–36.

Ward, Brian W., James M. Dahlhamer, Adena M. Galinsky, and Sarah S. Joestl. (2014). "Sexual Orientation and Health among US Adults: National Health Interview Survey, 2013." *National Health Statistics Report* 77, 1–10.

Weiss, Margot. (2005). "Mainstreaming Kink: The Politics of BDSM Representation in U.S. Popular Media." *Journal of Homosexuality* 50, 103–32.

———. (2011). *Techniques of Pleasure: BDSM and the Circuits of Sexuality.* Durham, NC: Duke University Press.

White, Andrea E. (2015). "The Nature of Taboo Contracts: A Legal Analysis of BDSM Contracts and Specific Performance." *UMKC Law Review* 84, 1163.

Whitney, Elizabeth. (2001). "Cyborgs among Us: Performing Liminal States of Sexuality." *Journal of Bisexuality* 2, 109–28.

Williams, D. J. (2009). "Deviant Leisure: Rethinking 'The Good, the Bad, and the Ugly.'" *Leisure Sciences* 31, 207–13.

Williams, D. J., Emily E. Prior, Thea Alvarado, Jeremy N. Thomas, and M. C. Christensen. (2016). "Is Bondage and Discipline, Dominance and Submission, and Sadomasochism Recreational Leisure? A Descriptive Exploratory Investigation." *Journal of Sexual Medicine* 13, 1091–94.

Xygalatas, Dimitris, Panagiotis Mitkidis, Ronald Fischer, Paul Reddish, Joshua Skewes, Armin W. Geertz, Andreas Roepstorff, and Joseph Bulbulia. (2013). "Extreme Rituals Promote Prosociality." *Psychological Science* 24: 1602.

Yingtai, Xiao. (2015, April 24). "It's a Bad Day for Rope Consent." *The University of Abject Submission.* https://abjectsub.com/it-is-a-bad-day-for-rope/

Yost, Megan R., and L. E. Hunter. (2012). "BDSM Practitioners' Understandings of their Initial Attraction to BDSM Sexuality: Essentialist and Constructionist Narratives." *Psychology & Sexuality* 3, 244–59.

YouGov. (2015). *Morality of Polyamory.* https://d25d2506sfb94s.cloudfront.net/cumulus_uploads/document/bz9id6ab5c/tabs_OPI_Poly_20150730.pdf

INDEX

Italicized page numbers indicate illustrations.

INDEX